From
INSTRUCTION
to *Delight*

From
INSTRUCTION
to *Delight*

AN ANTHOLOGY OF
CHILDREN'S LITERATURE TO 1850

Edited by Patricia Demers & Gordon Moyles

Toronto   Oxford University Press

Oxford University Press
70 Wynford Drive, Don Mills, Ontario M3C 1J9

Oxford New York
Athens Auckland Bangkok Bombay
Calcutta Cape Town Dar es Salaam Delhi
Florence Hong Kong Istanbul Karachi
Kuala Lumpur Madras Madrid Melbourne
Mexico City Nairobi Paris Singapore
Taipei Tokyo Toronto
and associated companies in
Berlin Ibadan
Oxford is a trademark of Oxford University Press

FOR ALISON
colleague, mentor, friend

The cover illustration, "The Village School in an Uproar" (c. 1820), is reproduced courtesy The Osborne Collection of Early Children's Books, Toronto Public Library. Photograph by VIDA/Saltmarche, Toronto

CANADIAN CATALOGUING IN PUBLICATION DATA
Main entry under title:
From instruction to delight
Bibliography: p.
Includes index.
ISBN 0-19-540384-3
1. Children's literature, English. I. Demers,
Patricia, 1946-   II. Moyles, R. G. (Robert
Gordon), 1939-
PR1109.F76   820'.8'09282   C82-094143-3

Cover design by Douglas V. Frank
Printed in Canada by Metrolitho

CONTENTS

ILLUSTRATIONS

PREFACE

He who combines the useful and the pleasing wins out by
both instructing and delighting the reader.—Horace

In his critical treatise, *The Art of Poetry*, Horace proposed a formula for literary success that has been the hallmark of the best children's books for over two centuries. Historians of children's literature have used his dictum as a sure means of charting the progress of that literature from its rude beginnings to its Golden Age. Prior to the middle of the eighteenth century, they maintain, the emphasis fell heavily and deliberately on instruction—so much so that before 1744 there were, properly speaking, no children's books. In that year John Newbery produced *A Little Pretty Pocket-Book*, which heralded the beginning of *delight* and, along with the ubiquitous chapbooks, ushered in a new era in children's reading. In the century that followed, the quality of works written for children varied according to the degree of their authors' acceptance or rejection of Horace's advice. But by 1850 there had emerged a literature whose unashamed *raison d'être* was to give pleasure to children. The Golden Age had dawned.

Although historians generally agree that children's literature developed "from instruction to delight", the search for examples to support this development can be a sometimes daunting task. Histories of children's books merely give brief quotations from early key works, which themselves can often be seen only in a few rare-book collections. It is the intention of this anthology to include—and discuss—enough important examples to illuminate the different approaches to writing for children that provide the basis for a historical tradition—one that is linked to the emergence of the child as an individual. From Aelfric's *Colloquy* (c. 1000) to the English version of Heinrich Hoffmann's Struwwelpeter (1848), we have chosen more than 150 literary "gems", arranged in historical groupings, that reveal the long, slow transition from instruction in various forms to the pleasing objective of amusement—with the occasional appearance of imaginative creativity and genuine literary quality anticipating the riches to come after 1850. While a few of the later selections are well known, most are drawn from works that are known by name or reputation only; a few have been rescued from obscurity. Collectively they represent an amazing variety of literary forms, including a charming Latin dialogue in a monastic school, Puritan exhortations, gentle Christian lyrics, psychologically intense narratives, and nonsense ditties. This wonderfully diverse literature reveals not only a steady increase in playful and entertaining features, which enliven both the content and the format of the stories and poems, but also the attitudes towards children and writing that form the basis of our understanding of modern children's literature.

The year 1850 is not merely an arbitrary frontier date: it marks the beginning of a period of high artistic productivity. Although most works for children at this time were still under the influence of Dr Watts and wagged a disapproving finger "against idleness and mischief"—which, incidentally, reach heights of joyous misrule in our cover subject, "The Village School in an Uproar" (c. 1820)—by the mid-nineteenth century their tone was less stern and more sympathetic than that of former children's books. As the balance shifted in favour of delight, striking changes occurred in the content. The tales of Perrault had been translated as early as 1729, but by the nineteenth century the compiling and composing of folk and fairy stories were vigorous activities. The Grimms' *Kinder -und Hausmarchen* was Englished in 1823, and by 1846 Andersen's collection of fairy tales, *Eventyr*, was also available in English. After the publication of the books discussed in our last chapter, "Harbingers of the Golden Age", the curtain was ready to rise on the fairy tales of Ruskin and Thackeray, the fantasies of Carroll and MacDonald, and the stylized art of Caldecott and Greenaway.

Happily, however, this anthology contains more than preparatory and formative material: much is still delightful and humorous—whether intentionally so or not. The early years of children's literature provide many surprises that do not deserve to languish on library shelves.

In compiling this anthology we have come to be grateful to many people and several institutions. A travel grant from the Faculty of Arts, University of Alberta, helped us to complete research at the Osborne and Lillian H. Smith Collections of the Toronto Public Library, where the knowledgeable and friendly assistance of Margaret Maloney, Dana Tenny, and Jill Shefrin made our stay both "useful and pleasing". The University Grants Office also assisted in defraying the costs of photographic reproductions. We are grateful to several librarians on our campus, particularly, John Charles, Head of Special Collections, and Angie Renville, Curator of the Library Science Collection, for their ready co-operation. Our retired colleague, Alison White, has been exceptionally generous—allowing us to browse through and borrow from her own valuable library. The typists in the Department of English have, as always, been patient in meeting our sometimes curious requests. Finally, for his encouragement and exacting care we are especially thankful to our editor, William Toye.

University of Alberta   PATRICIA DEMERS
October 1981   R. G. MOYLES

1. BOOKS OF COURTESY AND EARLY LESSONS

*Train up a child in the way he should go, and when
he is old he will not depart from it.*—Proverbs, 22.6.

If by the term "children's literature" we mean only those books written specifically for the entertainment of the young, we are forced to exclude from our consideration a great deal of material that, in the early centuries of English civilization, was the only kind of literature children ever knew. Books written for children prior to the middle of the eighteenth century were mainly of an educational kind—ABCs, primers, books of courtesy, and catechisms—and tell us much about how adults regarded children: as miniature vessels to be filled with imperial gallons of fact. These early books, therefore, provide the essential background against which the remarkable development in the mid-nineteenth century that we call the Golden Age of Children's Books can properly be appreciated.

Books of instruction written for children from Saxon times to the end of the Renaissance reflect the enormous social changes that occurred during more than six hundred years of English life. The Norman Conquest, the invention of printing, and the settlement of the New World all contributed to, and found expression in, the development of a literature for children. Before the eleventh century there were two types of educational establishments, both of which relied on Roman and, to a lesser extent, Alexandrian models of instruction. Song and Grammar Schools, or public clerical schools, were connected with the cathedrals and run by parish priests or deacons. Their pupils were either sons of the nobility or offspring of the poor who showed an aptitude for study and advancement in the Church; lessons included Latin grammar, rhetoric, logic, geometry, and music, and were aimed at creating an educated laity, along with candidates for the priesthood. Private monastic schools affiliated with specific orders were a second centre of education. Stressing an equally strong grounding in Latin, they usually prepared their pupils for membership in a religious community.

With the Norman Conquest and the new emphasis on chivalric manners and responsibilities, a third kind of seminary achieved prominence: the aristocratic home. Here nobly born children who might one day enter the service of the monarch acted as pages and squires while they learned courteous deportment as well as the rudiments of subjects normally taught in the Grammar School. This special school of etiquette groomed future advisers, administrators, and soldiers of the king.

In all these early schools the instruction was primarily oral—the rote-learned lessons were based on a manuscript manual usually possessed only by the Master or Tutor. With the establishment of William Caxton's printing press in the 1480s, however, the education of children could be textual as well as oral. The circulation of printed information, as opposed to the limited availability of manuscripts, made learning accessible to other than privileged children and contributed forcibly to the spread of literacy; more specifically, it introduced children's literature in embryonic form. Among Caxton's first publications were three books of moral instruction—*A Book of Curteyse* (1477), *The History of Reynard the Fox* (1481), and *Aesop's Fables* (1484)—that were designed for popular consumption. The concise text, pithy morals, and crude woodcuts (borrowed from a German edition) of the Aesop in particular were enjoyed by old and young alike.

By the early sixteenth century, when grammar schools acquired exercise books on various subjects, the printed word had entered the classroom. An inevitable commercial outcome of this publishing activity was the production and sale of lessons on single sheets pasted to a wooden board. Usually containing the alphabet and Lord's Prayer, these hornbooks conveyed the printed word to an eager and growing audience throughout the sixteenth and seventeenth centuries. With the spread of printing, even parents without any worldly standing began to realize that their offspring stood a better chance of gaining favour and, more important, their ultimate heavenly reward if they were taught to read.

The Puritan settlers of New England transplanted the notion of special publications for children to America. Hurt under Jacobean disfavour and persecuted after the close of Cromwell's Interregnum (1649-60), Puritans of both Congregational and Independent views emigrated in increasing numbers to a new and promisingly tolerant land. Among these early emigrants were university-educated preachers, who saw the formation of the young as an awesome responsibility, and London-trained printers who had suffered for their religious views. Together they not only brought current English primers and texts to the colonies but also encouraged the adaptation of these books to suit the religious and philosophical climate of New England. Since the colonies were originally experimental religious communities, it is not surprising that the literature they offered the young was intensely doctrinal. Presses and printing shops were among the first buildings erected, and Boston quickly became a focus of publishing activity.

The extracts that follow illustrate the distinctions between Latin and vernacular, noble and popular, oral and textual, English and colonial education. Collectively they provide their own evidence of the expansion of children's literature.

Aelfric's *Colloquy*, by a tenth-century Benedictine homilist, hagiographer, and teacher, is the earliest document that communicates directly with children rather than adults. It was probably composed as a manual for his pupils while Aelfric was instructing at Cerne Abbas (987-1002). A lesson in which Master and pupils talk about various occupations, the *Colloquy* is also, to our eyes, a revealing portrait of monastic instruction. The dialogue calls upon the respondents to answer, always in correct Latin, as a monk or a ploughman, an oxherd, a huntsman, a fowler, a merchant, a cook, or a blacksmith. As the title suggests, the exercise was meant to inject a colloquial flavour into the generally stern business of learning Latin and does so with a certain liveliness and charm.

Aelfric's account is a rarity; more numerous are documents describing Norman English education in courtesy. One of the earliest of these courtesy lessons, *The ABC of Aristotle*, is an alliterative catalogue of what not to do and shows just how many proscriptions could be packed into a short space. Its purpose was very direct: to encourage moderation in all things. True to the Aristotelian standard, the text enjoined the young page to know his place and to temper all activities.

The Babees Book sketches some of the specific duties of young gentlemanly attendants—or henchmen ("henxmen", as the manuscript calls them). They learned to carve and assist at table and to conduct themselves with mannerly grace. They served their lord in secular society much as altar boys or acolytes would assist the priest at the liturgy and movements of the Mass. After this preliminary training in courtesy, they could look forward to becoming Esquires. Some notable henchmen acquired even further distinctions. Thomas Howard became Duke of Norfolk; Thomas More rose to be Chancellor; Roger Ascham was enough of a courtier and scholar to serve in turn Princess Elizabeth as tutor and her Catholic half-sister Queen Mary as Latin Secretary. Sometimes these young gentlemen continued their studies at Oxford or Cambridge, or travelled on the Continent, taking lessons in Paris or Padua or Montpellier.

More universal, democratic, and numerous than the courtesy books were primers and hornbooks. The Prioress, one of the pilgrims in Chaucer's *Canterbury Tales*, gives us a glimpse of the first of these in describing the unfortunate "litel clergeon, seven yeer of age" who learns his alphabet and prayers:

This litel child, his litel book lernynge
As he sat in the scole at his prymer
(11.1706-7)

He was studying to be a cleric, a position that would require him to recite the Office and know the Psalms by heart. Although the child did not yet know his Latin, "for he was yong and tendre was of age", he learned hymns by rote and strove above all to praise Mary. Pre-Reformation primers usually contained the little Office of the Blessed Virgin, the beginnings of the four Gospels, the Athanasian and other Creeds, and prayers for Confession and Communion; post-Reformation primers deleted much of the Marian content. Offering preliminary religious instruction for every child attending a church school, the primer appeared in more than 180 editions between 1525 and 1560.

The hornbook, a smaller and less-sectarian tool, had an even wider distribution. It consisted of a single sheet, printed in either Black-letter (Gothic) or Roman type, pasted to a thin piece of wood in the shape of a paddle or batlet and covered with a sheet of transparent horn fixed by a narrow band of brass. Thus the content of the page, nearly always the Lord's Prayer and the alphabet, was protected from little soiled fingers. Nearly a century after the hornbook came into use another object of popular instruction was created: the battledore. It was a three-leaf cardboard lesson-book that contained a surprising variety of printed matter, including prayers, verses, and lists of vowels and consonants, often with some appealing wood-engravings. Its format was borrowed by monarchs in the Royal Primers they commissioned to promote literacy in the land.

The main purpose of the hornbook, and even of the later and more entertaining battledore, was to teach the child to read and thereby to pray, for the education of the young in Renaissance times was very strict. As Roger Ascham described grammar schools in *The Scolemaster* (1570), masters were often quicker to flog than to assist the student. Ascham himself held the uncommon view that education should inculcate "speciall pointes"—"trothe of Religion, honestie in living and right order in learning"—and believed the schoolhouse should be a "sanctuarie against feare". To him the child was an impressionable vessel:

For, the pure cleane witte of a sweete yong babe is like the newest wax, most hable to receive the best and fayrest printing: and like a new bright silver dishe never occupied, to receive and kepe cleane anie good thyng that is put into it. [1]

The grimly highminded Dissenters of New England were also aware of the receptiveness of children. Since many of the immigrant preachers had received a rigorous grammar-school and university education, they injected considerable severity into the lessons designed for the young. John Cotton's *Milk for Babes* offered spiritual nourishment in the form of a stern catechism. In contrast to the Tudors and Stuarts who commissioned Royal Primers

---

[1] *The Scholemaster*, ed. D.C. Whimster (London: Methuen, 1934), p. 25.

to promote literacy, the Dissenters eagerly seized on the primer as a forceful means of teaching doctrine. In its many variants, and over a long span of popularity, *The New England Primer* was lengthier than any of the Royal Primers; its catechism was supplemented by pictorial alphabets and imperative verses such as:

> *Have communion with few*
> *Be intimate with ONE*
> *Deal justly with all*
> *Speak evil of none.*

Rounding off the first section of this anthology is Johan Amos Comenius, Bishop of the Unity of Czech Brethren. A victim of repression and a continual wanderer because of his religion and nationality, he shines all the more remarkably as an enlightened innovator and ever-hopeful reformer. In his landmark text, *Orbis Sensualium Pictus* (1658), an attempt to improve and encourage the learning of Latin, the vernacular appears beside the parallel Latin text. The two columns describe a woodcut and its enumerated detail; the *Pictus* is thus

the first illustrated textbook. In addition to the encyclopaedic sweep of its lessons, the book shows the intelligence of a true pedagogue at work. Just as Aelfric realized that conversational exchanges helped in learning vocabulary, so Comenius affirms the value of the picture as an aid to understanding when he leads his pupils into a *Visible World; or, A Picture and Nomenclature of All the Chief Things That are in the World—* the 1659 English title of the *Pictus*.

This brief sketch of books written for children up to the late seventeenth century reveals the gradual widening of their young audience. All these books were meant to improve the child by enunciating religious doctrine, by laying down rules for righteous behaviour, or by passing on factual information. Though some efforts were made to accommodate lessons to the understanding of children, this literature was straightforward, dispassionate, and grave. It was not until well into the eighteenth century that books for children began to explore, and appeal openly to, their emotions.

ÆLFRIC (c. 955-c. 1020)
From the *Colloquy* (c. 1000)

The prominence given to the ploughman because he provides food underlines the solid common sense of the tenth-century monk who composed this Latin dialogue. The teacher Aelfric presents is stern, but kind as well; hence, while upholding his position of authority, he nevertheless accedes to the boys' requests that he use a vocabulary they can understand. Although a less scholarly contemporary of Aelfric wrote an interlinear gloss in Anglo-Saxon, the editors have provided a translation in modern English.

ÆLFRIC'S COLLOQUY

PUPILS. *Nos pueri rogamus te, magister, ut doceas nos loqui latialiter recte, quia idiote sumus et corrupte loquimur.*
We children ask you, oh master, that you will teach us to speak Latin correctly, because we are ignorant and speak brokenly.

MASTER. *Quid vultis loqui?*
What do you want to speak about?

PUPILS. *Quid curamus quid loquamur, nisi recta locutio sit et utilis, non anilis aut turpis.*

We are not concerned with what we talk about, except that it be correct and useful conversation, and not superstitious or foul.

MASTER. *Vultis flagellari in discendo?*

Are you willing to be flogged while learning?

PUPILS. *Carius est nobis flagellari pro doctrina quam nescire. Sed scimus te mansuetum esse et nolle inferre plagas nobis, nisi cogaris a nobis.*

It is dearer to us to be beaten for the sake of learning than not to know. But we know that you are gentle and unwilling to inflict blows on us unless we force you to.

MASTER. *Interrogo te, quid mihi loqueris? Quid habes operis?*

I ask you, what do you say to me? What sort of work do you do?

PUPIL 'MONK'. *Professus sum monachus, et psallam omni die septem sinaxes cum fratribus, et occupatus sum lectionibus et cantu, sed tamen vellem interim discere sermocinari latina langua.*

I am a professed monk, and I sing every day seven times with the brothers, and I am busy with reading and singing, but for all that I want in the meantime to learn to converse in the Latin language.

MASTER. *Quid sciunt isti tui socii?*

What do your comrades do?

PUPIL 'MONK'. *Alii sunt aratores, alii opiliones, quidam bubulci, quidam etiam venatores, alii piscatores, alii aucupes, quidam mercatores, quidam sutores, quidam salinatores, quidam pistores, coci.*

Some are ploughmen, others are shepherds, some oxherds, some again huntsmen, some fishermen, others fowlers, some merchants, some cobblers, some salters, some bakers.

MASTER. *Quid dicis tu, arator? Quomodo exerces opus tuum?*

What do you say, ploughman? How do you perform your work?

PUPIL 'PLOUGHMAN'. *O, mi domine, nimium laboro. Exeo diluculo minando boves ad campum, et iungo los ad aratrum; non est tam aspera hiems ut audeam latere domi pro timore domini mei, sed iunctis bobus, et confirmato vomere et cultro aratro, omni die debeo arare integrum agrum aut plus.*

Oh, my Lord, I work a great deal. I go out at dawn driving the oxen to the plain, and yoke them to the plough;

there is not so severe a winter that I would dare conceal myself at home for fear of my master, but having yoked the oxen and fastened the share and coulter to the plough, every day I must plough a whole acre or more. (The Pupils describe the occupations of the Shepherd, Oxherd, Huntsman, Fowler, Merchant, Shoemaker, Salter, Baker, and Cook.)

*   *   *

MASTER. *Quid dicis tu, sapiens? Que ars tibi videtur inter istas prior esse?*
What do you say, wise one? Which skill seems to you among all these to be of first importance?

PUPIL *Dico tibi, mihi videtur servitium Dei inter istas artes prima-*
'COUNSELLOR'. *tum tenere, sicut legitur in evangelio: "Primum querite regnum Dei et iustitiam eius, et haec omnia adicientur vobis."*
I tell you, it seems to me that the service of God among these skills holds the first place, just as it reads in the gospel: "Seek first the kingdom of God and his justice and all things will be added to you."

MASTER. *Et qualis tibi videtur inter artes seculares retinere primatum?*
And which among the secular crafts seems to you to hold the first place?

PUPIL *Agricultura, quia arator omnes pascit.*
'COUNSELLOR'. Agriculture, because the ploughman feeds everybody.

PUPIL *Ferrarius dicit: unde aratori vomer aut culter, qui nec stimu-*
'SMITH'. *lum habet nisi ex arte mea? Unde piscatori hamus, aut sutori subula sive sartori acus? Nonne ex meo opere?*
The blacksmith says: where does the ploughman get the ploughshare or coulter or even goad except through my skill? Where does the fisherman get his hook, or the cobbler his awl or the tailor his needle? Is it not from my work?

PUPIL *Consilarius respondit: Verum quidem dicis, sed omnibus nobis*
'COUNSELLOR'. *carius est hospitari apud te aratorem quam apud te, quia arator dat nobis panem et potum; tu, quid das nobis in officina tua nisi ferreas scintillas et sonitus tundentium malleorum et flantium follium?*
The Counsellor says: What you say is true, but it would be more esteemed by all of us to live near you, ploughman, than to live near to you, because the ploughman gives us bread and drink; you, what do you give us in your workshop except iron sparks and the noise of hammers beating and bellows blowing?

PUPIL
'CARPENTER'

Lignarius dicit: quis vestrum non utitur arte mea, cum domos et diversa vasa et naves omnibus fabrico?

The carpenter says: Which of you does not use my skill, when I make houses and different utensils and boats for everyone?

PUPIL
'SMITH'

Ferrarius respondit: O, lignare, cur sic loqueris, cum nec saltem unum foramen sine arte mea vales facere?

The blacksmith says: Oh, carpenter, why do you speak thus, when without my skill you could not pierce even one hole?

PUPIL
'COUNSELLOR'.

Consilarius dicit: O, socii et boni operarii, dissolvamus citius has contentiones, et sit pax et concordia inter vos, et prosit unusquisque alteri arte sua, et conveniamus semper apud aratorem, ubi victum nobis et pabula equis nostris habemus. Et hoc consilium do omnibus operariis, ut unusquisque artem suam diligenter exerceat, quia qui artem suam dimiserit, ipse dimittatur ab arte. Sive sis sacerdos, sive monachus, seu laicus, seu miles, exerce temet ipsum in hoc, et esto quod es; quia magnum dampnum et verecundia est homini nolle esse quod est et quod esse debet.

The counsellor says: Oh, comrades and good workmen, let us break up these arguments quickly, let peace and concord be between us, and let each one help the others by his skill, and let us always be in harmony with the ploughman from whom we have food for ourselves and fodder for our horses. And I give this counsel to all workmen, that each one perform his craft diligently, since the man who abandons his craft will be abandoned by his craft. Whoever you be, whether priest or monk, whether laymen or soldier, exercise yourself in this and be what you are; because it is a great injury and shame for a man not to want to be what he is and what he ought to be.

MASTER.

O, pueri, quomodo vobis placet ista locutio?

Oh, boys, how does this speech please you?

PUPIL.

Bene quidem placet nobis, sed valde profunde loqueris et ultra etatem nostram protrahis sermonem: sed loquere nobis uixta nostrum intellectum, ut possimus intelligere que loqueris.

It pleases us well, but you certainly talk profoundly and use discourse beyond our ability; but talk to us according to our perception, so that we can understand what you say.

MASTER.

Interrogo vos cur tam diligenter discitis?

I ask you, why are you learning so diligently?

PUPIL. *Quia nolumus esse sicut bruta animalia, que nihil sciunt, nisi herbam et aquam.*

Because we do not wish to be as stupid animals, who know nothing except grass and water.

MASTER. *Et quid vultis vos?*

And what do you want?

PUPIL. *Volumus esse sapientes.*

We wish to be prudent.

MASTER. *Qua sapientia? Vultis esse versipelles aut milleformes in mendaciis, astuti in loquelis, astuti, versuti, bene loquentes et male cogitantes, dulcibus verbis dediti, dolum intus alentes, sicut sepulchrum depicto mausoleo, intus plenum fetore?*

What sort of prudence? Do you want to be sly or cunning in lies, adroit in speech, clever, wily, speaking well and thinking evil, given to agreeable words, feeding anguish within, just like a sepulchre, painted like a splendid monument, and full of a stink inside?

PUPIL. *Nolumus sic esse sapientes, quia non est sapiens, qui simulatione semet ipsum decipit.*

We do not want to be clever in that way, because he is not clever who deceives himself with false show.

MASTER. *Sed quomodo vultis?*

But how do you want to be?

PUPIL. *Volumus esse simplices sine hipochrisi, et sapientes ut declinemus a malo et faciamus bona. Adhunc tamen profundius nobiscum disputas, quam etas nostra capere possit; sed loquere nobis nostro more, non tam profunde.*

We want to be upright without hypocrisy, and wise so that we avoid evil and do good. However, you are still debating with us more deeply than our years can take; therefore, speak to us in our own way, not so deeply.

MASTER. *Et ego faciam sicut rogatis. Tu, puer, quid fecisti hodie?*

And I will do as you ask. You, boy, what did you do today?

PUPIL. *Multas res feci. Hac nocte, quando signum audivi, surrexi de lectulo et exiui ad ecclesiam, et cantavi nocturnam cum fratribus; deinde cantavimus de omnibus sanctis et matutinales laudes; post haec primam et VII psalmos cum letaniis et primam missam; deinde tertiam, et fecimus missam de die; post haec cantavimus sextam, et manducavimus et bibimus et dormivimus, et iterum surreximus et cantavimus nonam; et modo sumus hic coram te, parati audire quid nobis dixeris.*

I did many things. Last night, when I heard the bell, I

got up from bed and went to church, and sang matins with the brothers; then we sang of all the holy ones and the morning praises; after this the six o'clock service and the seven psalms with the litanies and the first mass; then the nine o'clock service, and we celebrated the mass of the day; after this we sang the noon service, and ate and drank and slept, and we got up a second time and sang the three o'clock service; and now we are here in your presence, ready to hear what you will say to us.

*   *   *

MASTER.   *O, probi pueri et venusti mathites, vos hortatur vester eruditor ut pareatis divinis disciplinis et observetis vosmet eleganter ubique locorum. Inceditis morigerate cum auscultaveritis ecclesie campanas, et ingredimini in orationem, et inclinate suppliciter ad almas aras, et state disciplinabiliter, et concinite unanimiter, et intervenite pro vestris erratibus, et egredimini sine scurrilitate in claustrum vel in gimnasium.*

O, good boys and charming students, your teacher encourages you to obey the divine commandments and to conduct yourselves with taste in every situation. Proceed in a reverent fashion when you hear the church bells, and enter in prayer, and bow humbly towards the dear altars, and stand as you have been instructed, and sing all together, and pray for your wrongdoings and go out either into the cloister or school without any buffoonery.

ANONYMOUS
The ABC of Aristotle (c. 1430)

In some manuscripts this alliterative alphabet of courtesy bears the alternate title "Lerne or be Lewde" (ignorant). Despite' the claim that it is the work of a child (l. 11), this punctilious catalogue of traits to avoid was obviously penned by a demanding though practical adult. The abecedary is secular, yet its injunctions promoting conservative social conduct definitely comply with Christian teaching. Although emphasis on the ascetic life of the spirit is understandably absent, this lesson does uphold the Aristotelian mean of good sense and temperance.

In copying the British Museum manuscript, the editors have replaced the thorn (þ) with the letters "th".

THE ABC OF ARISTOTLE

Who-so wilneth to be wijs°, & worship desirith,   °wise
Lerne he oo° lettir, & looke on anothir   °one
Of the .a. b. c. of aristotil: argue not agen that:
4 It is councel for right manye clerkis & knyghtis a
    thousand,
And eek it myghte ameende° a man ful ofte   °amend
For to leerne lore of oo lettir, & his lijf save;
8 For to myche of ony thing was nevere holsum.
Reede ofte on this rolle, & rewle° thou ther aftir;   °rule
Who-so be greved° in his goost°, governe him   °grieved °ghost
    bettir;
Blame he not the barn° that this .a. b. c. made,   °bairn, child
12 But wite° he his wickid will & his werk aftir;   °blame
It schal nevere greve a good man though the gilti
    be meendid°.   °mended
Now herkeneth & heerith how y bigynne.

A to amerose°, to avnterose°, ne argue not to myche.   °amorous °adventurous
B to bolde, ne to bisi, ne boorde° not to large.   °babble
C to curteis, to cruel, ne care not to sore°.   °sorely
D to dul, ne to dreedful, ne drinke not to ofte.
E to elenge°, ne to excellent°, ne to eernesful° neither.   °melancholy °haughty °earnest
F to fers°, ne to famuler, but freendli of cheer.   °fierce
G to glad, ne to gloriose, & gelosie thou hate.
H to hasti, ne to hardi, ne to hevy in thine herte.
I to iettynge°, ne to iangeline°, ne iape° not to ofte.   °ostentatious °chattering °joke
K to kinde, ne to kepynge, & be waar° of knave tacchis°.   °wary °tricks
L to looth for to leene, ne to liberal of goodis.
M to medelus°, ne to myrie, but as mesure wole it meeve   °meddling
N to noiose°, ne to nyce, ne use to new iettis°.   °annoyed °devices
O to orped°, ne to overthwart°, & ooth° thou hate.   °overbold °obstinate °oaths
P to presing°, ne to prevy with princis ne with dukis;   °praising
Q to queynte, ne to quarelose, but queeme° well   °please
    youre sovereyns.
R to riotus, to reveling, ne rage not to rudeli.
S to straunge, ne to stirynge, ne straungeli to stare.
T to toilose°, ne to talewijs°, for temperaunce is beest.   °toiling °tale-bearing
V to venemose, ne to veniable°, & voide al vilonye.   °envious
W to wielde°, ne to wrathful, neither waaste, ne waade   °wild
    not to depe
For a mesurable meene° is evere the beste of alle.   °mean

ANONYMOUS
From *The Babees Book, or a 'Lytyl Reporte'* *of How Young People Should Behave* (c. 1475)

The author frequently calls upon his muse, "o lady myn, Facecia" (1. 50, from the Latin *facetia*), to guide his pen as he writes this fundamental lesson in courteous deportment for privileged children; *facetia* literally means "wit". The invocation of such a muse alludes to *Liber Faceti (The Book of the Polite Man)*, a thirteenth-century work by John Garland, of which *The Babees Book* purports to be a translation. Conveyed in rhyme-royal stanzas, these precepts about the etiquette of standing, sitting, and eating are concise and unambiguous. So too are the injunctions against joking at table, scratching one's body, and picking one's nose, teeth, or nails. The marginal paraphrase is taken from F.J. Furnivall's edition for the Early English Text Society (1868).

From THE BABEES BOOK

But, O yonge Babees, whome bloode Royalle
16 Withe grace, feture, and hyhe habylite°   °ability
Hathe enourmyd°, on yow ys that i calle   °endowed
To knowe this Book; for it were grete pyte°,   °pity
Syn that in yow ys sette sovereyne beaute,
20 But yf vertue and nurture were withe alle;
To yow therfore I speke in specyalle,

Young Babies, adorned with grace, I call on you to know this book (for nurture should accompany beauty),

And noughte to hem of elde that bene experte
in gouvernaunce, nurture, and honeste.
24 For what nedys to yeve° helle peynes smerte,   °give
Ioye vnto hevene, or water vnto the see,
Heete to the fyre that kan nat but hoote be?
It nedys nouhte: therfore, O Babees yynge°,   °young
28 My Book only is made for youre lernynge.

and not on aged men expert therein. Why add pain to hell, water to the sea, or heat to fire? Babies, my book is for you only,

    *   *   *

A, Bele° Babees, herkne now to my lore!   °beautiful
Whenne yee entre into your lordis place,
Say first, "god spede;" And alle that ben by-
   fore
60 Yow in this stede, salue° withe humble Face;   °greet
Stert nat Rudely; komme Inne an esy pace;
Holde vp youre heede, and knele but on oone
   kne
To youre sovereyne or lorde, whedir he be.

Fair Babies, when you enter your lord's place, say "God speed", and salute all there. Kneel on one knee to your lord.

64 And yf they speke withe you at youre komynge,
Withe stable° Eye loke vpone theym Rihte,   °steady
To theyre tales and yeve yee goode herynge
Whils they haue seyde; loke eke withe your
   myhte

If any speak to you, look straight at them, and listen well till they have finished;

68 Yee Iangle° nouht*e*, also caste nouht*e* your
      syht*e*   °chatter

Aboute the hovs, but take to theym entent
With*e* blyth*e* vysage, and spiryt diligent.

do not chatter
or let your
eyes wander
about the house.

*   *   *

Take eke noo seete, but to stonde be yee preste;
Whils forto sytte ye haue in komau*n*dement,
80 Youre heede, youre hande, y*ou*r feet, holde yee
      in reste;
Nor thurh*e* clowyng yo*ur* flesshe loke yee nat
      Rent;
Lene to no poste whils that ye stande present
Before yo*ur* lorde, nor handyll*e* ye no thyng
84 Als for that tyme vnto the hovs touching.

Stand till you are
told to sit: keep
your head, hands,
and feet quiet:

don't scratch
yourself,

or lean against
a post,
or handle
anything near.

*   *   *

92 Yiff that youre lorde also yee se drynkynge,
Looke that ye be in riht*e* stable sylence
With*e*-oute lowde lauht*e*re or Iangelynge,
Rovnynge°, Iapynge, or other Insolence.   °whispering
96 Yiff he komau*n*de also in his presence
Yow forto sytte, fulfill*e* his wylle belyve°,   °immediately
And for youre seete, looke nat with*e* other
      stryv*e*,

Be silent while
your lord drinks
not laughing,
whispering, or
joking.

If he tells you to
sit down, do
so at once.

*   *   *

Yif that youre lorde his owne coppe lyste com-°   °is pleased
      mende   to offer
121 To yow to drynke, ryse vp wha*n*ne yee it take,
And resseyve° it goodly with*e* booth*e* youre   °receive
      hende;
Of yt also to noone other profre ye make,
124 But vnto him that brouht*e* yt yee hit take
Whe*n*ne yee haue done, for yt in no kyn wyse
Auhte° comvne be, as techis vs the wyse.   °should be
                                               used commonly

If your lord
offers you his
cup, rise up,
take it with
both hands,

offer it to
no one else
but give it
back to him
that brought
it.

Now must I telle in shorte, for I muste so,
128 Youre observau*n*ce that ye shall*e* done at none°; °noon
Whe*n*ne that ye se youre lorde to mete shall*e*
      goo,
Be redy to fecche him water sone,
Som*m*e helle° water; su*m*me holde to° he hath*e*   °clear °until
      done
132 The cloth*e* to him, And from him yee nat pace
Whils he be sette, and haue herde sayde the
      grace.

At noon, when
your lord
is ready
for dinner,

fetch him some
clean water,
hold the
towel for him
till he has
finished, and
don't leave till
grace is said.

*   *   *

Kutte with*e* y*our* knyf y*our* brede, and breke
    yt nouht*e;*
A clene Trenchour° byfore yow eke ye lay,   °server
And when*ne* y*our* potage to yow shall*e* be
    brought*e,*
144 Take yow sponys, and soupe by no way,
And in youre dysshe leve nat y*our* spone, I
    pray,
Nor on the borde lenynge be yee nat sene,
But from embrowyng° the cloth*e* yee kepe clene. °soiling

Cut your bread, don't break it. Lay a clean trencher before you, and eat your broth with a spoon, don't sup it up. Don't leave your spoon in your dish. Don't lean on the table, or dirty the cloth.

Oute ou*er*e youre dysshe y*our* heede yee nat
    hynge,
149 And with*e* fulle mouth*e* drynke in no wyse;
Youre nose, y*our* teeth*e,* y*our* naylles, from
    pykynge,
Kepe At your mete, for so techis° the wyse.   °teach
152 Eke° or ye take in youre mouthe, yow avyse,   °also
So mekyl° mete but that yee riht*e* well*e* mowe   °much
Answere, And speke, when*ne* men speke to
    yow.

Don't hang your head over your dish, or eat with a full mouth, or pick your nose, teeth, and nails, or stuff your mouth so that you can't speak,

Whan*ne* ye shall*e* drynke, y*our* mouthe clence°   °clean
    with*e* A cloth*e;*
156 Youre handes eke that they in no manere
Imbrowe the cuppe, for than*ne* shull*e* noon*e* be
    loth*e*
With*e* yow to drynke that ben with*e* yow yfere.
The salte also touche nat in his salere°   °cellar
160 With*e* nokyns° mete, but lay it honestly   °any
On youre Trenchoure, for that is curtesy.

Wipe your mouth when you drink, and don't dirty the cup with your hands. Don't dip your meat in the salt-cellar,

Youre knyf with*e* mete to y*our* mouthe nat bere,
And in youre hande nor holde*n* yee yt no way,
164 Eke yf to yow be brought*e* goode metys sere°,   °diverse
Luke curteysly of ylke° mete yee assay,   °each
And yf y*our* dysshe with*e* mete be tane away
And better brought*e,* curtesye wole certeyne°   °demand
168 Yee late yt passe and calle it nat ageyne.

or put your knife in your mouth. Taste every dish that's brought to you, and when once your plate is taken away, don't ask for it again.

*   *   *

Whan*ne* that so ys that ende shall*e* kome of
    mete,
Youre knyffes clene, where they ouht*e* to be,
192 Luke yee putte vp*pe,* and holde eke yee y*our*
    seete
Whils yee hau*e* wasshe, for so wole honeste.

When the meal is over, clean your knives, and put them in their places: keep your seats till you've washed;

Whenne yee haue done, looke thanne goodly
that yee
Withe-oute lauhtere, Iapynge, or boystous°
worde,   °boisterous

196 Ryse vppe, and goo vnto youre lordis borde,

then rise up without laughing or joking, and go to your lord's table.

And stonde yee there, and passe yee him nat
fro
Whils grace ys sayde and brouhte vnto an ende,
Thanne somme of yow for water owe° to goo,   °ought
200 Somme holde the clothe, somme poure vppon
his hende.
Other service thanne this I myhte comende
To yow to done, but, for the tyme is shorte,
I putte theym nouhte in this lytyl Reporte,

Stand there till grace is said

Then some of you go for water, some hold the towel, some pour water over his hands. Other things I shall not put in this little report.

*   *   *

And, swete children, for whos love now I write,
212 I yow beseche withe verrey lovande° herte,   °loving
To knowe this book that yee sette your delyte;
And myhtefulle god, that suffred peynes smerte,
In curtesye he make yow so experte,
216 That thurhe° your nurture and youre
governaunce   °through
In lastynge blysse yee mowe° your self
auaunce!   °may

Sweet children, I beseech you know this book, and may God make you so expert therein that you may attain endless bliss.

Leather-covered hornbook
stamped with the effigy
of Charles II on horseback

Uncovered oaken hornbook
of the later period

THE HORNBOOK

Whether handwritten or printed from type, this little lesson book is known from manuscript evidence to have existed from the fourteenth century. The parchment or paper lesson-sheet pasted onto the board was protected by a leaf of horn. (This material was made from the horns of sheep and goats; after having been softened and then boiled in water, they yielded the true horn that could be pressed and cut into sheets.)

The covering was fixed to the small board by means of a brass or latten border held by minute tacks with raised heads; these slightly raised tacks protected the horn itself from scratches when the ''book'' was laid face down. In the earliest examples the alphabet was preceded by the Cross; hence, the format was called the Criss-Cross row. In later Puritan examples the Cross was omitted.

Early uncovered hornbook in black letter

Outside face of *Rosewarne's Royal Battledore* (c. 1800).
The inside face carried an alphabet, verses, and a syllabarium.

THE BATTLEDORE

The racquet in the game of battle-dore and shuttlecock, a forerunner of badminton, was modelled on the washerwoman's board or paddle ("batyldoure"). Just as the shuttle-cock evolved into a very light object, usually a cork stuck with feathers, so the battledore also became lighter; early ones consisted of parchment, inscribed with lessons, stretched over a wooden frame. A still lighter battledore, made of stiff paper, dis-played a pictorial alphabet and prayers on both sides. Since it was folded, this battledore held more in-formation than the hornbook sheet. The battledore was popular well into the nineteenth century, and devel-oped an increasingly sophisticated format.

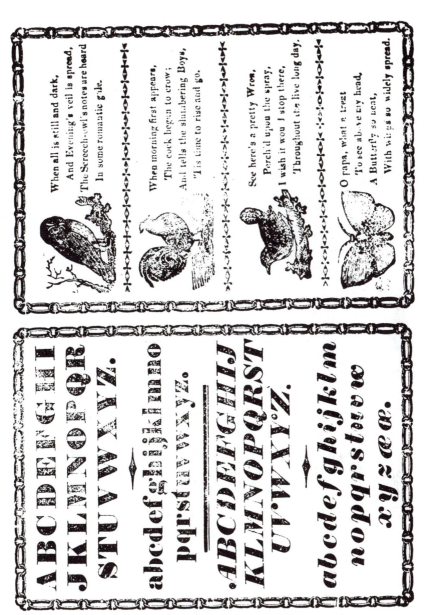

Inside face of Bloomer's *New Battledore*, Birmingham.

Go now to bed | Tim put the fox
For you are fed. | In to the box.
If Jem can run. | We had a cow,
He has a bun. | Cat, cur, and sow.
Now my new pen | You all may go
Is fit for Ben. | To see the doe.

THIS IS THE CAT,
That kill'd the Rat, that eat
the Malt, that lay in the House
that Jack built.

THIS IS THE ARK,
That did swim o'er the flood,
Till the dove did em-bark,
With the leaf or the bud.

A B C D E
F G H I J K
L M N O P
Q R S T U V
W X Y Z &

a b c d e f g
h i j k l m n
o p q r s t u
v w x y z &

A B
C D E
F G H
I J K
L M N
O P Q
R S T
U V W
X Y Z

a b c d
e f g h
i j k l
m n o p
q r s t
u v w x
y z &
1 2 3 4
5 6 7 8
9 0

Inside face of a nineteenth-century battledledore

had can had fat rag mad
hum mug den met him rid
mop who run gun dad lad
rod pop sop tip mut con tin

band	glad	have	sash	loss	sand
bank	milk	sing	mist	ment	fish
jump	plum	spun	pond	fond	sung
maid	nail	back	calm	baze	bull
earth	pearl	death	fierce	green	
stings	perch	wheat	young	guild	
bread	thread	touch	build	strong	
queen	yatch	range	quash	naugh	
cetch	vamp	inch	vague	waive	
dance	lance	learnt	plough	quake	

THE LORD'S PRAYER.

Our Father which art in heaven, hallowed be thy name; thy kingdom come; thy will be done on earth as it is in heaven, give us this day our daily bread; and forgive us our trespasses, as we forgive them that trespass against us. And lead us not into temptation, but deliver us from evil; for thine is the kingdom, the power, and the glory, for ever and ever, Amen.

GRACE BEFORE MEAT.

Give me a grateful heart O Lord, to remember that the provisions now set before me comes from thy bountiful goodness, and make me truly thankful.

Inside face of *Leighton's New Battledore*, Nottingham.

The Vulture is a very cruel, unclean, and indolent bird, and though unknown in England, is common in many parts of Europe.

The pig is a sloathful animal, and delights to wallow in its own mire.

THE GOOD BOY.

If you your task have learned true,
My pretty horse shall carry you
Unto the fair, so neat, so gay:
But naughty boys at home shall stay.

Then be for ever good and kind,
And walk betimes in wisdom's way,
For they will ne'er true pleasure find,
Who do not learn as well as play.

CHAIRS TO MEND.

This man may often be heard in the streets, crying, "Chairs to mend;" and now he seems to have got a job, at which his wife looks very well pleased.

Some children are apt to mimic the cries of these people, but that is very naughty, and none but a bad child will do so.

The man has seated himself on the ground, in the mode of Turkey, which of all countries is one of the most unfriendly to the chair maker and the hatter.

PRICE ONE PENNY.

Art and awl
Bat by ball
Can cat cry
Do dig dry
Eel egg eye
Fan for fly
Guy gun got
Her hat hot
Joe Jem Jay
Kit ken key
Lay lap lug
Me met mug
No not Nod
On old Odd
Pa put pin
Quit is Quin
Red rat run
Sam saw sun
Tom to turn
Ure use urn
Viz vie van
Wit we wan
Xen ox vex
Yet you yex
Zone of zest
& zeal is best

Outside face of an early-nineteenth-century battledore.

Ah I am in
If it is so
An ox is up
O ox go on
Go on by me
He is to go
I am by it

Am I to it
Oh he is up
Ah so am I
No ox is in
He or I go
We do as he
Of it to it
Ah wo to me

Ox go up
Go on ox
I am in
Is he up
Do go on
I am by
It is so

So it is
Be it so
Go by me
We go on
If ye go
Go ye in
Go to it
Go by us

A B C D E F G H
I J K L M N O
P Q R S T U
V W X Y Z

a b c d e f g h i j k
l m n o p q r s t
u v w x y z

1 2 3 4 5 6 7 8 9 0

This   thus
that   then
them   than
with   hath
moth   thin
when   rich
bush   rash
chat   lamb
comb   limb
dumb   calf
calm   talk
walk   meet
wrap   long
goat   work
meat   yolk

Inside face of *The Infant's Battledore; For a Good Child at School.*

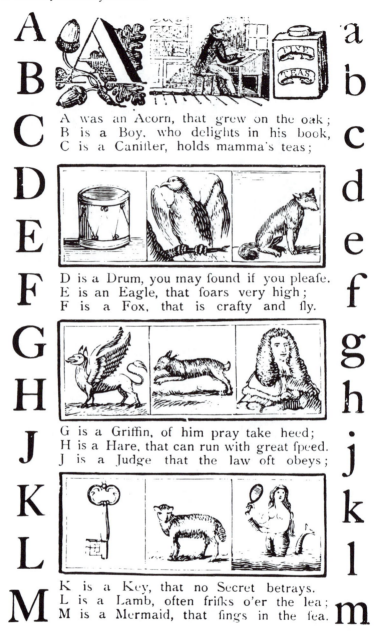

A was an Acorn, that grew on the oak;
B is a Boy, who delights in his book,
C is a Caniſter, holds mamma's teas;

D is a Drum, you may found if you pleaſe.
E is an Eagle, that ſoars very high;
F is a Fox, that is crafty and ſly.

G is a Griffin, of him pray take heed;
H is a Hare, that can run with great ſpeed.
J is a Judge that the law oft obeys;

K is a Key, that no Secret betrays.
L is a Lamb, often friſks o'er the lea;
M is a Mermaid, that ſings in the ſea.

Rusher's *English Spelling Book* (c. 1800)
relied on the time-proven battledore format.

N O P Q R S T V W X Y Z

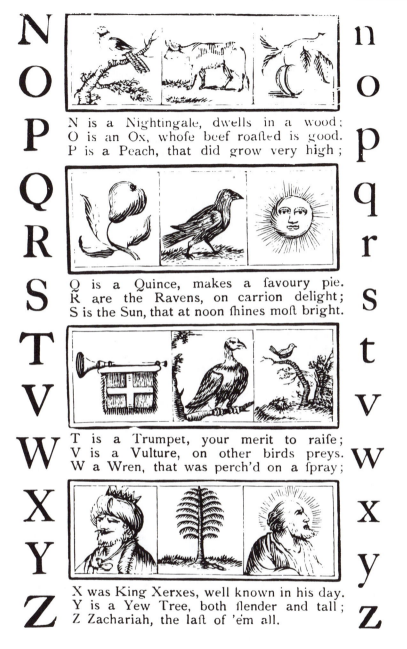

N is a Nightingale, dwells in a wood;
O is an Ox, whofe beef roafted is good.
P is a Peach, that did grow very high;

Q is a Quince, makes a favoury pie.
R are the Ravens, on carrion delight;
S is the Sun, that at noon fhines moft bright.

T is a Trumpet, your merit to raife;
V is a Vulture, on other birds preys.
W a Wren, that was perch'd on a fpray;

X was King Xerxes, well known in his day.
Y is a Yew Tree, both flender and tall;
Z Zachariah, the laft of 'em all.

n o p q r s t v w x y z

JOHN COTTON (1584-1652)

Milk for Babes, Drawn Out of the Breasts of Both Testaments. Chiefly for the spiritual nourishment of Boston babes in either England: but may be of like use for any children (1646)

John Cotton, the Vicar of Boston, Lincoln-shire, was one of many immigrant 'Rever-end Teachers', like Cotton Mather and Thomas Shepard, who wrote their own cat-echisms. A prolific writer, he composed *An Abstract of the Lawes of New England* (1641) and various expositions of the Books of Canticles, Ecclesiastes and Revelation; he also sought to bring about an accommoda-tion of Presbyterian and Congregationalist views in early Puritan New England. In the straightforward and strict religious instruc-tion of *Milk for Babes*, Cotton was both a stern legalist and a precise teacher. The complete title gives the only metaphorical description in the whole work. This Calvin-ist catechism insists unequivocally on the view of man as a sinning mortal whose hope of salvation lies both in obeying the Decalogue and the Gospels and in receiv-ing the two sacraments.

MILK FOR BABES

Q. *What hath God done for you?*

A. God hath made me, He keepeth me, and He can save me.

Q. *Who is God?*

A. God is a Spirit of himself and for himself.

Q. *How many Gods be there?*

A. There is but one God in three Persons, the Father, the Sonne, and the Holy Ghost.

Q. *How did God make you?*

A. In my first Parents, holy and righteous.

Q. *Are you then born holy and righteous?*

A. No, my first father sinned and I in him.

Q. *Are you then born a sinner?*

A. I was conceived in sinne, and born in iniquity.

Q. *What is your birth-sinne?*

A. Adams sinne imputed to me, and a corrupt Nature dwelling in me.

Q. *What is your corrupt Nature?*

A. My corrupt nature is empty of Grace, bent unto sinne, and only unto sinne, and that continually.

Q. *What is sinne?*

A. Sinne is the transgression of the Law.

Q. *How many commandments of the Law be there?*

A. Ten.

Q. *What is the first Commandement?*

A. Thou shalt have no other Gods but me.

Q. *What is the meaning of the commandement?*

A. That we should worship the only true God, and no other beside him.

Q. *What is the 2d. Commandement?*

A. Thou shalt not make to thy self any graven image, etc.

Q. *What is the meaning of the Commandement?*

A. That we should worship the true God with true worship: such as God hath ordained, not such as man hath invented.

Q. *What is the third commandement?*

A. Thou shalt not take the Name of the Lord thy God in vain, etc.

Q. *What is here meant by the Name of God?*

A. God himself and the good things of God, whereby he is known, as a man by his name; as his Attributes, worship, word and works.

Q. *What is it not to take his Name in vain?*

A. To make use of God, and the good things of God, to his glory, and our good; not vainly, not unreverently, not unprofitably.

Q. *What is the fourth Commandement?*

A. Remember that thou keep holy the Sabbath day, etc.

Q. *What is the meaning of the Commandement?*

A. That we should rest from labor and much more from play on the Lords day, that we may draw nigh to God in holy duties.

Q. *What is the fifth Commandement?*

A. Honour thy Father, and thy mother, that thy dayes may be long in the land, which the Lord thy God giveth thee.

Q. *Who are here meant by Father and Mother?*

A. All our superiours, whether in Family, School, Church, and Commonwealth.

Q. *What is the honour due to them?*

A. Reverence, obedience, and (when I am able) Recompence.

Q. *What is the Sixth Commandement?*

A. Thou shalt do no murder.

Q. *What is the meaning of this Commandement?*

A. That we should not shorten the life, or health of our selves or others, but preserve both.

Q. *What is the seventh Commandement?*

A. Thou shalt not commit Adultery.

Q. *What is the sinne here forbidden?*

A. To defile ourselves or others with unclean lusts.

Q. *What is the duty here commanded?*

A. Chastity, to possesse ourselves in holinesse and honour.

Q. *What is the eighth commandement?*

A. Thou shalt not steal.

Q. *What is the stealth here forbidden?*

A. To take away another mans goods, without his leave: or to spend our own without benefit to ourselves or others.

Q. *What is the duty here commanded?*

A. To get our goods honestly, to keep them safely, and to spend them thriftily.

Q. *What is the ninth Commandement?*

A. Thou shalt not bear false witnesse against thy Neighbour.

Q. *What is the sinne here forbidden?*

A. To lye falsly, to think or speak untruly of our selves, or others.

Q. *What is the duty here required?*

A. Truth and faithfulnesse.

Q. *What is the tenth Commandement?*

A. Thou shalt not covet, etc.

Q. *What is the coveting here forbidden?*

A. Lust after the things of other men: and want of contentment with our own.

Q. *Whether have you kept all these Commandements?*

A. No, I and all men are sinners.

Q. *What is the wages of sin?*

A. Death and damnation.

Q. *How look you then to be saved?*

A. Onely by Jesus Christ.

Q. *Who is Jesus Christ?*

A. The eternall Son of God, who for our sakes became man, that he might redeem and save us.

Q. *How doth Christ redeem and save us?*

A. By his righteous life, and bitter death, and glorious resurrection, to life again.

Q. *How do we come to have part and fellowship with Christ, in his Death And Resurrection?*

A. By the power of his Word and Spirit, which bring us to Christ, and keep us in him.

Q. *What is his Word?*

A. The Holy Scriptures of the Prophets and Apostles, the Old and New Testament, Law and Gospell.

Q. *How doth the Ministery of the Law bring you towards Christ?*

A. By bringing me to know my sinne, and the wrath of God against me for it.

Q. *What are you thereby the nearer to Christ?*

A. So I come to feel my cursed estate, and need of a Saviour.

Q. *How doth the Ministery of the Gospell help you in this cursed Estate?*

A. By humbling me yet more, and then raising me up out of the Estate.

Q. *How doth the ministery of the Gospell humble you more?*

A. By revealing the grace of the Lord Jesus, in dying to save sinners: and yet convincing me of my sinne, in not believing on him, and of mine utter insufficiency, to come to him; And so I feele my selfe utterly lost.

Q. *How then doth the Ministery of the Gospell raise you up out of this lost estate to come unto Christ?*

A. By teaching me the value and the vertue of the death of Christ, and the riches of his grace to lost sinners: By revealing the promise of grace to such, and by ministring the Spirit of grace, to apply Christ, and his promise of grace unto my selfe, and to keepe me in him.

Q. *How doth the spirit of Christ apply Christ, and his promise of grace unto you, and keepe you in him?*

A. By begetting in me faith to receive him: Prayer to call upon him: Repentance to mourne after him: and new obedience to serve him.

Q. *What is Faith?*

A. Faith is a grace of the spirit; whereby I deny my selfe: and believe on Christ for righteousnesse and salvation.

Q. *What is Prayer?*

A. It is calling upon God, in the Name of Christ, by the helpe of the Holy Ghost, according to the will of God.

Q. *What is Repentance?*

A. Repentance is a grace of the spirit, whereby I loath my sinnes, and my selfe for them, and confesse them before the Lord, and mourne after Christ for the pardon of them, and for grace to serve him in newnesse of life.

Q. *What is newnesse of life or new obedience?*

A. Newnesse of life is a grace of the spirit, whereby I forsake my former lusts, and vaine company, and walk before the Lord in the light of his word, and in the Communion of his Saints.

Q. *What is the communion of Saints?*

A. It is the fellowship of the Church in the blessings of the Covenant of grace, and the seales thereof.

Q. *What is the Church?*

A. It is a Congregation of Saints joyned together in the bond of the Covenant, to worship the Lord, and to edify one another, in all his Holy Ordinances.

Q. *What is the bond of the Covenant, in which the Church is joyned together?*

A. It is the profession of that Covenant, which God hath made with his faithfull people, to be a God unto them and to their seede.

Q. *What doth the Lord binde his people to in this Covenant?*

A. To give up themselves and their seede first to the Lord to be his people, and then to the Elders and Brethren of the Church, to set forward the worship of God and their mutuall edifycation.

Q. *How do they give up themselves and their seed to the Lord?*

A. By receiving through faith, the Lord, & his Covenant, to themselves, and to their seed, And accordingly walking themselves, and trayning up their Children in the wayes of his Covenant.

Q. *How do they give up themselves and their seed to the Elders and Brethren of the Church?*

A. By confession of their sinnes and profession of their faith, and of their subjection to the Gospell of Christ. And so they and their seede are received into the fellowship of the Church, and seales thereof.

Q. *What are the seales of the Covenant now in the dayes of the Gospel?*

A. Baptisme and the Lords Supper.

Q. *What is done for you in Baptism?*

A. In baptisme, the washing with water is a signe and seale of my washing with the blood and spirit of Christ, and thereby of my ingrafting into Christ: of the pardon and clensing of my sinnes: of my rising up out of Affliction: and also of my resurrection from the dead at the last day.

Q. *What is done for you in the Lords Supper?*

A. In the Lords Supper the receiving of the bread broken and the wine powred out, is a signe and a seal of my receiving the Communion of the body of Christ broken for me, and of his bloud shed for me. And thereby of my growth in Christ, of the pardon and healing of my sinnes: of the fellowship of his spirit: of my strengthening and quickning in Grace: and of my sitting together with Christ on his throne of glory at the last judgement.

Q. *What is the resurrection from the dead, which was sealed up to you in Baptisme?*

A. When Christ shall come to his last judgement, all that are in the graves shall arise again, both the just and unjust.

Q. *What is the last judgement, which is sealed up to you in the Lords Supper?*

A. At the last day we shall all appear before the judgement seat of Christ, to give an accompt of our works, and to receive our reward according to them.

Q. *What is the reward that shall then be given?*

A. The righteous shall go into life eternal, and the wicked shall be cast into everlasting fire with the Devill and his angels.

From *The New England Primer* (fl.1683-1830)

The *Primer* appeared in hundreds of editions, with many variants and additions, over its long span of popularity. Encased in a cover of thin sheets of oak spread with coloured paper, the book was literally read to pieces by its young owners. The earliest extant copy is dated 1727, but records indicate that it was printed as early as the 1680s. One of the first compilers of *The New England Primer* was the Boston book merchant Benjamin Harris. Formerly an enterprising London publisher, Harris had already printed *The Protestant Tutor* in England and had been pilloried in 1681 for issuing *The Protestant Petition. The New England Primer* was the staple lesson book for most young colonists and early Americans. It usually contained the alphabet and a syllabarium; prayers and promises to be memorized by all dutiful children; the antipapist testament of John Rogers, who was the first Smithfield martyr; a rhymed pictorial alphabet, which often summarized Bible history; and a Puritan catechism.

THE DUTIFUL CHILD'S PROMISES

I will fear God and honour the King.
I will honour my Father and Mother.
I will obey my Superiours.
I will submit to my Elders.
I will love my Friends.
I will hate no Man.
I will forgive my Enemies, and pray to God for them.
I will as much as in me lies, keep all God's holy Commandments.
I will learn my Catechism.
I will keep the Lord's Day Holy.
I will Reverence God's Sanctuary.

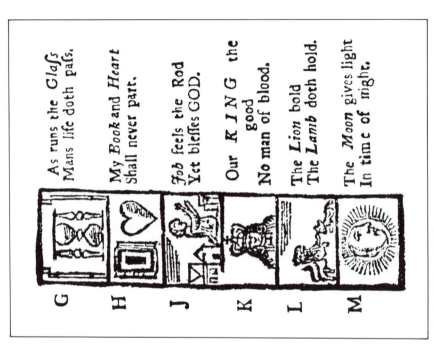

In *Adam's* Fall
We Sinned all.

Thy Life to Mend
This *Book* Attend.

The *Cat* doth play
And after flay.

A *Dog* will bite
A Thief at night.

An *Eagles* flight
Is out of fight.

The Idle *Fool*
Is whipt at School.

As runs the *Glaſs*
Mans life doth paſs.

My *Book* and *Heart*
Shall never part.

Job feels the Rod
Yet bleſſes GOD.

Our *K I N G* the
good
No man of blood.

The *Lion* bold
The *Lamb* doth hold.

The *Moon* gives light
In time of night.

Rhymed alphabet from *The New England Primer* (1727)

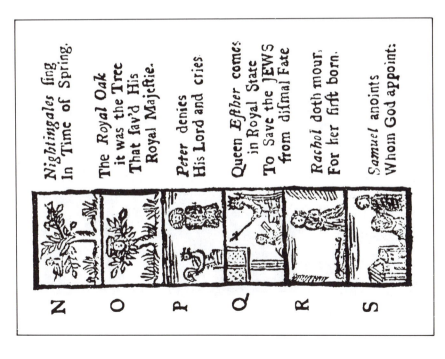

T — Time cuts down all
Both great and small.

U — Uriah's beauteous Wife
Made *David* seek his
Life.

W — Whales in the Sea
God's Voice obey.

X — Xerxes the great did
die,
And so must you & I.

Y — Youth forward slips
Death soonest nips.

Z — Zacheus he
Did climb the Tree
His Lord to see.

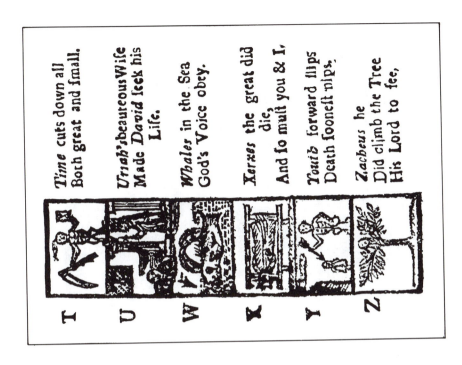

N — Nightingales sing
In Time of Spring.

O — The *Royal Oak*
it was the Tree
That sav'd His
Royal Majestie.

P — Peter denies
His Lord and cries.

Q — Queen *Esther* comes
in Royal State
To Save the JEWS
from dismal Fate.

R — Rachel doth mour,
For her first born.

S — Samuel anoints
Whom God appoint:

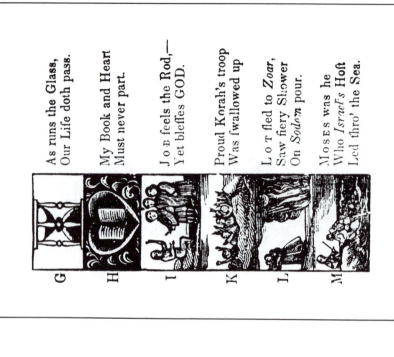

In ADAM's Fall
We finned all.

Heaven to find,
The Bible Mind.

Christ crucify'd
For finners dy'd.

The Deluge drown'd
The Earth around.

ELIJAH hid
By Ravens fed.

The judgment made
FELIX afraid.

As runs the Glass,
Our Life doth pass.

My Book and Heart
Must never part.

JOB feels the Rod,—
Yet bleffes GOD.

Proud Korah's troop
Was fwallowed up

LOT fled to Zoar,
Saw fiery Shower
On Sodom pour.

MOSES was he
Who Israel's Hoft
Led thro' the Sea.

Rhymed alphabet from *The New England Primer* (1777).

Young TIMOTHY
Learnt fin to fly.

VASTHI for Pride,
Was fet afide.

Whales in the Sea,
GOD's Voice obey.

XERXES did die,
And fo muft I.

While youth do chear
Death may be near.

ZACCHEUS he
Did climb the Tree
Our Lord to fee.

T U W X Y Z

NOAH did view
The old world & new.

Young OBADIAS,
DAVID, JOSIAS,
All were pious.

PETER deny'd
His Lord and cry'd.

Queen ESTHER fues
And faves the Jews.

Young pious RUTH,
Left all for Truth.

Young SAM'L dear
The Lord did fear.

N O P Q R S

JOHAN AMOS COMENIUS (1592-1670)
From *Orbis Sensualium Pictus* (1659)

Comenius, a Bishop of the Unity of Czech Brethren, strove throughout his life to prove the might of the pen and the mind. As rector of the German school at Fulnek, he conducted botany classes outdoors and added honey to the local diet by introducing beehives to the town. Eventually forced out of his homeland by the constant Hapsburg plundering of Bohemia—he found temporary homes in England, Sweden, Poland, and the Netherlands—this advocate of Pansophism, the harmonious system uniting all knowledge through education, still clung tenaciously to his motto: *omnia sponte fluant absit violentia rebus* (all things should develop of their own free will with complete absence of violence). Known to the royalty and *literati* of Europe for such works as *The Labyrinth of the World, Janua Linguarum Reserata/The Door to Languages Opened*, and *Via Lucis/The Way of Light*, Comenius enlivened and revolutionized the teaching of Latin with the *Pictus*. First published in a German-Latin version in Nuremburg in 1658, it was translated by the London schoolmaster Charles Hoole and made available in an English-Latin version by the next year.

X.

Terræ-Fœtûs.

The Fruits of the Earth.

A *meadow*, 1. yieldeth *grass* with *Flowers* and *Herbs*, which being cut down, are made *Hay*, 2.

A *Field*, 3. yieldeth *corn*, and *Pot-herbs*, 4.

Mushrooms, 5. *Straw-berries*, 6. *Myrtle-trees*, &c. *come up* in Woods.

Metals, Stones, and *Minerals* grow *under the earth.*

Pratum, 1. fert *Gramina*, cum *Floribus & Herbis* quæ defecta fiunt *Fœnum*, 2.

Arvum, 3. fert *Fruges*, & *Olera*, 4. *fungi*, 5. *Fraga*, 6. *Myrtilli*, &c. Proveniunt in Sylvis.

Metalla, Lapides, Mineralia, nascuntur sub terra.

XXV.

Infecta volantia.

Flying-vermin.

The *Bee*, 1. maketh honey which the *Drone*, 2. devoureth. The *Wasp*, 3. and the *Hornet*, 4. molest with a sting; and the *Gad-Bee* (or Breese), 5. especially *Cattel*; but the *Fly*, 6. and the *gnat*, 7. us.

The *Cricket*, 8. singeth.

The *Butterfly*, 9. is a winged *Caterpillar*.

The *Beetle*, 10. covereth her wings with *Cases*.

The *Glow-worm*, 11. shinest by night.

Aspis, 1. facit mel quod *Fucus*, 2. depascit *Vespa*, 3. & *Crabro*, 4. infestant oculeo; & *Oestrum* (Asilus), 5. imprimis *pecus*. autem *Musca*, 6. & *Culex*, 7. nos.

Gryllus, 8. *cantillat.*

Papillio, 9. est alata *Eruca.*

Scarabæus, 10. tegit alas *vaginis.*

Cicindela [Lampyris], 11. nitet noctu.

XXVIII.

Jumenta.

Labouring Beasts.

The *Ass*, 1. and the *Mule*, 2. carry burthens.

The *Horse*, 3. (which a *Mane*, 4. graceth) carryeth us.

The *Camel*, 5. carryeth the Merchant with his Ware.

The *Elephant*, 6. draweth his meat to him with his *Trunk*, 7.

He hath two *Teeth*, 8. standing out, and is able to carry full thirty men.

Asinus, 1. & *Mulus*, 2. gestant Onera.

Equus, 3. (quam *Juba*, 4. ornat) gestat nos ipsos.

Camelus, 5. gestat Mercatorem cum mercibus suis.

Elephas, (Barrus) 6. attrahit pabulum *Proboscide*, 7.

Habet duos *dentes*, 8. prominentes, & potest portare etiam triginta viros.

XXXVII.

Septem Ætates Hominis.

The Seven Ages of Man.

A *Man* is first an *Infant*, 1.
then a *Boy*, 2.
then a *Youth*, 3.
then a *Young-man*, 4.
then a *Man*, 5.
after that, an *Elderly-man*, 6.
and at last, a *decrepid old man*, 7.
   So also in the other, *Sex*, there are,
a *Girl*, 8.
A *Damosel*, a *Maid*, 10.
A *Woman*, 11.
an *elderly Woman*, 12. and
a *decrepid old Woman*, 13.

Homo est primum *Infans*, 1.
deinde *Puer*, 2.
tum *Adolescens*, 3.
inde *uvenis*, 4.
postea *Vir*, 5.
dehinc *Senex*, 6.
tandem *Silicernium*, 7.
   Sic etiam in altero *Sexu*,
sunt, *Pupa*, 8.
Puella, 9. *Virgo*, 10.
Mulier, 11.
Vetula, 12.
Anus decrepita, 13.

XLIV.

Deformes & Monstrosi.

Deformed and Monstrous People.

Monstrous and *deformed* People are those which differ in the Body from the ordinary shape, as the huge *Gyant*, 1. the little *Dwarf*, 2. One with *two bodies*, 3. One with *two Heads*, 4. and such like Monsters.

Amongst these are reckoned, The *Jolt-headed*, 5. The great *nosed*, 6. The *blubber-lipped*, 7. The *blub-cheeked*, 8. The *goggle-eyed*, 9. The *wry-necked*, 10. The *great-throated*, 11. The *Crump-backed*, 12. The *Crump-footed*, 13. The *steeple-crowned*, 15. add to these The *Bald-pated*, 14.

Monstrosi, & *deformes* sunt abeuntes corpore à communi formâ, ut sunt, immanis *Gigas*, nanus *(Pumilio)*, 2. *Bicorpor*, 3. *Biceps*, 4. & id genus monstra.

His accensentur, *Capito*, 5. *Naso*, 6. *Labeo*, 7. *Bucco*, 8. *Strabo*, 9. *Obstipus*, 10. *Strumosus*, 11. *Gibbosus*, 12. *Loripes*, 13. *Cilo*, 15. adde *Calvastrum*, 14.

XCVII.

Schola.

A School.

A *School*, 1. is a Shop in which *Young Wits* are fashion'd to vertue, and it is distinguish'd into *Forms*.

The *Master*, 2. sitteth in a *Chair*, 3. the *Scholars*, 4. in *Forms*, 5. he teacheth, they learn.

Some things are writ down before them with *Chalk* on a *Table*, 6.

Some sit at a Table, and write, 7. he mendeth their Faults, 8.

Some stand and rehearse things committed to memory, 9.

Some talk together, 10. and behave themselves wantonly and carelessly; these are chastised with a *Ferrula*, 11. and a *Rod*, 12.

Schola, 1. est Officina, in quâ *Novelli Animi* formantur ad virtutem, & distinguitur in *Classes*.

Præceptor, 2. sedet in *Cathedra*, 3. *Discipuli*, 4. in *Subselliis*, 5. ille docet, hi discunt.

Quaedam praescribuntur illis *Cretâ* in *Tabella*, 6.

Quidam sedent ad Mensam, & scribunt, 7. ipse corrigit Mendas, 8.

Quidam stant, & recitant mandata memoriae, 9.

Quidam confabulantur, 10. ac gerunt se petulantes, & negligentes; hi castigantur *Ferulâ* (baculo), 11. & *Virgâ*, 12.

CXX.

Societas Parentalis.

The Society betwixt Parents, and Children.

Married Persons (by the blessing of God) have *Issue*, and become *Parents*.

The *Father*, 1. begetteth and the *Mother*, 2. beareth *Sons*, 3. and *Daughters*, 4. (sometimes *Twins*).

The *Infant*, 5. is wrapped in *Swadling-cloathes*, 6. is laid in a *Cradle*, 7. is suckled by the Mother with her *Breasts*, 8. and fed with *Pap*, 9.

Afterwards it learneth to go by a *Standing-stool*, 10. playeth with *Rattles*, 11. and beginneth to speak.

As it beginneth to grow older, it is accustomed to *Piety*, 12. and *Labour*, 13. and is chastised, 14. if it be not dutiful.

Children owe to Parents Reverence and Service.

The Father maintaineth his Children *by taking pains*, 15.

Conjuges, (ex benedictione Dei) suscipiunt *Sobolem* (Prolem) & fiunt *Parentes*.

Pater, 1. generat & *Mater*, 2. parit *Filios*, 3. & *Filias*, 4. (aliquando *Gemellos*).

Infans, 5. involvitur *Fasciis*, 6. reponitur in *Cunas*, 7. lactatur a matre *Uberibus*, 8. & nutritur *Pappis*, 9.

Deinde discit incedere *Seperasto*, 10 ludit *Crepundiis*, 11. & incipit fari.

Crescente aetate, adsuescit *Pietati*, 12. & *Labori*, 13. & castigatur, 14. si non sit morigerus.

Liberi debent Parentibus Cultum & Officium.

Pater sustenat Liberos, *laborando*, 15.

CXXXVI.

Ludi Pueriles.

Boyes-Sport

Boys used to play either with *Bowling-stones* 1. or throwing a *Bowl*, 2. at *Nine-pins*, 3. or striking a *Ball*, through a *Ring*, 5. with a *Bandy*, 4. or scourging a *Top*, 6. with a *Whip*, 7. or shooting with a *Trunk*, 8. and a *Bow*, 9. or going upon *Stilts*, 10. or tossing and swinging themselves upon a *Merry-totter*, 11.

Pueri solent ludere vel *Globis fictilibus*, 1. vel jactantes *Globum*, 2. ad *Conas*, 3. vel *mittentes* Sphærulam per *Annulum*, 5. *Clava*, 4. versantes *Turbinem*, 6. *Flagello*, 7. vel jaculantes *Sclopo*, 8. & *Arcu*, 9. vel incidentes *Grallis*, 10. vel super *Petaurum*, 11. se agitantes & oscillantes.

2. THE 'HELL-FIRE' TALES OF THE PURITANS

Diverse children have their different natures: some are like flesh which nothing but salt will keep from putrefaction, some again like tender fruits that are best preserved with sugar. Those parents are wise that can fit their nurture according to their nature.
—*Anne Bradstreet,* Meditations Divine and Moral *(1664)*

Puritan writers believed that children, like their elders, were prone to sin and in need of exhortation. While the poet Anne Bradstreet (1612?-72), a Dissenting emigrant to the Massachusetts Bay Colony, saw children as needing, metaphorically, either salt or sugar, the main ingredient of most Puritan writings was salt, in the form of strong, almost corrosive injunctions, rather than anything in the nature of sweet reassurance or tenderness. And even Bradstreet, the fond and dedicated mother of "eight birds hatched in one nest", viewed the child as "conceived in sin and born with sorrow".

Stained from birth with Adam's sinful fact,
Thence I began to sin as soon as act:
A perverse will, a love to what's forbid,
A serpent's sting in pleasing face lay hid:
A lying tongue as soon as it could speak
And fifth commandment do daily break. [1]

She would have agreed with the Puritan clergyman and writer Cotton Mather (1663-1728) that it would be better for a child to be whipped than damned.

Since to the Puritans all mortal flesh was

infected with innate sinfulness, they chose their reading matter with the express purpose of forcefully reiterating this melancholy doctrine as a means of directing the reader to the path of salvation. Children were not exempt from this single-minded concern with sin and damnation. The following titles were included in *The Young Christian's Library* of 1701:

The Large Quarto Bible
The Christian's Daily Devotion
Bishop Kidder's *Young Man's Duty*
Bona's *Guide to Eternity*
Dr Sherlock's *On Judgement*
Milton's *Paradise Lost*

Puritans found abiding strength in the divine gift of sanctifying grace, which, through a rigorous and proscriptive code of behaviour, promised salvation to believers. This was the rock upon which their zeal was founded. They believed in a simple form of worship that focused not on the altar or the choir but on the pulpit, from which the preacher explicated a Biblical text. Presbyterians, Calvinists, Congregationalists, and Non-conformists—all degrees and temperaments of Puritans—demanded strict and sober standards of behaviour. They banned sabbath games and forbade instrumental music in their

---

[1] "Childhood", *The Works of Anne Bradstreet*, ed. J. Hensley (Cambridge, Mass: Harvard University Press, 1967), pp. 52, 54.

churches. New England Puritans outlawed the observance of Christmas, with its accompanying "profane" merriment, and replaced it with a celebration of Thanksgiving Day. Despite the severity of their beliefs, however, Puritans were very much men of this world: they permitted themselves to strive for both salvation and material success.

Although confident in their possession of grace, Puritans could never be smug. As the finest poetic, homiletic, and allegorical writing from within the tradition testifies, life for the Puritan was a continuing spiritual contest between conversion and backsliding. The various assaults on the town of Mansoul in Bunyan's The Holy War, and the sloughs and mountains over which Christian must journey in The Pilgrim's Progress, had equivalents in the daily lives of Puritans: they were constantly doubting, then restoring, their confidence in salvation.

For all the solemn finger-wagging of the Puritans, they were among the first to write specifically for children. In addition to the lessons of hornbooks and primers, Puritan children in the late seventeenth and early eighteenth centuries were familiar with little books of religious instruction designed specially for their benefit. Two well-circulated examples were James Janeway's A Token for Children (1672) and John Bunyan's A Book for Boys and Girls (1686). With their humourless preaching, fervent moral rectitude, and withering cautionary maxims, they seem frighteningly stern to today's reader. Both Janeway and Bunyan wrote to awaken and sustain children's penitence. As Bunyan observed in his address "To the Reader":

To shoot too high doth but make Children gaze
'Tis that which hits the man, doth him amaze.

James Janeway was an Oxford graduate and Nonconformist preacher who died before reaching the age of forty. John Bunyan was an itinerant mender, the father of six children, who gained a considerable reputation for his preaching as well as for his devotional books, notably his spiritual autobiography, Grace Abounding to the Chief of Sinners (1672), and two allegories of the quest for salvation: The Pilgrim's Progress (1678, 1684), and The Holy War (1682). Both men suffered for their beliefs—Janeway lost his indulgence to preach and Bunyan was imprisoned—and both wrote for children because they saw them as unformed diminutive adults who stood in urgent need of their soul-saving admonitions.

Like Anne Bradstreet, Janeway believed that children were "not too little to go to Hell". His A Token for Children is a Puritan martyrology composed of thirteen examples of the holy lives and joyful deaths of young Puritans. After catechizing the reader with eleven sorts of soul-battering questions, Janeway closes his Preface with this adjuration:

Children, if you love me, if you love your Parents, if you love your Souls, if you would scape Hell Fire, and if you would live in Heaven when you dye, do you go and do as these good children.

His virtuous children are obsessed by their faith. Their chilling life stories, which conclude with zealous, sometimes powerful sermons, were meant to frighten readers into submission: a breathless excited urgency pervades little Sarah Howley's admonitions, not only because she is aware of her approaching death but also because she is haemorrhaging; a dispirited urchin's self-abhorrence is so great that he sees himself as a toad. Janeway based his accounts, as he frequently affirms, on the testimony of real children. The epigraph to the last six states their purpose: "Out of the mouths of babes and sucklings hast thou ordained strength" (Psalms 8.2).

While Janeway's children are spiritually strong and physically weak, Bunyan's are often healthy reprobates. Using the medium of verse in A Book for Boys and Girls; or, Country Rhimes for Children, Bunyan meets his readers on their own ground:

. . . by their Play-things, I would them entice
To mount their thoughts from what are childish Toys,
To Heav'n, for that's prepar'd for Girls and Boys.

He also assures them that he knows the difference between "Boys" and "Men", and will temper his matter accordingly:

Our Ministers, long time by Word and Pen,
Dealt with them, counting them, not Boys but Men:
Thunder-bolts they shot at them, and their Toys:
But hit them not, 'cause they were Girls and Boys.

With the preacher's consciousness of analogies, Bunyan determines to hit the mark by extracting lessons from animal exempla, everyday occurrences, and childish pursuits. Domestic life, animals, and insects supply material for several rhymes, whether developed through prolonged metaphors, apt comparisons, or pointed one-for-one correspondences. When describing the life-cycle of the fertilized egg, for instance, he furnishes an extended gloss on man's spiritual condition; with contrasting brevity, he makes the swallow a pretty picture of serene faith and the bee an emblem of sweet yet mortal sin. Puritan beliefs are unmistakable in Bunyan's reduction of the sacraments to two ("Upon the Sacraments") and in his insistence on the interaction of grace and faith ("Upon a Lanthorn"). Soberly reflecting Puritan tenets in his manner as well as his matter, Bunyan makes no concessions to his young readers; despite his prefatory claim, he resembles very closely the thunderbolt-shooting ministers. The children Bunyan depicts are weighed down, like Christian in the City of Destruction, by such observations as these: *"With fears I am surrounded,/My spirit is confounded; Mercy I have neglected,/I fear I am rejected."* Echoing Anne Bradstreet, the lamenting child of one rhyme proclaims, *"Of late too I perceived,/I was in sin conceived."*

With this crushing perception of sinfulness as a constant motif, Bunyan utilizes the children in his rhymes to provide an assortment of behaviour models. They can be diligent and steadfast, like the reliable post-boy, or reckless and conceited, like the hobbyhorse rider. Young readers are meant to follow the example of the thoughtful boy who keeps his watch free of dust by frequent visits to the divine watchmaker, and to learn from the negative lesson of the boy who cannot see beyond the immediate pleasure of eating his "plumbs". In "Upon the Chalk-Stone" Bunyan portrays the ideal child as a "Child of God" and the sinful child as "one of whom men catch the Scab, or Itch". (His evangelistic zeal often prompted him to use repellent metaphors.)

Relying on a dour pedagogy, Janeway led his readers through a gallery of terrifying death-bed scenes, while Bunyan used ordinary objects and events as touchstones for his preaching. Whether these authors portrayed children as ideal or cautionary examples, they brought to their task of exhorting the young an impassioned solemnity and the threat of imminent doom—forceful ingredients that were not to be reserved for adults. We are uncertain of children's response. One assumes they merely suffered these accounts and rhymes depicting the fearful chasm that separates the City of Destruction from the heavenly reward. The books tell us little about them and their tastes, though much about the Puritan mind and the Puritan view of the young.

JAMES JANEWAY (1636-1674)

From *A Token For Children: Being An Exact Account of the Conversion, Holy and Exemplary Lives, and Joyful Deaths of Several young Children* (1672)

EXAMPLE I

Of one eminently converted between Eight and Nine years old, with an account of her Life and Death.

Mrs Sarah Howley, when she was between eight and nine years old, was carried by her Friends to hear a Sermon, where the Minister Preached upon *Matthew* 11.30. *My yoak is easie, and my burden is light*: In the applying of which Scripture, this Child was mightily awakened, and made deeply sensible of the condition of her Soul, and her need of a Christ; she wept bitterly to think what a case she was in; and went home and got by her self into a Chamber, and upon her knees she wept and cryed to the Lord, as well as she could, which might easily be perceived by her eyes and countenance.

2. She was not contented at this, but she got her little Brother and Sister into a Chamber with her, and told them of their condition by nature, and wept over them, and prayed with them and for them.

3. After this she heard another Sermon upon *Prov.* 29.1, *He that being often reproved, hardeneth his heart, shall suddenly be destroyed, and that without remedy*: At which she was more affected than before, and was so exceedingly solicitous about her Soul, that she spent a great part of the night in weeping and praying, and could scarce take any rest day or night for some time together; desiring with all her Soul to escape from everlasting flames, and to get an interest in the Lord Jesus; O what should she do for a Christ! what should she do to be saved!

4. She gave her self much to attending upon the Word Preached, and still continued very tender under it, greatly favouring what she heard.

5. She was very much in secret prayer, as might easily be perceived by those who listened at the Chamber Door, and was usually very importunate, and full of tears.

6. She could scarce speak of sin, or be spoke to, but her heart was ready to melt.

7. She spent much time in reading the Scripture, and a Book called *The best Friend in the worst times*; by which the work of God was much promoted upon her Soul, and was much directed by it how to get acquaintance with God, especially toward the end of that Book. Another Book that she was much delighted with, was Mr. *Swinnocks Christian Mans Calling*, and by this she was taught in some measure to make Religion her business. The *Spiritual Bee* was a great companion of hers.

8. She was exceeding dutiful to her Parents, very loath to grieve them in the least; and if she had at any time (which was very rare) offended them, she would weep bitterly.

9. She abhorred lying, and allowed her self in no known sin.

10. She was very Conscientious in spending of time, and hated idleness, and spent her whole time either in praying, reading, instructing her little Brothers, and working at her Needle, at which she was very ingenious.

11. When she was at School, she was eminent for her diligence, teachableness, meekness and modesty, speaking very little; but when she did, it was usually very spiritual.

12. She continued in this course of Religious Duties for some years together.

13. When she was about fourteen years old, she brake a Vein in her Lungs (as is supposed), and oft did spit blood, yet did a little recover again, but had several dangerous relapses.

14. At the beginning of *January* last she was taken very bad again, in which sickness She was in great distress of Soul. When she was first taken, she said, O Mother, pray, pray, pray, for me, for Satan is so busie that I cannot pray for my self, I see I am undone without a Christ, and a pardon! O I am undone! undone to all Eternity!

15. Her Mother knowing how serious she had been formerly, did a little wonder that she should be in such agonies; upon which her Mother asked her what sin it was that was so burdensome to her spirit: O Mother, said she, it is not any particular Sin of Omission or Commission, that sticks so close to my Conscience, as the Sin of my nature; without the blood of Christ, that will damn me.

16. Her Mother asked her what she should pray for, for her? she answered, that I may have a saving knowledge of Sin and Christ; and that I may have an assurance of Gods love to my Soul. Her Mother asked her, why she did speak so little to the Minister that came to her? She answered, that it was her duty with patience and silence to learn of them: and it was exceeding painful to her to speak to any.

17. One time when she fell into a fit, she cried out, O I am going, I am going: But what shall I do to be saved? Sweet Lord Jesus, I will lye at thy feet, and if I perish, it shall be at the Fountain of thy mercy.

18. She was much afraid of presumption, and dreaded a mistake in the matters of her Soul, and would be often putting up ejaculations to God, to deliver her from deceiving her self. To instance in one: Great and mighty God, give me faith, and true faith, Lord, that I may not be a foolish Virgin, having a Lamp and no Oyl.

19. She would many times be laying hold upon the Promises, and plead them in prayer. That in *Mat.* 11.28, 29. was much in her Tongue, and no small relief to her spirit. How many times would she cry out, Lord, hast thou not said, *Come unto me all ye that are weary and heavy laden, and I will give you rest*.

20. Another time her Father bid her be of good cheer, because she was going to a better Father; at which she fell into a great passion, and said, but how do I know that? I am a poor sinner that wants assurance: O, for assurance! It was still her Note, O, for assurance! This was her great, earnest, and constant request to all that came to her, to beg assur-

ance for her; and, poor heart, she would look with so much eagerness upon them as if she desired nothing in the world so much, as that they would pity her, and help her with their prayers; never was poor creature more earnest for any thing, than she was for an assurance, and the Light of Gods Countenance: O the piteous moan that she would make! O the agonies that her Soul was in!

21. Her Mother askt her, if God should spare her life, how she would live; truly Mother, said she, we have such base hearts that I can't tell; we are apt to promise great things; when we are sick, but when we are recovered, we are as ready to forget our selves, and to turn again unto folly; but I hope I should be more careful of my time and my soul, than I have been.

22. She was full of natural affection to her Parents, and very careful least her Mother should be tired out with much watching. Her Mother said, how shall I bear parting with thee, when I have scarce dryed my eyes for thy Brother? She answered, The God of love support and comfort you; it is but a little while, and we shall meet in Glory, I hope. She being very weak, could speak but little; therefore her Mother said, Child, if thou hast any comfort, lift up thy hand, which she did.

23. The Lords day before that in which she died, a Kinsman of hers came to see her, and asking of her, whether she knew him, she answered; yes, I know you, and I desire you would learn to know Christ: you are young, but you know not how soon you may die; and O to die without a Christ, it is a fearful thing: O redeem Time, O Time, Time, Time, precious Time! Being requested by him not to spend her self: she said, she would fain do all the good she could while she lived, and when she was dead too, if possible; upon which account, she desired that a Sermon might be Preached at the Funeral concerning the preciousness of Time. O that young ones would now remember their Creator!

24. Some Ministers that came to her, did with earnestness, beg that the Lord would please to give her some token for good, that she might go off triumphing; and Bills of the same Nature were sent to several Churches.

25. After she had long waited for an answer of their prayers, she said, *Well, I will venture my soul upon Christ.*

26. She carried it with wonderful patience, and yet would often pray that the Lord would give her more patience, which the Lord answered to astonishment; for considering the pains and agonies that she was in, her patience was next to a wonder; Lord, Lord give me patience, said she, that I may not dishonour thee.

27. Upon Thursday, after long waiting, great fears, and many Prayers, when all her Friends thought she had been past speaking, to the astonishment of her Friends she broke forth thus with a very audible voice, and chearful Countenance: Lord, thou hast promised that whosoever comes unto thee, thou wilt in no wise cast out; Lord, I come unto thee, and surely thou wilt in no wise cast me out. O so sweet! O so glorious is Jesus! O I have the sweet and glorious Jesus; he is sweet, he is

sweet, he is sweet! O the admirable love of God in sending Christ! O free grace to a poor lost Creature! And thus she ran on repeating many of these things a hundred times over; but her Friends were so astonished to see her in this Divine Rapture, and to hear such gracious words, and her prayers and desires satisfied, that they could not write a quarter of what she spoke.

28. When her soul was thus ravished with the love of Christ, and her tongue so highly engaged in the magnifying of God; her Father, Brethren, and Sisters, with other of the Family were called, to whom she spake particularly, as her strength would give leave. She gave her Bible as a Legacy to one of her Brothers, and desired him to use that well for her sake, and added to him and the rest, O make use of time to get a Christ for your Souls; spend no time in running up and down in playing; O get a Christ for your Souls while you are young, remember now your Creator before you come to a sick-bed; put not off this great work till then, for then you will find it a hard work indeed. I know by experience, the Devil will tell you it is time enough; and ye are young, what need you to be in such haste? You will have time enough when you are old. But there stands one (meaning her Grand-mother) that stayes behind, and I that am but young, am going before her. O therefore make your Calling and Election sure, while you are in health. But I am afraid this will be but one nights trouble to your thoughts; but remember, these are the words of a dying Sister. O if you knew how good Christ were! O if you had but one taste of his sweetness, you would rather go to him a thousand times, than stay in this wicked world. *I would not for ten thousand, and ten thousand worlds part with my interest in Christ.* O how happy am I that am going to everlasting Joyes! I would not go back again for twenty thousand worlds; And will not you strive to get an interest in Christ?

29. After this, looking upon one of her Fathers Servants, she said, What shall I do? What shall I do at that great day, when Christ shall say to me, *Come thou Blessed of my Father inherit the Kingdom prepared for thee?* and shall say to the wicked, *Go thou cursed into the Lake that burns for ever*: What a grief is it to me to think that I shall see any of my friends that I knew upon Earth turned into that Lake that burns for ever! O that word for ever! Remember that for ever; I speak these words to you, but they are nothing, except God speak to you too. O pray, pray, pray, that God would give you grace! and then she prayed, O Lord finish thy work upon their Souls. It will be my comfort to see you in glory; but it will be your everlasting happiness.

30. Her Grandmother told her she spent her self too much; she said, I care not for that, if I could do any Soul good. O with what vehemency, did she speak, as if her heart were in every word she spoke.

31. She was full of Divine Sentences, and almost all her discourse from the first to the last in the time of her sickness, was about her Soul, Christs sweetness, and the Souls of others, in a word, like a continued Sermon.

32. Upon *Friday*, after she had had such lively discoveries of Gods love, she was exceeding desirous to die, and cryed out, Come Lord Jesus, come quickly, conduct me to thy Tabernacle; I am a poor creature without thee: but Lord Jesus, my soul longs to be with thee: O when shall it be? Why not now, dear Jesus? Come Lord Jesus, come quickly; but why do I speak thus? Thy time dear Lord is the best; O give me patience.

33. Upon *Saturday* she spoke very little (being very drowsie) yet now and then she dropt these words, How long sweet Jesus, finish thy work sweet Jesus, come away sweet dear Lord Jesus, come quickly; sweet Lord help, come away, now, now dear Jesus, come quickly; Good Lord give patience to me to wait thy appointed time; Lord Jesus help me, help me, help me. Thus at several times (when out of her sleep) for she was asleep the greatest part of the day.

34. Upon the Lords Day she scarce spoke any thing, but much desired that Bills of Thanksgiving might be sent to those who had formerly been praying for her, that they might help her to praise God for that full assurance that he had given her of his love; and seemed to be much swallowed up with the thoughts of Gods free love to her Soul. She oft commended her spirit into the Lords hands, and the last words which she was heard to speak, were these, Lord Help, Lord Jesus help, Dear Jesus, Blessed Jesus—And thus upon the Lords Day, between Nine and Ten of the Clock in the Forenoon, she slept sweetly in Jesus, and began an everlasting Sabbath, *February 19, 1670.*

EXAMPLE VII

Of a notorious wicked child, who was taken up from begging, and admirably converted; with an account of his holy Life and joyful Death, when he was nine years old.

1. A Very poor Child of the Parish of *Newington-Butts* came begging to the door of a dear Christian friend of mine, in a very lamentable case, so filthy and nasty, that he would even have turned ones stomack to have looked on him: But it pleased God to raise in the heart of my friend, a great pity and tenderness towards this poor child, so that in Charity he took him out of the streets, whose Parents were unknown, who had nothing at all in him to commend him to any ones Charity, but his misery. My friend eying the glory of God, and the good of the immortal soul of this wretched Creature, discharged the Parish of the Child, and took him as his own, designing to bring him up for the Lord Christ. A noble piece of Charity! And that which did make the kindness far the greater was, that there seemed to be very little hopes of doing any good upon this Child, for he was a very Monster of wickedness, and a thousand times more miserable and vile by his sin, than by his poverty. He was running to Hell as soon as he could go, and was old in naughtiness when he was young in years; and one shall scarce hear of one so like the Devil in his infancy, as this poor Child was. What sin was there (that his

age was capable of) that he did not commit? What by the corruption of his Nature, and the abominable example of little beggar boyes, he was arrived to a strange pitch of impiety. He would call filthy Names, take Gods Name in vain, curse and swear, and do almost all kind of mischief; and as to any thing of God, worse than an Heathen.

2. But his sin and misery was but a stronger motive to that gracious man to pity him, and to do all that possibly he could to pluck this fire-brand out of the fire; and it was not long before the Lord was pleased to let him understand that he had a design of everlasting kindness upon the Soul of this poor child: for no sooner had this good man taken this creature into his house, but he prays for him, and labours with all his might to convince him of his miserable condition by Nature, and to teach him something of God, the worth of his own Soul, and that Eternity of Glory or Misery that he was born to; and blessed by Free-grace, it was not long before the Lord was pleased to let him understand, that it was himself which put it into his heart to take in this Child, that he might bring him up for Christ. The Lord soon struck in with his godly instructions, so that an amazing change was seen in the Child, in a few weeks space he was soon convinced of the evil of his ways; no more news now of his calling of Names, Swearing, or Cursing; no more taking of the Lords Name in vain; now he is civil, and respectful, and such a strange alteration was wrought in the child, that all the Parish that rung of his villany before, was now ready to talk of his reformation, his company, his talk, his imployment is now changed, and he is like another creature; so that the glory of Gods Free-grace began already to shine in him.

3. And this change was not only an eternal one, and to be discerned abroad, but he would get by himself, and weep and mourn bitterly for his horrible wicked life, as might easily be perceived by them that lived in the house with him.

4. It was the great care of his godly Master to strike in with those convictions which the Lord had made, and to improve them all he could; and he was not a little glad to see that his labour was not in vain in the Lord; he still experiences that the Lord doth carry on his own work mightily upon the heart of the Child, he is still more and more broken under a sense of his undone state by nature; he is oft in tears and bemoaning his lost and miserable condition. When his Master did speak of the things of God, he listened earnestly, and took in with much greediness and affection what he was taught. Seldom was there any discourse about Soul-matters in his hearing, but he heard it as if it were for his life, and would weep greatly.

5. He would after his Master had been speaking to him or others of the things of God, go to him, and question with him about them, and beg of him to instruct and teach him further, and to tell him those things again, that he might remember and understand them better.

6. Thus he continued seeking after the knowledge of God and Christ, and practising holy duties, till the sickness came into the house, with

which the child was smitten; at his first sickning, the poor child was greatly amazed and afraid, and though his pains were great, and the distemper very tedious, yet the sense of his sin, and the thoughts of the miserable condition that he feared his soul was still in, made his trouble ten times greater; he was in grievous agonies of spirit, and his former sins stared him in the face, and made him tremble; the poison of Gods Arrows did even drink up his spirits; the sense of sin and wrath was so great, that he could not tell what in the world to do; the weight of Gods displeasure, and the thoughts of lying under it to all eternity, did even break him to pieces, and he did cry out very bitterly, what should he do? he was a miserable sinner, and he feared that he should go to Hell; his sins had been so great and so many that there was no hopes for him. He was not by far so much concerned for his life, as for his Soul, what would become of that for ever. Now the plague upon his body seemed nothing to that which was in his soul.

7. But in this great distress the Lord was pleased to send one to take care for his Soul, who urged to him the great and precious promises which were made to one in his condition, telling him that there was enough in Christ for the chiefest of sinners, and that he came to seek and save such a lost creature as he was. But this poor Child found it a very difficult thing for him to believe that there was any mercy for such a dreadful sinner as he had been.

8. He was made to cry out of himself, not only for his swearing and lying, and other outwardly notorious sins; but he was in great horrour for the sin of his Nature, for the vileness of his heart, and original corruption; under it he was in so great anguish, that the trouble of his spirit made him in a great measure to forget the pains of his body.

9. He did very particularly confess and bewail his sins with tears; and some sins so secret that none in the world could charge him with.

10. He would condemn himself of sin, as deserving to have no mercy, thought that there was not a greater sinner in all *London* than himself, and he abhorred himself as the vilest creature he knew.

11. He did not only pray much with strong cries and tears himself, but he begged the prayers of Christians for him.

12. He would ask Christians, whether they thought there were any hopes for him, and would beg of them to deal plainly with him, for he was greatly afraid of being deceived.

13. Being informed how willing and ready the Lord Christ was to accept of poor sinners upon their repentance and turning, and being counselled to venture himself upon Christ for mercy and salvation, he said he would fain cast himself upon Christ, but he could not but wonder how Christ should be willing to dye for such a vile wretch as he was, and he found it one of the hardest things in the world to believe.

14. But at last it pleased the Lord to give him some small hopes that there might be mercy for him, for he had been the chiefest of sinners; and he was made to lay a little hold upon such promises, as that, *Come unto me all ye that are weary and heavy laden, and I will give you rest.* But O

how did this poor boy admire and bless God for the least hopes! How highly did he advance free and rich grace that should pity and pardon him! and at last he was so full of praise, and admiring of God, so that (to speak in the words of a precious man, that was an eye and ear-witness) to the praise and glory of God be it spoken, the house at that day, for all the sickness in it, was a little lower Heaven, so full of joy and praise.

15. The Child grew exceedingly in knowledge, experiences, patience, humility, and self-abhorrency, and he thought he could never speak bad enough of himself; the Name that he would call himself by, was a Toad.

16. And though he prayed before, yet now the Lord poured out upon him the Spirit of prayer in an extraordinary manner, for one of his age, so that now he prayed more frequently, more earnestly, more spiritually than ever. O how eagerly would he beg to be washed in the Blood of Jesus; and that the King of Kings, and Lord of Lords, that was over Heaven and Earth, and Sea, would pardon and forgive him all his sins, and receive his Soul into his Kingdom! and what he spoke, it was with so much life and fervour of Spirit, as that it filled the hearers with astonishment and joy.

17. He had no small sense of the use and excellency of Christ, and such longings and breathings of his Soul after him, that when mention hath been made of Christ, he hath been ready almost to leap out of his bed for joy.

18. When he was told that if he should recover, he must not live as he list; but he must give up himself to Christ, and to be his Child and Servant, to bear his Yoke, and be obedient unto his Laws, and live a holy life, and take his Cross and suffer mocking and reproach, it may be persecution for his Name sake. Now Child (said one to him) are you willing to have Christ upon such terms? He signified his willingness by the earnestness of his looks and words, and the casting up of his eyes to Heaven, saying, yes, with all my Soul, the Lord helping me, I will do this.

19. Yet he had many doubts and fears, and was ever and anon harping upon that, that though he were willing, yet Christ he feared was not willing to accept him, because of the greatness of his sin, yet his hopes were greater than his fears.

20. The *Wednesday* before he died, the Child lay as it were in a trance for about half an hour, in which time he thought he saw a Vision of Angels: When he was out of his Trance, he was in a little pett, and asked his Nurse, why she did not let him go; go, whither child, said she? why along with those brave Gentlemen (said he); but they told me they would come and fetch me away for all you, upon *Friday* next, those brave Gentlemen will come for me; and upon that day the Child dyed joyfully.

21. He was very thankful to his Master, and very sensible of his great kindness in taking him up out of the streets when he was a begging, and he admired at the goodness of God, which put it into the mind of a

stranger to look upon, and to take such fatherly care of such a pitiful sorry creature as he was. O my dear Mother (said he) and child of God, I hope to see you in Heaven, for I am sure you will go thither. O blessed, blessed be God that made you to take pity upon me, for I might have dyed, and have gone to the Devil, and have been damned for ever, if it had not been for you.

22. The Thursday before he dyed he asked a very godly friend of mine, what he thought of his condition, and whither his soul was now going? for he said he could not still but fear least he should deceive himself with false hopes, at which my friend spoke to him thus, Child, for all that I have endeavoured to hold forth the grace of God in Christ to thy Soul, and given you a warrant from the Word of God, that Christ is as freely offered to you, as to any sinner in the world; if thou art but willing to accept of him, thou mayest have Christ and all that thou dost want, with him; and yet thou givest way to these thy doubtings and fears, as though I told thee nothing but lyes. Thou sayest thou fearest that Christ will not accept of thee; I fear thou art not heartily willing to accept of him. The Child answered, indeed I am: Why then Child, if thou art unfeignedly willing to have Christ, I tell thee he is a thousand times more willing to have thee, and wash thee, and save thee, than thou art to desire it. And now at this time Christ offers himself freely to thee again; therefore receive him humbly by Faith into thy heart, and bid him welcome, for he deserveth it: Upon which words the Lord discovered his love to the Child, and he gave a kind of a leap in his bed, and snapt his fingers and thumb together with abundance of joy, as much as to say, Well, yea all is well, the match is made, Christ is willing, and I am willing too; and now Christ is mine, and I am his for ever. And from that time forward, in full joy and assurance of Gods love, he continued earnestly praising God, with desiring to die, and be with Christ. And on Friday morning he sweetly went to rest, using that very expression, Into thy hands Lord I commit my Spirit. He died punctually at that time which he had spoke of, and in which he expected those Angels to come to him; he was not much above nine years old when he dyed.

This Narrative I had from a judicious holy man un-related to him, who was an eye and ear-witness to all these things.

JOHN BUNYAN (1628-88)
From *A Book for Boys and Girls; or, Country Rhimes for Children* (1686)

Bunyan's originally unillustrated book went through several editions in the eighteenth century. In an abridged form, which reduced its rhymes from seventy-four to forty-nine, *Divine Emblems: or, Temporal Things Spiritualized* often appeared adorned with woodcuts.

III
MEDITATIONS UPON AN EGG

The Egg's no Chick by falling from the Hen;
   Nor man a Christian, till he's born agen.
  The Egg's at first contained in the Shell;
Men afore Grace, in sins, and darkness dwell.
  The Egg when laid, by Warmth is made a Chicken;
And Christ, by Grace, those dead in sin doth quicken.
  The Egg, when first a Chick, the shell's its Prison;
So's flesh to th'Soul, who yet with Christ is risen.
  The Shell doth crack, the Chick doth chirp and peep;
The flesh decays, as men do pray and weep.
  The Shell doth break, the Chick's at liberty;
The flesh falls off, the Soul mounts up on high.
  But both do not enjoy the self-same plight;
The Soul is safe, the Chick now fears the Kite.

2

  But Chick's from rotten Eggs do not proceed;
Nor is an Hypocrite a Saint indeed.
  The rotten Egg, though underneath the Hen,
If crack'd, stinks, and is loathsome unto men.
  Nor doth her Warmth make what is rotten sound,
What's rotten, rotten will at last be found.
  The Hyppocrite, sin has him in Possession,
He is a rotten Egg under Profession.

3

Some Eggs bring Cockatrices; and some men
Seem hatcht and brooded in the Vipers Den.
  Some Eggs bring wild-Fowls; and some men there be
As wild as are the wildest Fowls that flee.
  Some Eggs bring Spiders; and some men appear
More venom than the worst of Spiders are.
  Some Eggs bring Piss ants; and some seem to me
As much for trifles as the Piss-ants be.
  Thus divers Eggs do produce divers shapes,
As like some Men as Monkeys are like Apes.
But this is but an Egg, were it a Chick,
Here had been Legs, and Wings, and Bones to pick.

VIII
UPON THE SWALLOW

This pretty Bird, oh! how she flies and sings!
But could she do so had she not Wings?
Her Wings, bespeak my Faith, her Songs my Peace;
When I believe and sing, my Doubtings cease.

IX
UPON THE BEE

The Bee goes out and Honey home doth bring;
And some who seek that Honey find a sting.
Now wouldst thou have the Honey and be free
From stinging; in the first place kill the Bee.

Comparison
This Bee an Emblem truly is of sin
Whose sweet unto a many death hath been.
Now wouldst have Sweet from sin, and yet not dye,
Do thou it in the first place mortifie.

XI
UPON A LOW'RING MORNING

Well, with the day, I see, the Clouds appear,
    And mix the light with darkness everywhere:
This threatning is to Travellers, that go
Long Journeys, slabby Rain, they'l have or Snow.
    Else while I gaze, the Sun doth with his beams
Belace the Clouds, as 'twere with Bloody Streams;
This done, they suddenly do watry grow,
And weep, and pour their tears out where they go.

Comparison

Thus 'tis when Gospel-light doth usher in
To us, both sense of Grace, and sense of Sin;
Yea when it makes sin red with Christ's blood,
Then we can weep, till weeping does us good.

XIV
UPON THE SACRAMENTS

Two Sacraments I do believe there be,
Baptism and the Supper of the Lord:
Both Mysteries divine, which do to me,
By Gods appointment, benefit afford:
But shall they be my God? or shall I have
Of them so foul and impious a Thought,
To think that from the Curse they can me save?
Bread, Wine, nor Water me no ransom bought.

XXI
OF THE BOY AND BUTTER FLY

Behold how eager this our little Boy,
Is of this Butter Fly, as if all Joy,
All Profits, Honours, yea and lasting Pleasures,
Were wrapt up in her, or the richest Treasures,
Found in her would be bundled up together,
When all her all is lighter than a feather.
　He hollo's, runs, and cries out here Boys, here,
Nor doth he Brambles or the Nettles fear:
He stumbles at the Mole-Hills, up he gets,
And runs again, as one bereft of wits;
And all this labour and this large Out-cry,
Is only for a silly Butter-fly.

Comparison

This little Boy an Emblem is of those,
Whose hearts are wholly at the World's dispose.
The Butter-fly doth represent to me,
The World's best things at best but fading be.
All are but painted Nothings and false Joys,
Like this poor Butter-fly to these our Boys.
　His running through Nettles, Thorns and Bryers,
To gratifie his boyish fond desires,
His tumbling over Mole-hills to attain
His end, namely, his Butter-fly to gain;
Doth plainly shew, what hazards some men run,
To get what will be lost as soon as won.
Men seem in Choice, then children far more wise,
Because they run not after Butter flies:
When yet alas! for what are empty Toys
They follow Children, like to beardless Boys.

XXIX
UPON A RING OF BELLS

Bells have wide mouths and tongues, but are too weak,
   Have they not help, to sing, or talk, or speak.
But if you move them they will mak't appear,
By speaking they'l make all the Town to hear.
   When Ringers handle them with Art and Skill,
They then the ears of their Observers fill,
With such brave Notes, they ting and tang so well
As to out strip all with their ding, dong, Bell.

Comparison

   These Bells are like the Powers of my Soul;
Their Clappers to the Passions of my mind:
The Ropes by which my Bells are made to tole,
Are Promises (I by experience find.)
   My body is the Steeple, where they hang,
My Graces they which do ring ev'ry Bell:
Nor is there any thing gives such a tang,
When by these Ropes these Ringers ring them well.
   Let not my Bells these Ringers want, nor Ropes;
Yea let them have room for to swing and sway:
To toss themselves deny them not their Scopes.
Lord! in my Steeple give them room to play.
If they do tole, ring out, or chime all in,
They drown the tempting tinckling Voice of Vice:
Lord! when my Bells have gone, my Soul has bin
As 'twere a tumbling in this Paradice!
   Or if these Ringers do the Changes ring,
Upon my Bells, they do such Musick make,
My Soul then (Lord) cannot but bounce and sing,
So greatly her they with their Musick take.
But Boys (my Lusts) into my Belfry go,
And pull these Ropes, but do no Musick make
They rather turn my Bells by what they do,
Or by disorder make my Steeple shake.
   Then, Lord! I pray thee keep my Belfry Key,
Let none but Graces meddle with these Ropes:
And when these naughty Boys come, say them Nay,
From such Ringers of Musick there's no hopes.
   O Lord! If thy poor Child might have his will,
And might his meaning freely to thee tell;
He never of this Musick has his fill,
There's nothing to him like thy ding, dong, Bell.

XXXVII
UPON THE WHIPPING OF A TOP

Tis with the Whip the Boy sets up the Top,
  The Whip makes it run round upon it's Toe;
The Whip makes it hither and thither hop:
Tis with the Whip, the Top is made to go.

Comparison

Our Legalist is like unto this Top,
Without a Whip, he doth not Duty do.
Let *Moses* whip him, he will skip and hop;
Forbear to whip, he'l neither stand nor go.

XLVI
THE BOY AND WATCH-MAKER

This Watch my Father did on me bestow,
  A Golden one it is, but 'twill not go,
Unless it be at an Uncertainty;
But as good none, as one to tell a Lye.
  When 'tis high Day, my Hand will stand at nine;
I think there's no man's Watch so bad as mine.
Sometimes 'tis sullen, 'twill not go at all,
And yet 'twas never broke, nor had a Fall.

Watch-maker

Your Watch, tho it be good, through want of skill,
May fail to do according to your will.
Suppose the Ballance, Wheels, and Spring be good,
And all things else, unless you understood
To manage it, as Watches ought to be,
Your Watch will still be at Uncertainty.
Come, tell me, do you keep it from the Dust?
Yea wind it also duly up you must.
Take heed (too) that you do not strain the String;
You must be circumspect in ev'ry thing.
Or else your Watch, were it as good again,
Would not with Time, and Tide you entertain.

Comparison

This Boy an Emblem is of a Convert;
His Watch of th'work of Grace within his heart.
The Watch-maker is Jesus Christ our Lord,
His Counsel, the Directions of his Word.
Then Convert, if thy heart be out of frame,
Of this Watch-maker learn to mend the same.
  Do not lay ope'thy heart to Worldly Dust,
Nor let thy Graces over grow with Rust.
Be oft renew'd in th' Spirit of thy mind,
Or else uncertain thou thy Watch wilt find.

XLIX
UPON A LANTHORN

The Lanthorn is to keep the Candle Light,
  When it is windy, and a darksome Night.
Ordain'd it also was, that men might see
By Night their way, and so in safety be.

Comparison

  Compare we now our Lanthorn to the man,
That has within his heart a Work of Grace.
As for another let him, if he can,
Do as this Lanthorn, in its time and place:
  Profess the Faith, and thou a Lanthorn art:
But yet if Grace has not possessed thee:
Thou want'st this Candle Light within thy heart,
And art none other, than dark Lanthorns be.

LIV
UPON THE CHALK-STONE

This Stone is white, yea, warm, and also soft,
  Easie to work upon, unless 'tis naught.
It leaves a white Impression upon those,
Whom it doth touch, be they its Friends or Foes.

  The Child of God, is like to this Chalk-Stone,
White in his Life, easily wrought upon:
Warm in Affections, apt to leave impress,
On whom he deals with, of true Godliness.

  He is no sulling Coal, nor daubing Pitch,
Nor one of whom men catch the Scab, or Itch;
But such who in the Law of God doth walk,
Tender of heart, in Life whiter than Chalk.

LXXII
UPON TIME AND ETERNITY

Eternity is like unto a Ring.
Time, like to Measure, doth it self extend;
Measure commences, is a finite thing.
The Ring has no beginning, middle, end.

3. THE LYRICAL INSTRUCTION
OF ISAAC WATTS

The Sorrows of the mind
Be banish'd from the place
Religion never was design'd
To make our pleasures less.
—*Watts,* Hymns and Spiritual Songs *(1709)*

I have often tried to strip death of its frightful
colours, and make all the terrible airs of it vanish
into Softness and Delight.—*Watts,* Reliquiae
Juveniles *(1734)*

*Divine Songs Attempted in Easy Language for
the Use of Children* (1715) by Isaac Watts provides a lyrical complement to the frequently alarming stories and verses of his fellow Puritan writers for children. Like Bunyan and Janeway, this Dissenting tutor and pastor made religious instruction his paramount aim. But unlike his predecessors, he relied on the engaging lyric and on metrical dexterity to reach his audience. While always upholding Puritan doctrine, his poetry gently softens the Christian message of repentance and gracefully attenuates the stress on fire and brimstone.

The son of an Independent deacon, Watts was born in the year of Milton's death and probably came under the spell of the great Puritan poet's writings at an early age. He studied Latin, Greek, French, and Hebrew at King Edward VI School in

Southampton, after which he spent four years at London's Newington Green Academy under the principalship of the Reverend Thomas Rowe, a Calvinist. But even though Watts was brought up strictly within the Puritan tradition, and even though he moved with ease among the learned Puritan élite, he remained free of sectarian bias—unaffected by the extremes of such enclaves as Arminianism, Arianism, and Trinitarianism. What is so remarkable about his poetry is its universal appeal born of a conscious desire to praise. In the preface to his *Divine Songs* Watts makes it very clear that "you will find here nothing that savours of a Party: the children of high and low degree, of the Church of England and Dissenters, baptized in infancy or not, may all join together in these Songs."

A clear indication that Watts had no intention of following the example of the unremittingly admonitory Janeway can be seen by comparing their choice of Biblical quotations. Watts chose as his epigraph "Out of the Mouths of Babes and Sucklings Thou hast perfected Praise" (Matt. 21.16), which certainly echoes Janeway's use of Psalm 8.2: "Out of the mouths of Babes and Sucklings Thou hast ordained Strength." But the difference between *ordaining strength* and *perfecting praise* is significant, and it accounts for the palpable contrasts between the lyrics of Watts and the writings of Janeway, Bunyan, and the Puritan primers.

Watts deliberately proposed to divert, amuse, and entertain in all his poetry for children. "There is a great delight", he says in the preface to the *Divine Songs*, "in the very learning of truths and duties this way. There is something so amusing and entertaining in rhymes and metre, that will incline children to make this part of their business a diversion." And in the preface to the two "Moral Songs" that were included in the 1715 edition of the *Divine Songs*, he hoped that "children might find Delight and Profit together." Prior to the composition of the songs, Watts had already written *Horae Lyricae* (1706), early experiments with psalms and hymns, and *Hymns and Spiritual Songs* (1707, 1709), which made a long-lasting contribution to English hymnody. A few years later in the *Divine Songs* (1715) he demonstrated his ability to employ simple diction, rhymes, and rhythms to fashion Christian lyrics for children that artfully combine instruction, admonition, and praise. Often announcing his "lessons" in his titles—"Love Between Brother and Sister", "Against Idleness and Mischief"—he claims the young reader's attention with homely, familiar subjects before introducing fearful depictions of the wages of sin. The God-fearing, sin-obsessed children in Watts's hymns reflect the Puritan view of the child as a miniature adult, capable of an adult's conception of death and damnation, yet Watts's severity is tempered by his graceful prosody and sweetness of tone. His inimitable gentleness is most evident in his treatment of the Incarnation, Crucifixion, and Resurrection in "A Cradle Hymn". Only a poet of great compassion and delicacy would have attempted to relate the highlights of the Christian story in the form of a lullaby. While the infant is rocked and soothed to sleep, the mother or nurse sings of the Christ Child whose "softest bed was hay", and who came to earth "to save thee, child, from dying/Save my dear from burning flame." Hell-fire, a plain fact in Watts's creed, has been woven naturally and unobtrusively into this lilting cradle-song.

In the 1740 edition of the *Divine Songs* the number of "Moral Songs" had increased to seven. (The title was changed to *Divine and Moral Songs* in the 1812 edition.) These lessons by example show a more benign Watts. Prominent motifs in these songs are animals and plants (which in the *Divine Songs* were used only occasionally), employed to provide ideal moral comparisons. "The Rose" extends the lilies-of-the field theme of the Divine Song "Against Pride in Clothes", laying its stress on the enduring "scent" of dutiful goodness. Watts shows in his "Moral Songs" his closest affinity to Bunyan's *Country Rhimes*; there is a difference, however, in the fact that, while Bunyan's sinner is catechized by the articulate spider, Watts's "The Ant" inculcates its lesson simply by describing that insect's activities.

The importance of Watts's *Divine and Moral Songs* is not difficult to document. In Victorian times the freshness and power of his imagery made his children's poems not only effective inducements to piety and virtue but comforting memory exercises as well. Lewis Carroll in *Alice in Wonderland* recognized the hold of Watts on the popular imagination when he submitted "Against Idleness and Mischief" to the brilliant parody of "How doth the little crocodile". Historians of church music readily acknowledge a general indebtedness to Watts, and some pay specific tribute to his works for the young. Louis Benson in *The English Hymn* (1915; rpt., 1962) regards these poems as "the fountainhead of . . . Children's Hymnody in the English Language". *The Oxford Book of Carols* (1928) contains Martin Shaw's setting of the "Cradle Song". Finally, many of Watts's poetic maxims about the Christian's responsibility to be always busy, obedient, and clean—often accepted as direct biblical injunction—have exerted an influence on Sunday School parlance to this day.

ISAAC WATTS (1674-1748)
From *Divine Songs Attempted in Easy Language for the Use of Children* (1715)

THE EXCELLENCY OF THE BIBLE

Great God, with wonder and with praise
    On all thy works I look;
But still thy wisdom, power, and grace,
    Shine brighter in thy book.

The stars, that in their courses roll,
    Have much instruction given;
But thy good Word informs my soul
    How I may climb to heaven.

The fields provide me food, and show
    The goodness of the Lord;
But fruits of life and glory grow
    In thy most holy Word.

Here are my choicest treasures hid,
    Here my best comfort lies;
Here my desires are satisfied,
    And hence my hopes arise.

Lord, make me understand thy law;
    Show what my faults have been;
And from thy gospel let me draw
    Pardon for all my sin.

Here would I learn how Christ has died
    To save my soul from hell:
Not all the books on earth beside
    Such heavenly wonders tell.

Then let me love my Bible more,
    And take a fresh delight
By day to read these wonders o'er,
    And meditate by night.

PRAISE TO GOD
FOR LEARNING TO READ

The praises of my tongue
   I offer to the Lord,
That I was taught and learnt so young
   To read his holy Word.

That I am brought to know
   The danger I was in,
By nature and by practice too
   A wretched slave to sin.

That I am led to see
   I can do nothing well;
And whither shall a sinner flee
   To save himself from hell?

Dear Lord, this book of thine
   Informs me where to go,
For grace to pardon all my sin,
   And make me holy too.

Here I can read, and learn
   How Christ, the Son of God,
Has undertook our great concern;
   Our ransom cost his blood.

And now he reigns above,
   He sends his Spirit down
To show the wonders of his love,
   And make his gospel known.

O may that Spirit teach,
   And make my heart receive,
Those truths which all thy servants preach,
   And all thy saints believe.

Then shall I praise the Lord
   In a more cheerful strain,
That I was taught to read his Word,
   And have not learnt in vain.

THE ALL-SEEING GOD

Almighty God, thy piercing eye
   Strikes through the shades of night,
And our most secret actions lie
   All open to thy sight.

There's not a sin that we commit,
   Nor wicked word we say,
But in thy dreadful book 'tis writ,
   Against the judgment-day.

And must the crimes that I have done
   Be read and published there?
Be all expos'd before the sun,
   While men and angels hear?

Lord, at thy foot asham'd I lie;
   Upward I dare not look;
Pardon my sins before I die,
   And blot them from thy book.

Remember all the dying pains
   That my Redeemer felt,
And let his blood wash out my stains,
   And answer for my guilt.

O may I now for ever fear
   To indulge a sinful thought,
Since the great God can see and hear,
   And writes down every fault.

HEAVEN AND HELL

There is beyond the sky
   A heaven of joy and love;
And holy children, when they die,
   Go to that world above.

There is a dreadful hell,
   And everlasting pains;
There sinners must with devils dwell,
   In darkness, fire, and chains.

Can such a wretch as I
   Escape this cursed end?
And may I hope, whene'er I die,
   I shall to heaven ascend?

Then will I read and pray,
   While I have life and breath:
Lest I should be cut off to-day,
   And sent to eternal death.

THE ADVANTAGES OF EARLY RELIGION

Happy's the child whose youngest years
    Receive instructions well;
Who hates the sinner's path, and fears
    The road that leads to hell.

When we devote our youth to God,
    'Tis pleasing in his eyes:
A flower, when offer'd in the bud,
    Is no vain sacrifice.

'Tis easier work if we begin
    To fear the Lord betimes;
While sinners that grow old in sin
    Are harden'd in their crimes.

'Twill save us from a thousand snares,
    To mind religion young;
Grace will preserve our following years,
    And make our virtue strong.

To thee, almighty God, to thee,
    Our childhood we resign;
'Twill please us to look back and see
    That our whole lives were thine.

Let the sweet work of prayer and praise
    Employ my youngest breath;
Thus I'm prepar'd for longer days,
    Or fit for early death.

LOVE BETWEEN BROTHERS AND SISTERS

Whatever brawls disturb the street,
　　There should be peace at home;
Where sisters dwell and brothers meet,
　　Quarrels should never come.

Birds in their little nests agree;
　　And 'tis a shameful sight,
When children of one family
　　Fall out, and chide, and fight.

Hard names at first, and threatening words,
　　That are but noisy breath,
May grow to clubs and naked swords,
　　To murder and to death.

The devil tempts one mother's son
　　To rage against another;
So wicked Cain was hurried on
　　Till he had kill'd his brother.

The wise will make their anger cool,
　　At least before 'tis night;
But in the bosom of a fool
　　It burns till morning light.

AGAINST QUARRELLING AND FIGHTING

[handwritten: Warning for children not to fight]

Let dogs delight to bark and bite,
　　For God hath made them so;
Let bears and lions growl and fight,
　　For 'tis their nature too.

[handwritten: most famous]

But, children, you should never let
　　Such angry passions rise;
Your little hands were never made
　　To tear each other's eyes.

Let love through all your actions run,
　　And all your words be mild;
Live like the blessed Virgin's Son,
　　That sweet and lovely child.

His soul was gentle as a lamb;
　　And as his stature grew,
He grew in favour both with man,
　　And God his Father too.

Now Lord of all he reigns above,
　　And from his heavenly throne
He sees what children dwell in love,
　　And marks them for his own.

AGAINST IDLENESS AND MISCHIEF

For our
purposes
most
important
one

in
Alice &
Wonderland

How doth the little busy bee
  Improve each shining hour,
And gather honey all the day
  From every opening flower!

How skilfully she builds her cell!
  How neat she spreads the wax!
And labors hard to store it well
  With the sweet food she makes.

In works of labour or of skill,
  I would be busy too;
For Satan finds some mischief still
  For idle hands to do.

In books, or work, or healthful play,
  Let my first years be past,
That I may give for every day
  Some good account at last.

AGAINST PRIDE IN CLOTHES

Why should our garments, made to hide
Our parents' shame, provoke our pride?
The art of dress did ne'er begin,
Till Eve, our mother, learn'd to sin.

When first she put the covering on,
Her robe of innocence was gone;
And yet her children vainly boast
In the sad marks of glory lost.

How proud we are! how fond to shew
Our clothes, and call them rich and new!
When the poor sheep and silkworm wore
That very clothing long before.

The tulip and the butterfly
Appear in gayer coats than I;
Let me be drest fine as I will,
Flies, worms, and flowers, exceed me still.

Then will I set my heart to find
Inward adornings of the mind;
Knowledge and virtue, truth and grace,
These are the robes of richest dress.

No more shall worms with me compare;
This is the raiment angels wear;
The Son of God, when here below,
Put on this blest apparel too.

It never fades, it ne'er grows old,
Nor fears the rain, nor moth, nor mould;
It takes no spot, but still refines;
The more 'tis worn, the more it shines.

In this on earth would I appear,
Then go to heaven and wear it there;
God will approve it in his sight,
'Tis his own work, and his delight.

OBEDIENCE TO PARENTS

Let children that would fear the Lord
   Hear what their teachers say;
With reverence meet their parents' word,
   And with delight obey.

Have not you heard what dreadful plagues
   Are threaten'd by the Lord,
To him that breaks his father's law,
   Or mocks his mother's word?

What heavy guilt upon him lies!
   How cursed is his name!
The ravens shall pick out his eyes,
   And eagles eat the same.

But those who worship God, and give
   Their parents honour due,
Here on this earth they long shall live,
   And live hereafter too.

THE CHILD'S COMPLAINT

Why should I love my sport so well,
  So constant at my play,
And lose the thoughts of heaven and hell,
  And then forget to pray?

What do I read my Bible for,
  But, Lord, to learn thy will?
And shall I daily know thee more,
  And less obey thee still?

How senseless is my heart, and wild!
  How vain are all my thoughts!
Pity the weakness of a child,
  And pardon all my faults!

Make me thy heavenly voice to hear,
  And let me love to pray,
Since God will lend a gracious ear
  To what a child can say.

A MORNING SONG

My God, who makes the sun to know
  His proper hour to rise,
And to give light to all below,
  Doth send him round the skies.

When from the chambers of the east
  His morning race begins,
He never tires, nor stops to rest,
  But round the world he shines.

So, like the sun, would I fulfil
  The business of the day:
Begin my work betimes, and still
  March on my heavenly way.

Give me, O Lord, thy early grace,
  Nor let my soul complain
That the young morning of my days
  Has all been spent in vain.

AN EVENING SONG

And now another day is gone,
　I'll sing my Maker's praise;
My comforts every hour make known
　His providence and grace.

But how my childhood runs to waste!
　My sins, how great their sum!
Lord, give me pardon for the past,
　And strength for days to come.

I lay my body down to sleep;
　Let angels guard my head,
And through the hours of darkness keep
　Their watch around my bed.

With cheerful heart I close my eyes,
　Since thou wilt not remove;
And in the morning let me rise
　Rejoicing in thy love.

From *The Moral Songs*

By 1740 Watts's edition of *Divine Songs* included seven "Moral Songs" as well.

THE SLUGGARD

'Tis the voice of the sluggard; I heard him complain,
"You have waked me too soon, I must slumber again."
As the door on its hinges, so he on his bed,
Turns his sides, and his shoulders, and his heavy head.

"A little more sleep, and a little more slumber;"
Thus he wastes half his days and his hours without number;
And when he gets up, he sits folding his hands,
Or walks about sauntering, or trifling he stands.

I pass'd by his garden, and saw the wild brier,
The thorn and the thistle, grow broader and higher;
The clothes that hang on him are turning to rags;
And his money still wastes, till he starves, or he begs.

I made him a visit, still hoping to find
He had took better care for improving his mind:
He told me his dreams, talk'd of eating and drinking,
But he scarce reads his Bible, and never loves thinking.

Said I then to my heart, "Here's a lesson for me;
That man's but a picture of what I might be;
But thanks to my friends for their care in my breeding,
Who taught me betimes to love working and reading."

THE ANT, OR EMMET

These emmets, how little they are in our eyes!
We tread them to dust, and a troop of them dies,
   Without our regard or concern;
Yet as wise as we are, if we went to their school,
There's many a sluggard and many a fool
   Some lessons of wisdom might learn.

They don't wear their time out in sleeping or play
But gather up corn in a sunshiny day,
   And for winter they lay up their stores:
They manage their work in such regular forms,
One would think they foresaw all the frost and the storms,
   And so brought their food within doors.

But I have less sense than a poor creeping ant,
If I take no due care for the things I shall want,
   Nor provide against dangers in time:
When death or old age shall stare in my face,
What a wretch shall I be in the end of my days,
   If I trifle away all their prime!

Now, now, while my strength and my youth are in bloom,
Let me think what will serve me when sickness shall come,
   And pray that my sins be forgiven:
Let me read in good books, and believe, and obey,
That when death turns me out of this cottage of clay,
   I may dwell in a palace in heaven.

THE ROSE

How fair is the Rose! what a beautiful flower.
   The glory of April and May!
But the leaves are beginning to fade in an hour,
   And they wither and die in a day.

Yet the Rose has one powerful virtue to boast,
   Above all the flowers of the field;
When its leaves are all dead, and fine colours are lost,
   Still how sweet a perfume it will yield!

So frail is the youth and the beauty of man,
   Though they bloom and look gay like the Rose;
But all our fond care to preserve them is vain;
   Time kills them as fast as he goes.

Then I'll not be proud of my youth or my beauty,
   Since both of them wither and fade;
But gain a good name by well-doing my duty;
   This will scent, like a Rose, when I'm dead.

A SUMMER EVENING

How fine has the day been! how bright was the sun,
How lovely and joyful the course that he run!
Though he rose in a mist when his race he begun,
    And there followed some droppings of rain;
But now the fair traveller's come to the west,
His rays are all gold, and his beauties are best;
He paints the skies gay as he sinks to his rest,
    And foretells a bright rising again.

Just such is the Christian: his course he begins,
Like the sun, in a mist, while he mourns for his sins,
And melts into tears; then he breaks out and shines,
    And travels his heavenly way:
But when he comes nearer to finish his race,
Like a fine setting sun he looks richer in grace,
And gives a sure hope at the end of his days
    Of rising in brighter array.

In the 1727 edition of *Divine Songs* "A Cradle Hymn" appeared after two "Moral Songs".

A CRADLE HYMN

Hush, my dear, lie still and slumber!
    Holy angels guard thy bed!
Heavenly blessings without number
    Gently falling on thy head.

Sleep, my babe; thy food and raiment,
    House and home, thy friends provide;
All without thy care or payment,
    All thy wants are well supplied.

How much better thou'rt attended
    Than the Son of God could be,
When from heaven he descended,
    And became a child like thee!

Soft and easy is thy cradle;
    Coarse and hard thy Saviour lay,
When his birthplace was a stable,
    And his softest bed was hay.

Blessed babe! what glorious features,
    Spotless fair, divinely bright!
Must he dwell with brutal creatures?
    How could angels bear the sight!

Was there nothing but a manger
   Cursed sinners could afford,
To receive the heavenly Stranger?
   Did they thus affront their Lord?

Soft, my child; I did not chide thee,
   Though my song might sound too hard;
'Tis thy { mother* / nurse that } sits beside thee,
   And her arms shall be thy guard.

Yet to read the shameful story,
   How the Jews abus'd their King,
How they serv'd the Lord of Glory,
   Makes me angry while I sing.

See the kinder shepherds round him,
   Telling wonders from the sky;
There they sought him, there they found him,
   With his virgin mother by.

See the lovely babe a-dressing;
   Lovely infant, how he smil'd!
When he wept, the mother's blessing
   Sooth'd and hush'd the holy child.

Lo, he slumbers in his manger,
   Where the horned oxen feed;
Peace, my darling, here's no danger,
   Here's no ox a-near thy bed.

'Twas to save thee, child, from dying,
   Save my dear from burning flame,
Bitter groans, and endless crying,
   That thy blest Redeemer came.

Mayst thou live to know and fear him,
   Trust and love him all thy days;
Then go dwell for ever near him,
   See his face, and sing his praise!

I could give thee thousand kisses,
   Hoping what I most desire;
Not a mother's fondest wishes
   Can to greater joys aspire.

* Here you may use the words, brother, sister, neighbour, friend, &c. [Author's note.]

4. CHAPBOOKS AND PENNY HISTORIES

Oh! give us once again the wishing cap
Of Fortunatus, and the invisible coat
Of Jack the Giant Killer, Robin Hood,
And Sabra in the forest with St. George!
The child, whose love is here, doth reap
One precious gain, that he forgets himself.
—Wordsworth, The Prelude *(1805)*

Although the austere Puritan influence exerted by Janeway and Bunyan persisted well into the nineteenth century, the emphasis gradually shifted in the eighteenth century away from their dogmatic and fearful lessons towards the more subdued moralizing adopted by Isaac Watts. Prominent among the changing attitudes in British society were those concerning childhood. Children were no longer always viewed as miniature adults but as "rational creatures" who should be allowed "liberties and freedom suitable to their ages", in the words of the philosopher John Locke, whose *Some Thoughts Concerning Education* (1693) exerted an influence throughout the eighteenth century. Locke wrote that children should not "be hindered from being children, nor from playing and doing as children. . . . They love to be busy, change and variety are what they delight in; curiosity is but an appetite for knowledge, the in-

strument nature has provided to remove ignorance" (Section 118).

Not everyone agreed with Locke, of course, nor did change come unchallenged. The anonymous author of *The Parental Instructor; or, A Father's Present to His Children* (1820) clung to the Puritan conception of children as little adults. But while he admitted that they "may be amused and instructed at the same time", he considered such reading as the fairy tales of Charles Perrault, which had been available in English translation for nearly a century, unedifying and therefore without value.

"Come, papa," said the little Charles, "you must favour us either with the tale of Cinderella, Ass-skin, Tom Thumb, or Bluebeard."

"What!" said Mr Elliot, "at your age—would you wish me to relate stories which have not even the shadow of common sense in them? It would really be ridiculous, to see a great big

boy of ten years of age, and a young lady of nine, listening, with open mouths, to the adventures of an Ogre who ate little children, or the Little Gentleman with his Seven-league Boots; I could only pardon it in a child, who requires to be rocked asleep by his nurse."

"But papa," said Charles, "these stories are very amusing." "Yes, my dear, but what benefit can you derive from them? Absurdities like these only serve to vitiate your taste and weaken your mind, while some of them excite terror and disgust." "Oh, papa, I know very well that there are neither ogres nor fairies." "When that is the case," returned his father, "why are you so anxious to hear about these chimeras? What benefit can you derive from the story of the Beautiful Princess who sleeped an hundred years? I fear that, by accustoming yourself to learn such stories, you will be disgusted with what is useful and of real importance, and relinquish beneficial conversations and instructive reading, to run after frivolous books, or listen to childish tales."

"Papa," replied Charles, "you know better what is suitable for us than we do ourselves; but may I venture to inquire why you make us learn the Fables of La Fontaine by heart, in which there are ravens and foxes that speak? These animals are quite as extra-ordinary as fairies and ogres; for instance, the stork who gives the alarm of famine at the hillock of the ants, her neighbours, exists no more than the wolf which converses with Little Red-Riding-Hood!"

"Charles," returned Mr Elliot, "you are now reasoning like a man; therefore let us discourse together a little. What you have said is very true, for the speaking stork does not exist any more than the blue bird and the cat in boots; but the story of the bird does not contain any moral; that is, there is nothing results from the reading of it that can afford you instruction, while the stork gives a very important lesson, by making us sensible of the necessity of preparing, during our youth, resources which may be of the most essential service in old age,—and here lies the difference between the fables of La Fontaine and the fairy tales."

In spite of such widely held views, however, fairy tales survived and proliferated. Aided by the popularity, among young and old alike, of such new novels as *Robinson Crusoe* (1719) and *Gulliver's Travels* (1726), adventure and delight soon gained an undisputed place in children's reading and continued to find an ever-expanding audience—even when they were presented in the form of crude formula writing.

The first entrepreneurs to take advantage of this development were a group of low-class itinerant salesmen, known as chapmen, who had peddled their pins, needles, ribbons, and broadside ballads since the days of Shakespeare, and now added to their wares small paperbound books supplied by publishers. The compilers of these chapbooks—or penny histories, as many were called—borrowed from jestbooks, broadsides, and ballads in offering stories of the adventures of Guy of Warwick and Bevis of Southampton, Dick Whittington and Tom Thumb, Jack Horner and Cock Robin; such legends as that of Faust in *Fortunatus*, abridged from medieval romance; and native English folklore, popularizing the prophecies of Mother Shipton and the deeds of Robin Hood. The chapmen were greeted eagerly, and their books were read voraciously by both children and adults.

Chapbooks (the term is possibly derived from the Anglo-Saxon *ceap*, meaning "trade") were all the more successful because they were inexpensive, attractive, and small. They could be purchased for as little as a penny, although the price rose slightly in the nineteenth century with improved bindings, leather covers, and hand-coloured copperplate illustrations. Originally they were paper-covered booklets, produced by folding a single sheet several times. They often consisted of twenty-four uncut pages, though lengths of eight and sixteen pages were also common, and they were adorned with woodcut illustrations on the title-page and throughout the text.

While few chapbooks could make any claim to literary value, they have enduring importance in the history of children's literature. Satisfying the human desire for stories, conducting readers into the realm of fancy, celebrating heroes, they uncovered and pleased a new market for books. For generations of children to whom little else was available they provided their first, and therefore formative, reading matter and as a result contributed to the spread of literacy. Chapbooks were also an archive of fairy mythology that might have been lost if these publications had not existed. Finally the popularity of chapbooks drew to the attention of serious writers the fact that there was a specific audience, young and keen, waiting to be introduced to new works of the imagination.

An Elegy on the Death and Burial of Cock Robin

The first four verses of "Cock Robin" appeared in *Tommy Thumb's Pretty Song-Book* (1744); by the 1780s the entire rhyme had been published. In *The Oxford Dictionary of Nursery Rhymes* Iona and Peter Opie present two theories about its origin. It may describe the "intrigues attending the downfall of Robert Walpole's ministry (1742)"; or it may be of much earlier provenance, possibly deriving from the Norse tale of the death of Balder. These two theories are not incompatible. It could have been an old rhyme rewritten to fit the political situation in Walpole's day.

COCK ROBIN.

WHO kill'd Cock Robin ?
I, says the Sparrow,
    With my bow and arrow,
And I kill'd Cock Robin.

This is the Sparrow,
With his bow and arrow.

5

Who saw him die?
  I, said the Fly,
  With my little eye,
And I saw him die.

This is the Fly,
With his little eye.

6

Who caught his blood?
  I, said the Fish,
  With my little dish,
And I caught his blood.

This is the Fish,
That held the dish.

7

Who made his shroud?
  I, said the Beetle,
  With my little needle,
And I made his shroud.

This is the Beetle,
With his thread and needle.

(handwritten) Beetle made his shroud

8

Who shall dig the grave?
  I, said the Owl,
  With my spade and shov'l,
And I'll dig his grave.

This is the Owl so brave,
That dug Cock Robin's grave.

(handwritten) Owl is only brave bird.

9

Who will be the Parson?
I, said the Rook,
With my little book,
And I will be the Parson.

Here's parson Rook,
A reading his book.

10

Who will be the clerk?
I, said the Lark,
If 'tis not in the dark,
And I will be the clerk.

Behold how the Lark,
Says Amen, like a clerk.

mocking
people In the
Church.

11

Who'll carry him to the grave?
  I, said the Kite,
  If 'tis not in the night,
And I'll carry him to the grave.

Behold now the Kite,
How he takes his flight.

Fear ot Dark, ghost + grave yards

12

Who will carry the link,
  I, said the Linnet,
  I'll fetch it in a minute,
And I'll carry the link.

— torch

super stitious

Here's the Linnet with a light
Altho' 'tis not night.

13

Who'll be the chief mourner?
I, said the Dove,
For I mourn for my love,
And I'll be the chief mourner.

Here's a pretty Dove,
That mourns for her love.

love birds

14

Who'll bear the pall?
We, says the Wrens,
Both the cock and the hen,
And we,ll bear the pall.

See the Wrens so small,
Who bore Cock Robin's pall.

15

Who'll sing a psalm?
I, says the Thrush,
As he sat in a bush,
And I'll sing a psalm.

Here's a fine Thrush,
Singing psalms in a bush.

[handwritten note: Bird singing psalms]

16

Who'll toll the bell?
I, says the Bull,
Because I can pull,
So Cock Robin farewell.

All the birds in the air,
Fell a sighing and sobbing,
When they heard the bell toll
For poor Cock Robin.

[handwritten note: the bell is a signal for birds to mourn for cock robin]

The Interesting Story of the Children in the Wood

Also known as *The Babes in the Wood*, this story appeared in book form as early as 1595. It was a favourite ballad with minstrels. Mrs Trimmer recalled reading a chapbook version in her childhood during the 1740s.

THE CHILDREN IN THE WOOD

Now ponder well, ye parents dear,
  The words which I shall write,
A dismal story you shall hear,
  In time brought forth to light.

A merchant of no small account,
  In England dwelt of late,
Who did in riches far surmount
  Most men of his estate.

Yet sickness came, and he must die,
  No help his life could save;
In anguish too his wife did lie,
  Death sent them to the grave.

No love between this pair was lost,
  For each was mild and kind;
Together they gave up the ghost,
  And left two babes behind.

The one a fine and pretty boy,
  Not passing six years old;
A girl the next, the mother's joy,
  And cast in beauty's mould.

The father left his little son,
  As it was made appear,
When at the age of twenty-one,
  Three hundred pounds a year.

And to his daughter, we are told,
  Six hundred pounds to pay,
In value full of English gold,
  Upon her wedding day.

But if these children chanced to die,
  As death might soon come on,
The uncle then (none can deny)
  Made all the wealth his own.

Pisarius call'd his brother near,
    As on his bed he lay:
Remember, oh! my brother dear,
    Remember what I say?

This life I quit, and to your care
    My little babes commend:
Their youth in hopeful virtue rear;
    Their guardian, uncle, friend.

Their parents both you must supply,
    They do not know their loss,
And when you see the tear-swoln eye,
    For pity be not cross:

'Tis in your power (now alone)
    Their greatest friend to be;
To give them, when we're dead & gone,
    Or bliss, or misery.

If you direct their steps aright,
    From God expect reward;
All actions are within His sight,
    Of which He takes regard.

With clay-cold lips the babes they kiss'd,
    And gave their last adieu!
A heart of stone would melt, I wist,
    So sad a scene to view.

With tears, Androgus did reply—
    Dear brother, do not fear;
Their ev'ry wish I will supply,
    And be their uncle dear.

God never prosper me nor mine,
    In whatsoe'er I have,
If e'er I hurt them with design,
    When you are in the grave!

The parents being dead and gone,
    The children home he takes,
And seems to soften all their moan,
    So much of them he makes:

But had not kept the little souls
    A twelvemonth and a day,
But in his breast a scheme there rolls,
    To take their lives away.

He bargain'd with two ruffians strong,
    Who were of furious mood,
To take away these children young,
    And slay them in a wood.

Then gave it out both far and near,
    That he them both did send
To town for education there,
    To one who was their friend.

Away the little babes were sent,
    Rejoicing with much pride;
It gave them both no small content,
    On horseback for to ride:

They prate and prattle pleasantly,
    As they ride on the way,
To those who should their butchers be,
    And work their lives decay.

The pretty speeches which they said,
    Made one rogue's heart relent;
For though he undertook the deed,
    He sorely did repent.

The other still more hard of heart,
    Was not at all aggriev'd,
And vow'd that he would do his part,
    For what he had receiv'd.

The other wont thereto agree,
    Which caused no little strife;
To fight they go right suddenly,
    About the children's life.

And he that was in mildest mood,
    Did slay the other there,
Within an unfrequented wood,
    The babes did quake with fear.

He took the children by the hand,
   While tears were in their eyes;
And for a scheme which he had planned,
   He bid them make no noise:

Then two long miles he did them lead,
   Of hunger they complain;
Stay here, says he, I'll bring you bread,
   And soon be back again.

Then hand in hand they took their way,
   And wander'd up and down;
But never more did they survey
   The man come from the town.

Their pretty lips with blackberries
   Were all besmear'd and dy'd,
And when the shades of night arose,
   They sat them down and cry'd.

imagination is used.

These pretty babes thus wander'd long,
   Without the least relief,
The woods, the briers, and thorns among,
   Till death did end their grief.

the birds bury them.

These pretty babes from any man,
   No funeral rite receives;
But Robin Redbreast forms the plan,
   To cover them with leaves.

And now the heavy wrath of God
   Upon their uncle fell;
The furies haunt his curst abode,
   And peace bade him farewell.

spirits that are outside your house

His barns consum'd, his house was fired,
   His lands were barren made,
His cattle in the fields expired,
   And nothing with him staid.

His ships, which both were gone to sea,
    Were on their voyage lost,
And fate did order him to be
    With wants and sorrows crost.

His lands or sold or mortgag'd were,
    Ere seven years were past,
Attend, and you shall quickly hear
    How prosper'd guilt at last.

The fellow who did take in hand
    The children both to kill,
To die was judged by the land,
    For murder—by God's will.

The guilty secret in his breast
    He could no more contain:
So all the truth he then confess'd,
    To ease him of his pain.

The uncle did in prison die,
    Unpitied was his fate:
Ye guardians, warning take hereby,
    And never prove ingrate.

To helpless infants still be kind,
    And give to each his right;
For, if you do not, soon you'll find
    God will your deeds requite.

From *The Life and Death of Tom Thumb*

The adventures of a miniature man are part of international folklore. The earliest known text of the story in English (1621) is attributed to Richard Johnson (1573-1659?). The English versions of the tale, in both prose and verse, have such details as Tom's finding favour with the Fairy Queen and performing service in King Arthur's court.

This version is from a chapbook in the collection of Samuel Pepys (1663-1703), which he called "Penny Merriments".

THE LIFE AND DEATH OF TOM THUMB

Of the Birth, Name, and bringing up of Tom Thumb,
with the merry Pranks he play'd in his Child-hood.

In Arthurs Court Tom Thumb did live,
a man of mickle might,
The best of all the Table round,
and eke a doughty Knight:
In stature but an inch in height,
or quarter of a span,
Then think you not this worthy Knight,
was prov'd a valiant man.

[handwritten: Didn't speak any more this way — used humorously]

His Father was a Plow-man plain,
his mother milkt the Cow,
And yet a way to get a Son,
these couple knew not how:
Until such time the good old man
to learned Merlin goes,
And there to him in deep distress,
in secret manner show.

How in his heart he wisht to have
a Child in time to come,
To be his heir, though it might be,
no bigger then his Thumb:
Of which Old Merlin was foretold,
that he his wish should have,
And so his Son of Stature small,
the Charmer to him gave.

No blood nor bones in him should be,
in shape, and being such,
That he should hear him speak, but not
his wandring shaddow touch,
But so unseen to go or come,
whereas it pleas'd him well,
Begot and born in half an hour,
to fit his Fathers will.

And in four minutes grew so fast,
that he became so tall,
As was the Plow-mans Thumb in length,
and so she did him call:
Tom Thumb, the which the Fairy Queen,
there gave him to his name,
Whom with her train of Goblins grim,
unto the Christening came.

Whereas she cloath'd him richly brave,
in Garments richly fair,
The which did serve him many years
in seemly sort to wear:
His hat made of an Oaken leaf,
his Shirt a Spiders web,
Both light and soft for these his limbs,
which was so smally bred.

His hose and Doublet thistle down,
together weav'd full fine,
His Stockins of an apple green,
made of the outward Rhine:[1]
His Garters were two little hairs,
pluckt from his Mothers eye,
His Shooes made of a Mouses skin,
and tann'd most curiously.

Thus like a valiant gallant he,
adventures forth to go,
With other Children in the streets,
his pretty tricks to show;
Where he for Counters, Pins and Points,[2]
and cherry-stones did play,
Till he amongst those Gamesters young,
had lost his stock away.

Yet he could soon renew the same,
when as most nimbly he,
Would dive into the cherry bags,
and there partaker be:
Unseen or felt of any one,
until a Schollar shut,
This nimble youth into a box,
wherein his Pins were put.

Of whom to be reveng'd, he took,
in mirth and pleasant game,
Black pots and Glasses, which he hung
upon a bright Sun beam,
The other Boys to do the same;
in pieces broke them quite,
For which they were most soundly whipt,
whereat he laught out-right.

[1] Finest quality hemp.
[2] Ribbons.

From *The Pleasant History of Thomas Hickathrift*

Tom Hickathrift is only one English example of the type of the strong giant. The motif of the strong man's labour contract also occurs in the story of another folk hero, the Lincolnshire muscle-man William of Lindholme. Like the *Tom Thumb*, the following is taken from a chapbook in Pepys's collection, "Penny Merriments".

THE PLEASANT HISTORY OF THOMAS HICKATHRIFT

His Birth and Parentage, and the true manner of his performing many Many Acts, and how he Killed a Gyant.

Young man, here thou mayest behold what Honour Tom came unto.

And if that thou dost buy this Book,
Be sure that thou dost in it look;
And read it o're, then thou wilt say,
Thy money is not thrown away.

Tall tale

In the Reign before William the Conqueror, I have read in ancient Histories, that there dwelt a Man in the Marsh of the Isle of Ely, in the County of Cambridge whose Name was Thomas Hic-ka-thrift, a poor Man, and day labourer, yet he was a very stout Man, and able to perform two days works instead of one, he having one Son, and no more Children in the world, he called him by his own Name Thomas Hickathrift; this old Man put his Son to good Learning, but he would take none, for he was, as we call them now in this Age, none of the wisest sort, but something soft, and had no docity[1] at all in him: God calling this Old Man his Father out of the world, his Mother being tender of him, and maintained him by her hand labour as well as she could: he being sloathful and not willing to work to get a penny for his living, but all his delight was to be in the Chimney corner, and would eat as much at one time as might very well serve four or five ordinary men, for he was in length when he was but Ten years of age, about eight foot, and in Thickness five foot, and his Hand was like unto a shoulder of Mutton, and in all parts from top to toe, he was like a Monster and yet his great Strength was not known.

How Tom Hic-ka-thrift's Strength came to be known; the which if you please but to read, will give you full satisfaction.

The first time that his Strength was known, was by his Mothers going to a Rich Farmers House, (she being but a poor Woman) to desire a Bottle[2] of Straw to shift[3] her self and her Son Thomas: the Farmer being an honest Charitable Man, bid her take what she would: she going home to her Son Tom, said, I pray thee to go to such a place and fetch me a Bottle of Straw, I have asked him leave: he swore a great Oath he would not go; nay, prithee Tom go, said his old Mother, he swore again he would not go, unless she would borrow him a Cart-rope, she being willing to please him, because she would have some Straw, went and borrowed

[1] Gumption.   [2] Bundle, bale.   [3] In order to replace the old straw.

How the world comes to Know his Strength.

him a Cart-rope to his desire, he taking went his way; so coming to the Farmers House, the Master was in the Barn, and two men a Thrashing: said Tom, I am come for a Bottle of Straw: Tom, said the Master, take as much as thou canst carry; he laid down his Cart-rope, and began to make his Bottle; but, said they, Tom thy rope is too short, and jeer'd poor Tom, but he fitted the man well for it, for he made his bottle, and when he had made it, there was supposed to be a Load of Straw in it for two thousand weight; but, said they, what a great fool art thou? thou canst not carry the Tith[4] on't; but Tom took the Bottle and flung it on his shoulder, and made no more of it then we do of an hundred weight, to the great admiration of Master and Men. Tom Hic-ka-thrift's strength being known in the Town, then they would not let him any longer lye basking by the fire in the Chimney-corner, every one would be hiring him to work, they seeing him to have so much strength, told him that it was a shame for him to live such a lazy course of life, and to lye idle day after day as he did. So Tom seeing them bait at him in such a manner as they did, he went first to one work, then to another, but at length came a Man to Tom, and desired him to go with him unto the Wood, for he had a Tree to bring home, and he would content him. So Tom went with him, and he took with him four Men beside; but when they came to the Wood, they set the Cart by the Tree and began to draw it up with Pullies, but Tom seeing them not able to lift it up, said Stand away you Fools, and takes the Tree and sets it on one end, and lays it in the Cart, now says he, see what a Man can do; Marry, it is true, said they: so when they had done, coming through the Wood they met the Wood-man, Tom asked him for a stick to make his Mother a fire with; I, said the Woodman, take one that thou canst carry: so Tom espyed a Tree bigger then was in the Cart, and lays it on his Shoulder, and goes home with it as fast as the Cart went and six Horses could draw it: This was the second time that Toms Strength was known: so when Tom began to know that he had more strength then twenty Men had, he then began to be Merry with Men, and very tractable, and would Run, or Go, or Jump; and took great delight to be amongst Company, and to go to Fairs and Meetings, and to see Sports and Pastime: So going to a Feast, the Young Men were all met, some to Cudgels, some to Wrastling, some throwing the Hammer, and the like; So Tom stood a little to see their Sport, and at last goes to them that were a throwing the Hammer, and standing a little by to behold their Man-like Sport, at last he takes the Hammer in his hand, to feel the weight of it, and bid them stand out of the way, for he would throw it as far as he could: I, said the Smith, and jeer'd poor Tom, you'l throw it a great way i'le warrant you: but Tom took the Hammer and flung it, and there was a River about five or six furlungs off, and flung it into that: so when he had done he bid the Smith go fetch his Hammer again, and laught the Smith to scorn; but when Tom had done that, he would go to Wrastling, though he had no more skill than an Ass

---

[4] Tenth.

had, but what he did by Strength, yet he flung all that came, for if once he laid hold they were gone: some he would throw over his head, some he would lay down slyly and how he pleased: he would not lock nor strike at their Heels, but flung them two or three Yards from him, ready to break their Necks asunder: so that none at last durst go into the Ring to wrastle with him, for they took him to be some Devil that was come amongst them, so Tom's fame was spread more in the Country.

The Trial of an Ox, for Killing a Man (late eighteenth century)

The animal court is a common scene in many fables. This late eighteenth-century chapbook version of "The Trial of an Ox" contrasts strikingly with the less lenient and more dishonest court depicted by La Fontaine in "The Animals Sick of the Plague" (Bk. VII.1).

TRIAL
OF THE OX.

An Ox was seized by the Dogs, and brought to trial, for having gored his Driver in such a brutal manner, in Smithfield Market, as caused his death. His trial was held at Quadruped Court, Beast Park, near the Pedestrian Hotel. The Lion sat as

TRIAL OF THE OX.   **7**

Judge. The Dogs offered themselves as witnesses, which the Judge refused, as they were thief-takers, and interested. Here the council too began to arrangue, which the Judge would not admit of; he told them, indeed, if a point of law should arise, they might speak to it, but he would have no witness brow-beaten or misled in that court.

The Horse and Ass were then
called up; who deposed, that
they saw the Ox go to a Man
and gore him, near Smithfield,
and that his life was despaired of.

To this the Ox pleaded ignorance, and said, that he had been
ill-used and deprived of his senses,
and knew not what happened in
consequence thereof; but, provided that were not the case, he
certainly would have lost his life

by the murdering Butcher, who
deals death and destruction to
our race, to procure subsistence
for himself and family, by the
sale of our carcases. So now,
my lord, I stand here, arraigned
for the accidental offence of gor-
ing an inhuman drover, whose
only business it was to dispose of
me to the keeper of the slaugh-
ter house.

A Bee, that had been perched
on the Oxes head, offered his
evidence,—and deposed, that he
had been an eye witness of the
whole affair.

" This poor Ox, my Lord,"
says he, " was taken from his
friends and relations in the country, where he led a peaceful innocent life, and put under the
care of a cruel and inhuman
drover, who pricked him all the
way to London, with a nail at
the end of a pole ; and when he
was lame, and unable to walk so

fast as the savage driver designed,
he beat him about the legs, with
a stick, with a great knob at the
end of it, which still made him
more lame. When he came to
Smithfield, he stood, with his
head tied on the rails, from 4
o'clock on Monday morning, till
8 on Monday night, which was
sixteen hours, when the anguish
he was in affected his head so
much, that he lost his senses, and

12   TRIAL OF THE OX,

committed the act for which he stands indicted. Who is to blame, my Lord? It is true, the Man lost his life, but the innocent Ox is not to suffer for it: because from ill treatment the Ox had lost his senses, and therefore could not be accountable for his actions. Those are too blame, my Lord, who encourage drivers in such acts of inhumanity; and suffer a market for wild and mad beasts, to be held in the middle of a large and opulent city: do you

FOR KILLING A MAN.   13

think the queen of my hive would suffer us to bring home what we make boot upon? No, in order to prevent mischief and confusion, we prepare our meat before we are let into the city, and so would these people, had they half the sense they pretend to have!"

Then the Judge interrogated several other witnesses, who corroborated the fact of the former, and the Bear, as counsel, cross-

14   TRIAL OF THE OX,

examined them, in a mild and friendly manner, so as not to confuse their evidence.

Then the Tiger arose, and having commanded silence, spoke as follows:

"*Gentlemen of the Jury,*

You hear what a distinct and clear evidence the Bee has given, in behalf of the prisoner, and you seem sensible of the truth of it. 'Tis amazing that mankind should

FOR KILLING A MAN.   15

complain of cruelty in animals, when their own minds are productive of such scenes of inhumanity: Are not the Ox and other creatures murdered for their emolument? Are not we hunted to death for their amusement, as well as the Stag and the Hare? Are not the Bees burnt, and their houses plundered for their use?

What have you Mr. Horse, for
carrying the boobies on your
back, but stripes and ill treatment? And what have you, Mr.
Ass, who are their nurse and doctor, but lashes and ill language?
Man, the two legged Tiger man,
is the most ungrateful of beasts.''

Then the Judge recapitulated
the evidence, which appeared too
clear to admit of a doubt, that
the poor Ox was pricked and

beaten in a most inhuman manner, by the drover, and that being
driven to desparation by the cruel
treatment, he turned suddenly
round, and gored the heard-
hearted Drover. Upon which,
the Jury returned a *Verdict of
Manslaughter*, and the Judge
Fined him a Blade of Grass,
ordered him to be *Imprisoned
an Hour*, and then *Discharged
him*, amid general acclamations.

Upon which, the Cock clapped
his wings, and crowed applause
to the verdict; and the spectators
departed, perfectly satisfied with
the sentence.

THE END.

From *A New Riddle Book; or A Whetstone for Dull Wits*
(mid-eighteenth century)

(2)

A

New Riddle-Book.

QUESTION I.

INTO this World I came hanging,
And when from the fame I was ganging,
I was bitterly batter'd and fqueez'd,
And then with my Blood they are pleas'd.

Anfwer. *Tis a Pipping pounded into Cyder.*

Q. I am white and ftiff it is well known,
  Likewife my Nofe is red ;
Young Ladies will, as well as **Joan**,
  Oft take me to their Bed.

A. *It is a Candle.*

Q. A wide

(3)

Q. A wide Mouth, no Ears or Eyes,
　No fcorching Flames I feel ;
I fwallow more than may fuffice
　Full forty at a Meal.

A. *It is an Oven.*

Q. Tho' of a great Age,
I am kept in a Cage,
　Having a long tail and one Ear ;
My Mouth it is round,
And when Joys do abound,
　O then I fing wonderful clear.

A. *It is a Bell in a Steeple; the Rope be-*
tokens a Tail, and the wheel an Ear.
　　　　　　　　Q. The

From *The Riddle Book; or Fireside Amusements*, printed by
and for Thomas Richardson, Derby (late eighteenth
century).

7

My face is smooth and wondrous bright,
Which mostly I keep out of sight
Within my house; how that is made
Shall with much brevity be said:
Compos'd with timber and with skin,
Cover'd with blankets warm within:
Here I lie snug, unless in anger,
I look out sharp suspecting danger;
For I'm a blade of mighty wrath,
Whene'er provok'd I sally forth;
Yet quarrels frequently decide,
But n'er am known to change my side,
Tho e'er so much our party vary,
In all disputes my point I carry.
Thousands by me are daily fed,
As many laid among the dead.
I travel into foreign parts;
But not in coach convey'd, or carts.
Ladies, for you I often war,
Then in return my name declare.

7. A SWORD.

10

With words unnumber'd I abound,
  In me mankind take much delight,
In me great store of learning's found,
  Yet I can neither read nor write.

10. A BOOK.

13

In places where mirth and good-humour abound,
Who so welcome as I, or so commonly found?
If I get among gamblers, I never am winner;
Eat nothing, yet who can afford better dinner.
At church of my privilege n'er bate an ace;
Not e'en to churchwarden or parson give place.
In verse or in prose, there are few who indite,
But to me they apply e'er they venture to write.
In council I'm present, nor absent at sea,
Nymphs who're courted by all, come and pay court to me.
Then seek out my title, each spirit lover,
Who dares such a favourite rival discover:
If I move not on four, as I usually do,
You may find me on one leg, but never on two.

13. A TABLE.

14

Ever eating, never cloying,
All devouring, all destroying,
Never finding full repast
'Till I eat the world at last.

14. TIME.

CONUNDRUMS

Q. Why is a good tragedy like a good onion?
A. Because it will make you cry.
Q. Why is a barber like a pepper-box?
A. Because he often takes people by the nose.
Q. Why is a bad woman like a good epigram?
A. Because she carries a sting in her tail.
Q. Why is a large wig like a fierce engagement?
A. Because it consumes much powder.
Q. Why are submissive husbands
   like barleycorns given to poultry?
A. Because they are hen-pecked.
Q. Why is a diverting novel like a canister of tea?
A. Because the leaves afford pleasure to the ladies.
Q. Why is ink like scandal?
A. Because it blackens the fairest things.

Delectando monemus

Instruction with Delight

5. JOHN NEWBERY:
"INSTRUCTION WITH DELIGHT"

*Good counsel is the best legacy a Father can leave to a child; and it
is still the better, when it is so wrapt up, as to beget a curiosity as
well as an inclination to follow it.—Samuel Richardson,* Aesop's
Fables, Fable 86 (1740)

On 18 June 1744 this seemingly inauspicious advertisement appeared in the pages of the *London Penny Advertiser*:

A LITTLE PRETTY POCKET-BOOK, intended for the Instruction and Amusement of little Master Tommy and pretty Miss Polly; with an agreeable Letter to each from *Jack the Giant-Killer*; as also a Ball and Pincushion, the Use of which will infallibly make Tommy a good Boy and Polly a good Girl.

That book, published by the enterprising London businessman John Newbery, stands today as a landmark in children's literature. Its explicit pronouncement regarding the "amusement" of Master Tommy and Miss Polly, and its success in fulfilling that aim, have made it the embodiment of the enlightened eighteenth-century view of literature for the young.

As well as being knowledgeable and sol-

vent, John Newbery had the happy fortune to enter the London publishing business at the right time in 1743. In addition to the thriving chapbook trade, two children's books were gaining more and more readers: Mrs Cooper's *The Child's New Plaything* (1742) and Thomas Boreman's *Gigantick Histories* (1740-3). The former was a small manual of instruction flavoured with stories and rhymes; the latter a curious guidebook explaining the gargoyles and other architectural features of various London buildings. For a man like Newbery—an ambitious middle-class book merchant and family man, acquainted with Locke's principles regarding the rational upbringing of children and blessed with an instinct for business opportunities—a large market for children's books was waiting to be exploited.

In 1744, then—the same year in which Mrs Cooper offered the first collection of nursery rhymes in *Tommy Thumb's Song-Book*—John Newbery launched his revolutionary work, *A Little Pretty Pocket-Book*, which boldly asserted the motto: "Delectando monemus: Instruction with Delight". Newbery, of course, was not blind to the opposition such a book might encounter, and he introduced his book with calculated caution. First he lectured parents, guardians, and nurses on the ways to make a child "strong, hardy, healthy, virtuous, wise and happy" in the acquisition of a "method of reasoning"—echoing Locke's educational theories. Then, casting aside this role as parental adviser, he became a salesman in the guise of Jack the Giant-Killer, addressing Master Tommy and Miss Polly about the toys that could be purchased to accompany his book: for the boy a red-and-black ball, for the girl a red-and-black pincushion, in both of which pins could be stuck to record good and bad behaviour. The book cost sixpence and each toy tuppence.

The *Pocket-Book* is an illustrated catalogue of children's amusements based on the alphabet. Newbery (or a hack writer employed by him) begins instructively, attaching a "moral" or a "rule of life" to the homely rhymes; but he soon indulges in some fun:

> Here's great K, and L,
> Pray Dame can you tell,
> Who put the Pig-Hog
> Down into the Well?

and introduces a few fables, an illustrated "catalogue" of the actions of good children, a "Poetical Description of the Four Seasons", and "Select Proverbs for the Use of Children". Even when the verses are pre-eminently didactic, they are all composed with a light touch. Furthermore, the book is visually attractive. *The Little Pretty Pocket-Book*, which was published in a facsimile edition in 1966, *is* pretty, with original woodcuts and a handsomely designed small-page layout. It was intended for middle-class children who said their prayers, sought their parents' blessing, learned their lessons, and bestowed charity—and whose parents could afford to buy it. Its subtle introduction of the element of delight would be essential to books for children forever after.

The composition of his audience had changed little in 1755 when Newbery offered them *Nurse Truelove's New Year's Gift; or, The Book of Books for Children*. Always instinctively aware of what prospective buyers wanted, by this time he had sharpened his skills as an advertiser. This gift book cost only tuppence ("for the Binding") and was "designed for a present to every little Boy who would become a great Man, and ride upon a fine horse, and to every little Girl who would become a fine Woman, and ride in a Governour's gilt coach." Accordingly, the first story recounted the good match Miss Polly Friendly made in marrying Mr Alderman Foresight, "who was always of the opinion that virtue and industry was the best portion with a wife." Virtue was more than its own reward in most of Newbery's stories; it usually netted some recognizable social gain as well. Copiously illustrated, the *New-Year's Gift* marked the first appearance of the cumulative nursery rhyme, "The House that Jack Built".

The book most often associated with Newbery's name is *The History of Little Goody Two-Shoes* (1765). Ornamented with thirteen woodcuts, which the title page attributed to 'Michael Angelo', it describes the rise to renown and fortune of the ever-virtuous Margery Meanwell, more popularly known as Goody Two-Shoes. (The proper names label the story's personified abstractions of evil and good.) As with most of Newbery's books for children, its authorship remains uncertain; the publisher himself may have had a hand in it, but unsubstantiated attributions to Oliver Goldsmith and Giles Jones are still current. Little Margery, possessing only one shoe, and her fully shod brother Tommy were orphaned at an early age. Their father had succumbed to a "violent Fever" because, alas, the Meanwells lived in an area "where Dr James's Powder was not to be had" (this being a product sold by Newbery). Satire directed against idle landed gentry, avaricious farmers, and the movement to consolidate and enclose farms was scarcely concealed. The landowner was Sir Timothy Gripe, the "overgrown Farmer" Mr Graspall. Although Newbery dedicated the book "To all young Gentlemen and Ladies, who are good, or intend to be good", he hoped his burlesque of adult foibles would appeal to "Children of six Feet high, of which . . . there are many Millions in the Kingdom", and he addressed his introduction to them.

The pace of this lengthy (140 pp.) story is mercifully rapid. Little in the way of obstacles is allowed to interfere with Margery's sure and steady rise, with the result that there is a minimum of conflict and suspense. When Margery's first benefactors, the Smiths, are put under threat of seizure by the nefarious Sir Timothy and send her away, the girl does not mope but promptly teaches herself to read, and because of her great natural abilities helps others to learn too. Just as her goodness prompts the generous Smiths to order a pair of shoes for Margery, her aptitude as an instructor ensures her success as a travelling tutor. She acquires a reputation among old and young as both "a cunning little Baggage" and "a sensible Hussey". She allays fears of ghosts and, true to the beliefs of her publisher, censoriously deflates the importance of fairies, "for the Tales of Ghosts, Witches, and Fairies, are the Frolicks of a distempered Brain." In Part Two she presides over A.B.C. College, teaches a devoted menagerie many strange tricks, escapes charges of witchcraft, is reunited with her brother, marries Sir Charles Jones, and survives as his widow, the esteemed benefactress of the Manor of Mouldwell. While Sir Timothy and Graspall are suitably mortified, the ever-thoughtful Lady Margery makes provision for the annual planting of potatoes "for all the Poor of any Parish who could come and fetch them for the Use of their Families."

It cannot be denied that the ever-virtuous Goody Two-Shoes is often too good to be believed. Nevertheless her adventure-filled (but always didactic) story was one of the most successful Newbery publications. Today Goody Two-Shoes is valued as another landmark in the development this anthology is charting. Though prolix and repetitive, it is one of the first full-length English stories written expressly for the amusement of children. In addition it pictures an utterly vanished, if idealized, rural way of life.

Newbery is a focal character in this anthology for several reasons. Publishing and marketing dozens of titles, he did more than any other single publisher of his day to encourage the production of books for children. In the century that followed the establishment of his shop at the Bible and Crown, many writers of widely differing philosophies and talents began to cater for the market Newbery had uncovered. Thanks to his example, the production of children's books increased a hundredfold. His name and importance have been commemorated by the American Library Association, whose Newbery Medal is awarded annually to the outstanding juvenile book published in the United States.

Joining the accelerated publishing activity that Newbery began were at least three distinct groups of writers: the Rational Moralists, influenced by Locke and Rousseau; the Sunday School and Evangelical writers; and a number of poets and storytellers whose daring and individuality ushered in the Golden Age of children's literature. The following chapters will examine their contributions at closer range.

From *A Little Pretty Pocket-Book* (1744)

The little a Play.

Flying the KITE.

UPHELD in Air, the gaudy Kite
High as an Eagle takes her Flight;
But if the Winds their Breath refrain,
She tumbles headlong down again.

RULE *of* LIFE.

Soon as thou feeft the Dawn of Day,
To God thy Adoration pay.

Dancing

The great A Play.

CHUCK-FARTHING.

AS you value your Pence,
At the *Hole* take your Aim;
Chuck all fafely in,
And you'll win the Game.

MORAL.

Chuck-Farthing, like Trade,
Requires great Care;
The more you obferve,
The better you'll fare.

B 3   *Flying*

The little b Play.

T A W.

KNUCKLE down to your *Taw*,
Aim well, fhoot away ;
Keep out of the *Ring*,
And you'll foon learn to play.

M O R A L.

Time rolls like a *Marble*,
And awes ev'ry State ;
Then hufband each Moment,
Before 'tis too late.

HOOP

The great B Play.

Dancing round the MAY-POLE.

WITH Garlands here the May-Pole's
crown'd,
And all the Swains a dancing round
Compofe a num'rous jovial Ring,
To welcome in the chearful Spring.

RULE *of* LIFE.

Leave God to manage, and to grant
That which his Wifdom fees thee want.

B 4   TAW.

The little d Play.

BLINDMAN'S BUFF.

BEREFT of all Light,
I ſtumble alone;
But, if I catch you,
My Doom is your own.

MORAL.

How blind is that Man,
Who ſcorns the Advice
Of Friends, who intend
To make him more wiſe!

SHUTTLE-

The great D Play.

FISHING.

THE artful Angler baits his Hook,
and throws it gently in the Brook;
Which the Fiſh view with greedy Eyes,
And ſoon are taken by Surpriſe.

RULE of LIFE.

Learn well the Motions of the Mind;
Why you are made, for what deſign'd.

BLIND-

The little e Play.

KING I AM.

AMBITION here fires every Heart,
And all aſſume the Monarch's Part;
For a few Minutes, though in Play,
Each rules with arbitrary Sway.

RULE of LIFE.

Deſcend into thyſelf, to find
The Imperfections of thy Mind.

Pig-

The great E Play.

SHUTTLE-COCK.

THE Shuttle-Cock ſtruck
Does backward rebound;
But, if it be miſs'd,
It falls to the Ground.

MORAL.

Thus chequer'd in Life,
As Fortune does flow;
Her Smiles lift us high,
Her Frowns ſink us low.

KING

The great O Play.

All the BIRDS *in the* AIR.

HERE various Boys ſtand round the Room,
Each does ſome favourite Bird aſſume;
And if the *Slave* once hits his Name,
He's then made free, and crowns the Game.

RULE *of* LIFE.

Live well, and then, die ſoon or late,
For ever happy is your State.　　Hor-

The little o Play.

HOP-HAT.

O'ER this *Hat*, and that,
Boys hop to the laſt;
Which, once in their Mouths,
Behind them is caſt.

MORAL.

Thus Men often ſtruggle,
Some Bliſs to obtain;
Which, once in their Pow'r,
They treat with Diſdain.

SHOOTING.

The little p Play.

Hop-Scotch.

FIRST make with Chalk an oblong Square,
With wide Partitions here and there;
Then to the firſt a *Tile* convey;
Hop in—then kick the *Tile* away.

Rule of Life.

Strive with good Senſe to ſtock your Mind,
And to that Senſe be Virtue join'd.

Who

The great P Play.

Shooting.

THO' ſome *Birds*, too heedleſs,
Dread no Danger nigh;
Yet ſtill by the *Fowlers*
They inſtantly die.

Moral.

From hence we may learn
That, by one thoughtleſs Trip,
Strange Accidents happen
'Twixt the Cup and the Lip.

D   Hop-

The little q Play.

RIDING.

IN Quest of his Game,
 The *Sportsman* rides on ;
But falls off his Horse
 Before he has done.

MORAL.

Thus Youth without Thought,
 Their Amours pursue ;
Tho' an Age of Pain
 Does often accrue.

Great

The great Q Play.

Who will play at my SQUARES ?

THIS well-invented *Game's* defign'd
 To strike the *Eye* and form the *Mind*;
And he most doubtless aims aright,
Who joins *Instruction* with *Delight.*

RULE of LIFE.

So live with Men, as if God's Eye
Did into every Action pry.

D 2   RIDING.

Nurse Truelove's New-Year's Gift: or, The Book of Books for Children. Designed for a Present to every little Boy who would become a great Man, and ride upon a fine Horse; and to every little Girl who would become a great Woman, and ride in a Governour's gilt Coach. (1755)

THE HISTORY OF MISS POLLY FRIENDLY

You may remember, my dear, to have read at the end of my Christmas Box, the history of Master *Friendly*; and this is the history of Miss *Polly*, his Sister, who you must know was altogether as good as her brother; for indeed she imitated him in everything. She was dutiful to her Papa and Mamma, loving to her brothers and sisters, kind to her play-mates, and very complaisant and obliging to everybody. Then she never miss'd saying her prayers morning and evening, as some naughty girls do. —No, no! She always *remembered her Creator in the days of her Youth*; and asked a blessing of her Papa and Mamma every morning and night. Then she was so fond of going to church and to school; so ready and willing to do as she was bid, and so ready at her work, that I think she was the best little girl I ever knew; and everybody lov'd her. Then she never told a lie in her life. No, no! She knew that was a naughty pau-pau trick. Why I remember once she by accident, poor girl, broke a whole set of the finest China I ever saw; and for fear her Mamma should be angry, truly she hid the pieces in the coal-hole. All the servants were called to account for it, and they all affirmed they were innocent; so the fault laid upon No-body; for there is an old imaginary fellow of that name in every family, who generally does a great deal of mischief. However, to make short of my story, the broken pieces were found two days afterwards in the coal-hole in the kitchen; and that being the province of *Dolly* the cook-maid, the poor girl was again taxed with the crime, and threaten'd to be turned away, when in comes Miss *Polly* with tears in her eyes, and falling on her knees to her Mamma, begged she would not be angry with *Dolly* the cook, or any body else; for 'twas she that broke the China, and hid it there, to avoid her displeasure. Her Mamma was so pleased with her open and generous confession, that she took her up in her arms, and kissed her a thousand times. "Now, my dear, says she, I love you better than ever I did, because you would not tell me a lie nor suffer your own faults to be laid upon another; and as a reward for your honesty and love of truth, here, d'ye see I will give you this fine watch." Little *Polly* took the watch indeed, and thanked her Mamma, with a curtsey down to the ground, but would not wear it: "For, says she, as none of the other children at school have watches, Mamma, they may think I am proud; and you know, Mamma, you always told me it was a very naughty thing to be proud."

As she grew up she made it her business to visit the poor, and to make every body happy in the neighbourhood; by which means she obtained such a good character, and was so esteemed, that a great many gentlemen made their addresses to her, though her fortune was but small; and among the rest of her admirers came Mr. Alderman *Foresight*, who was always of opinion, that virtue and industry was the best portion with a wife. He therefore married Miss *Polly*, who made him a dutiful, obedient and loving wife; and he in return proved to her a kind, indulgent and affectionate husband. Soon after the wedding Mr. Alderman was chosen Lord-Mayor; and now she is the great Lady-Mayoress, and rides in the grand gilt coach which you have seen drawn by fine prancing horses.

THE HOUSE THAT JACK BUILT

This is the house that Jack built.

This is the malt
That lay in the house that Jack built.

This is the rat,
That ate the malt
That lay in the house that Jack built.

This is the cat,
That killed the rat,
That ate the malt
That lay in the house that Jack built.

This is the dog,
That worried the cat,
That killed the rat,
That ate the malt
That lay in the house that Jack built.

This is the cow with the crumpled horn,
That tossed the dog,
That worried the cat,
That killed the rat,
That ate the malt
That lay in the house that Jack built.

This is the maiden all forlorn,
That milked the cow with the crumpled horn,
That tossed the dog,
That worried the cat,
That killed the rat,
That ate the malt
That lay in the house that Jack built.

This is the man all tattered and torn,
That kissed the maiden all forlorn,
That milked the cow with the crumpled horn,
That tossed the dog,
That worried the cat,
That killed the rat,
That ate the malt
That lay in the house that Jack built.

This is the priest all shaven and shorn,
That married the man all tattered and torn,
That kissed the maiden all forlorn,
That milked the cow with the crumpled horn,
That tossed the dog,
That worried the cat,
That killed the rat,
That ate the malt
That lay in the house that Jack built.

This is the cock that crowed in the morn,
That waked the priest all shaven and shorn,
That married the man all tattered and torn,
That kissed the maiden all forlorn,
That milked the cow with the crumpled horn,
That tossed the dog,
That worried the cat,
That killed the rat,
That ate the malt
That lay in the house that Jack built.*

* Iona and Peter Opie note that "The House that Jack Built" may have originated in the
Hebrew chant, "Had Gaddyo", from an early Prague edition of the *Haggadah* (EDITORS).

From Part I of *The History of Little Goody Two-Shoes;*
Otherwise called Mrs. Margery Two-Shoes (1765)

CHAPTER IV

How Little Margery learned to read, and by Degrees taught others.

Little *Margery* saw how good, and how wise Mr. *Smith* was, and concluded, that this was owing to his great Learning, therefore she wanted
of all Things to learn to read. For this Purpose she used to meet the little
Boys and Girls as they came from School, borrow their Books, and sit
down and read till they returned; By this Means she soon got more
Learning than any of her Playmates, and laid the following Scheme for
instructing those who were more ignorant than herself. She found, that
only the following Letters were required to spell all the Words in the
World; but as some of these Letters are large and some small, she with
her Knife cut out of several Pieces of Wood ten Setts of each of these:

a b c d e f g h i j k l m n o p q r s

t u v w x y z.

And six Setts of these:

A B C D E F G H I J K L M N O P Q R S

T U V W X Y Z.

And having got an old Spelling-Book, she made her Companions set up
all the Words they wanted to spell, and after that she taught them to
compose Sentences. You know what a Sentence is, my Dear, *I will be
good*, is a Sentence; and is made up, as you see, of several Words.

The usual Manner of Spelling, or carrying on the Game, as they called
it, was this: Suppose the Word to be spelt was Plumb Pudding (and who
can suppose a better) the Children were placed in a Circle, and the first
brought the Letter *P*, the next *l*, the next *u*, the next *m*, and so on till the
Whole was spelt; and if any one brought a wrong Letter, he was to pay a
Fine, or play no more. This was at their Play; and every Morning she
used to go round to teach the Children with these Rattle-traps in a Basket, as you see in the Print. I once went her Rounds with her, and was
highly diverted, as you may be, if you please to look into the next
Chapter.

CHAPTER V

*How Little Two-Shoes became a trotting Tutoress, and how she taught her
young pupils.*

It was about seven o'Clock in the Morning when we set out on this important Business, and the first House we came to was Farmer *Wilson's*.
See here it is. Here *Margery* stopped, and ran up to the Door, *Tap, tap,
tap*. Who's there? Only little goody *Two-Shoes*, answered *Margery*, come
to teach *Billy*. Oh Little *Goody*, says Mrs. *Wilson*, with Pleasure in her
Face, I am glad to see you, *Billy* wants you sadly, for he has learned all

his Lesson. Then out came the little Boy. *How do doody Two-Shoes*, says he, not able to speak plain. Yet this little Boy had learned all his Letters; for she threw down this Alphabet mixed together thus:

b d f h k m o q s u w y z
a c e g i l n p r t v x j

and he picked them up, called them by their right Names, and put them all in order thus:

a b c d e f g h i j k l m n o
p q r s t u v w x y z

She then threw down the Alphabet of Capital Letters in the Manner you here see them.

B D F H K M O Q S U W Y Z
A C E G I L N P R T V X J

and he picked them all up, and having told their Names, placed them thus:

A B C D E F G H I J K L M
N O P Q R S T U V W X Y Z

Now, pray little Reader, take this Bodkin, and see if you can point out the Letters from these mixed Alphabets, and tell how they should be placed as well as little Boy *Billy*.

From Part II of *The Renowned History of Mrs. Margery Two-Shoes* (1765)

CHAPTER V

The whole History of the Considering Cap, set forth at large for the Benefit of all whom it may concern.

The great Reputation Mrs. *Margery* acquired by composing Differences in Families, and especially, between Man and Wife, induced her to cultivate that Part of her System of Morality and Economy, in order to render it more extensively useful. For this Purpose, she contrived what she called a Charm for the Passions; which was a considering Cap, almost as large as a Grenadier's, but of three equal Sides; on the first of which was written, I MAY BE WRONG; on the second, IT IS FIFTY TO ONE BUT YOU ARE; and on the third, I'LL CONSIDER OF IT. The other Parts on the out-side, were filled with odd Characters, as unintelligible as the Writings of the old *Egyptians*; but within Side there was a Direction for its Use, of the utmost Consequence; for it strictly enjoined the Possessor to put on the Cap, whenever he found his Passions begin to grow turbulent, and not to deliver a Word whilst it was on, but with great Coolness and Moderation. As this Cap was an universal Cure for Wrong-headedness, and prevented numberless Disputes and Quarrels, it greatly hurt the Trade of the poor Lawyers, but was of the utmost Service to the rest of the Community. They were bought by Husbands and Wives, who had themselves frequent Occasion for them, and sometimes lent them to their Children: They were also purchased in large Quantities by Masters and Servants; by young Folks, who were intent on Matrimony, by Judges, Jurymen, and even Physicians and Divines; nay, if we may believe History, the Legislators of the Land did not disdain the Use of them; and we are told, that when any important Debate arose, *Cap, was the Word*, and each House looked like a grand Synod of *Egyptian Priests*. Nor was this Cap of less Use to Partners in Trade, for with these, as well as with Husband and Wife, if one was out of Humour, the other threw him the Cap, and he was obliged to put it on, and keep it till all was quiet. I myself saw thirteen Caps worn at a Time in one Family, which could not have subsisted an Hour without them; and I was particularly pleased at Sir *Humphry Huffum's*, to hear a little Girl, when her Father was out of Humour, ask her Mamma, *if she should reach down the Cap*? These Caps, indeed, were of such Utility, that People of Sense never went without them; and it was common in the Country, when a Booby made his Appearance, and talked Nonsense, to say, *he had no Cap in his Pocket*.

What was *Fortunatus's* Wishing Cap, when compared to this? That Cap, is said to have conveyed People instantly from one Place to another; but, as the Change of Place does not change the Temper and Disposition of the Mind, little Benefit can be expected from it; nor indeed is much to be hoped from his famous Purse: That Purse, it is said, was never empty, and such a Purse, may be sometimes convenient; but as Money will not purchase Peace, it is not necessary for a Man to encumber himself with a great deal of it. Peace and Happiness depend so much upon the State of a Man's own Mind, and upon the Use of the considering Cap, that it is generally his own Fault, if he is miserable. One of these Caps will last a Man his whole Life, and is a Discovery of much greater Importance to the Public than the Philosopher's Stone. Remember what was said by my Brazen Head, *Time is, Time was, Time is past*: Now the *Time is*, therefore buy the Cap immediately, and make a proper Use of it, and be happy before the *Time is past*.

Yours, ROGER BACON.

6. RATIONAL MORALISTS

The great Work of a Governor, *is to fashion the Carriage, and form the Mind; to settle in his Pupil good Habits and the Principles of Virtue and Wisdom; to give him little by little a View of Mankind, and work him into a Love and Imitation of what is excellent and praise-worthy; and, in the Prosecution of it, to give him Vigour, Activity, and Industry.—John Locke,* Some Thoughts Concerning Education *(1693)*

There is only one science for children to learn—the duties of man. This science is one and . . . indivisible. Besides, I prefer to call the man who has this knowledge master rather than teacher, since it is a question of guidance rather than instruction. He must not give precepts, he must let the scholar find them out, for himself.—Jean-Jacques Rousseau, Émile *(1762)*

Both John Locke (1632-1704) and Jean-Jacques Rousseau (1712-78) refused to think of education as a series of imposed dictates. For them it was a process of discovery whose main instrument was not the book but usually the tutor or preceptor who stimulated the exercise of innate perceptions and judgements. Such beliefs may appear commonplace today, but in their time Locke's *Some Thoughts Concerning Education* (1693) and Rousseau's *Émile; ou de l'éducation* (1762) caused a considerable stir.

Locke's work was the less controversial of the two. Oxford don and medical practitioner, philosopher and essayist, Locke was a well-travelled and respected intellectual who had served as both private tutor and travelling "governor" to sons of the nobility. Hence he brought to his educational treatise direct experience of children and an impressive knowledge of books and men. Like Montaigne before him, he was most concerned with the complete education of young gentlemen, which should have both rigorous and sympathetic aspects. He believed that anyone who has "A Sound Mind in a sound Body . . . has little more to wish for". *Some Thoughts Concerning Education* opens with a long disquisition about the need for, and the ways to obtain, a sound body; a plain, sugarless diet, fresh air, swimming, cold foot-baths, and shoes "that let in water" were prominent in the hardening regimen he advocated. The curriculum was eminently sensible, beginning with the learning of the alphabet as "a Sport", recreational literature that was also instructional (Aesop, Reynard the Fox, some Old Testament stories), and graduating to calligraphy, drawing, composition, French and Latin, and the sciences. Necessary to the educational process was one person to act as an unassertive all-wise guide and counseller— a hired tutor chosen for his "Sobriety, Temperance, Tenderness, Diligence, and Discretion". This paragon was required above all to set the stamp of good breeding on his pupil: "without good Breeding his other Accomplishments make him pass but for proud, conceited, vain or foolish". Locke's system was fundamentally one of character formation, to which health, knowledge, and habits of mind that are rational, moral, and just, all contributed.

Locke's pronouncements, buttressed with a wealth of classical examples, have a more theoretical cast than Rousseau's text, which is much more personal, approachable—and controversial. An unsuccessful apprentice and self-educated wanderer, Rousseau as a child had been an omnivorous reader and an attentive listener to adult conversation. Disapproving in retrospect of this uncritical and indiscriminate introduction to books, he advocated keeping his hypothetical pupil, Émile, illiterate until the age of twelve, to protect him from the negative and corrupting effects of adults' received opinions; in contrast to Rousseau's own unsupervised childhood,

Émile's was constantly monitored by a dedicated tutor *(maître)*. Judicious tutelage, not doctrinal proscriptions, was to guide the pupil's activities and intellectual development, and this was to be undertaken (until the age of twenty!) apart from the possibly restrictive influences of family, and protected from the negative influences of society and books—of civilization in general. Respect for the nature of the child, as Rousseau understood it, meant introducing nothing that would alter his primitive innocence. Rousseau's goal in *Émile* was to re-create the natural man.*

Émile was a radical antidote for the ills of what its revolutionary author saw as a degenerating society. He had intended it as an introduction to *The Social Contract*, also published in 1762, though separate publication by two rival firms destroyed this interdependence. Both books were written in opposition to all doctrinaire influences, and advocated a new liberating basis for human development and for society: a new social contract. They so scandalized his native city of Geneva, as well as his adopted country France, that Rousseau was banished from both. Sales of them were forbidden and the Sorbonne condemned them; they were burned in the public squares of Geneva and Paris.

Cultivating rational thought and moral judgment along the general lines proposed by Locke and Rousseau was the paramount concern of a large group of authors who wrote improving books for children between 1750 and 1850. These writers were keen believers in the power of carefully designed narratives, and of positive as well as negative examples to shape children's understanding. All emphasized tutelage: most of their stories feature a hired tutor, but sometimes a parent is the principal dispenser of information. The purpose remains the same whoever the instructor: to make learning an active, engaging pursuit.

In the books here excerpted by Sarah-Fielding, Thomas Day and Mary Wollstonecraft, the tutor is all-important. Fielding's Mrs Teachum runs her "little fe-

---

* While Locke ignored the education of girls, Rousseau devoted the fifth book of his treatise to Émile's helpmeet, Sophie, who was properly docile and restrained—a competent embroiderer, lacemaker, singer, and dancer—whose "mind knows little, but is trained to learn; it is well-tilled soil ready for the sower [her husband]".

male academy" with strictness and common sense; her response to a quarrel among the girls that breaks out in her absence is both severe and humane. Day's omnipresent Mr Barlow is endlessly patient and loquaciously instructive as he superintends the learning of Harry Sandford and Tommy Merton. Mary Wollstonecraft's Mrs Mason lucidly and tirelessly directs the girls' attention to the proper awareness of "conscious worth", "simple elegance", and "a most excellent understanding and feeling heart".

Among writers who give parents the formative role in their children's early education, Lady Fenn dedicates her simple dialogues to fond mothers who, in the nursery, teach children "the first rudiments of knowledge". The parent characterized by Maria Edgeworth in "The Purple Jar" oversees her impulsive seven-year-old daughter with a determination that borders on heartlessness, insisting that the child not only make her own decisions but also accept the consequences of her impulsiveness. If she is intransigent, the "affectionate" parent of the versifier Henry Horsley is positively frightening. Having announced his intention to promote "temporal Prosperity and eternal Happiness" in his two sons, a father provides cautionary examples by conducting visits to Newgate Prison and the "Lunatic Asylum". Nevertheless Horsley was also capable of indulging in strong sentiment in his poem about a dying mother, whose prolonged death-bed scene is intended to redouble a reader's love for parents.

Instruction, of course, was the primary aim of these Rational Moralists, not instruction with delight. But some of their books have modest though effective literary qualities (obscured, at times, by their open didacticism), for the authors were anxious to engage and hold the reader's attention. In attempting to enliven the information and moral principles they wished to con-

vey, they reveal varying degrees of literary skill in the handling of narrative, dialogue, characterization, and incident.

The most skilful writer in this section is Maria Edgeworth, the author of "The Purple Jar". Her Rosamond is a well-rounded, believable character, and the conversation she has with her mother is spritely and well developed. Thomas Day's Tommy Merton is a wonderfully reluctant pupil who articulates his selfish desires confidently, and is almost impervious to Mr Barlow's laborious moralizing. Barbara Hofland's Janetta, while as "good" as Goody Two-Shoes, is also engaging, and has the unusual experience of being shown the errors of her admirable generosity. The fray in which Mrs Teachum's female pupils pull "one another to Pieces, for a sorry Apple" is described by Sarah Fielding with fast-paced action and spirited dialogue. And the anguished soliloquy that is the climax of Miss Sukey's realization of her guilt is an effective emotional outburst that clears the way for the concluding reconciliation.

One thing that strikes the modern reader about these books is that they seem to have been written for adults. The diction, for the most part, is uncompromisingly elevated, the arguments are adult, and each child is an adult's idealized conception. The interests and activities of the children, who soberly enter into rational discussions with their seniors, are coloured by adult emotions and viewpoints. Nevertheless these books *were* written for children. However, they were purchased by well-intentioned parents (those who did not object to the slighting of religious topics), who pressed them on their offspring. They, poor lambs, were conditioned to accept and profit by such gifts. Like the hell-fire tales of the Puritans, these books of the Rational Moralists tell us more about their authors and other like-minded adults than about the true interests of the children for whom they were written.

SARAH FIELDING (1710-1768)
From *The Governess; or, Little Female Academy* (1749)

Sister and devoted admirer of the novelist Henry Fielding, Sarah published her first novel, *The Adventures of David Simple in Search of a Faithful Friend*, in 1744. Since she and her three sisters were sent to a Protestant boarding school where they acquired a gentlewoman's knowledge of reading, writing, dancing, and French conversation, she could write about a "little Female Academy' from her own experience. The Governess is Mrs Teachum, and the book relates how she instructed and entertained her nine girls over a period of nine days. The first full-length original story for children in English, *The Governess* is an educative mixture of realism and romance. On the first day the girls engage in a pitched battle over an apple; Fielding manages the battle and the reconciliation with a psychological acuteness quite unique in children's stories of the mid-eighteenth century. Incidentally, after concord is assured, Miss Jenny Peace is permitted to regale the others with an exemplary tale about the "cruel Giant Barbarico" and the "good Giant Benefico"—a story that is allowed by Mrs Teachum because of its "very good moral".

AN ACCOUNT OF A FRAY

Begun and carried on for the sake of an Apple: In which are shewn the sad Effects of Rage and Anger.

It was on a fine Summer's Evening, when the School-hours were at an End, and the young Ladies were admitted to divert themselves for some time as they thought proper, in a pleasant Garden adjoining to the House, that their Governess, who delighted in pleasing them, brought out a little Basket of Apples, which were intended to be divided equally amongst them: But Mrs *Teachum* being hastily called away (one of her poor Neighbours having had an Accident which wanted her Assistance), she left the Fruit in the Hands of Miss *Jenny Peace*, the eldest of her Scholars, with a strict Charge to see that every one had an equal Share of her Gift.

But here a perverse Accident turned good Mrs *Teachum's* Design of giving them Pleasure into their Sorrow, and raised in their little Hearts nothing but Strife and Anger: For, alas! there happened to be one Apple something larger than the rest, on which the whole Company immediately placed their desiring Eyes, and all at once cried out, 'Pray, Miss *Jenny*, give me that 'Apple.' Each gave her Reasons why she had the best Title to it: The youngest pleaded her Youth, and the eldest her Age; one insisted on her Goodness, another from her Meekness claimed a Title to Preference; and one, in confidence of her Strength, said positively, she would have it; but all speaking together, it was difficult to distinguish who said this, or who said that.

Miss *Jenny* begged them all to be quiet: But in vain: For she could not be heard: They had all set their Hearts on that fine Apple, looking upon those she had given them as nothing. She told them, they had better be contented with what they had, than be thus seeking what it was impossible for her to give to them all. She offered to divide it into Eight Parts, or to do any-thing to satisfy them: But she might as well have been silent; for they were all talking, and had no Time to hear. At last, as a Means to quiet the Disturbance, she threw this Apple, the Cause of their Contention, with her utmost Force, over a Hedge into another Garden, where they could not come at it.

At first they were all silent, as if they were struck dumb with Astonishment with the Loss of this one poor Apple, tho' at the same time they had Plenty before them.

But this did not bring to pass Miss *Jenny's* Design: For now they all began again to quarrel which had the most Right of it, and which *ought* to have had it, with as much Vehemence as they had before contended for the Possession of it: And their Anger by degrees became so high, that Words could not vent half their Rage; and they fell to pulling of Caps, tearing of Hair, and dragging the Cloaths off one another's Backs. Tho' they did not so much strike, as endeavour to scratch and pinch their Enemies.

Miss *Dolly Friendly* as yet was not engaged in the Battle: But on hearing her Friend Miss *Nanny Spruce* scream out, that she was hurt by a sly Pinch from one of the Girls, she flew on this sly Pincher, as she called her, like an enraged Lion on its Prey; and not content only to return the Harm her Friend had received, she struck with such Force, as felled her Enemy to the Ground. And now they could not distinguish between Friend and Enemy; but fought, scratch'd, and tore, like so many Cats, when they extended their Claws to fix them in their Rival's Heart.

Miss *Jenny* was employed in endeavouring to part them.

In the Midst of this Confusion, Mrs *Teachum*, who was returning in Hopes to see them happy with the Fruit she had given them, appeared: But she was some time there before either her Voice or Presence could awaken them from their Attention to the Fight; when on a sudden they all faced her, and Fear of Punishment began now a little to abate their Rage. Each of the Misses held in her Right-hand, fast clenched, some Marks of Victory; for they were beat and beaten by Turns. One of them held a little Lock of Hair, torn from the Head of her Enemy: Another grasped a Piece of a Cap, which, in aiming at her Rival's Hair, had deceived her Hand, and was all the Spoils she could gain: A third clenched a Piece of an Apron; a fourth, of a Frock. In short, every one unfortunately held in her Hand a Proof of having been engaged in the Battle. And the Ground was spread with Rags and Tatters, torn from the Backs of the little inveterate Combatants.

Miss *Teachum* stood for some time astonished at the Sight: But at last she required Miss *Jenny Peace*, who was the only Person disengaged, to tell her the Truth, and to inform her of the Cause of all this Confusion.

Miss *Jenny* was obliged to obey the Commands of her Governess; tho' she was so good-natured, that she did it in the mildest Terms; and endeavoured all she could to lessen, rather than increase, Mrs *Teachum's* Anger. The guilty Persons now began all to excuse themselves as fast as Tears and Sobs would permit them.

One said, "Indeed, Madam, it was none of my Fault; for I did not
"begin; for Miss *Sukey Jennett*, without any Cause in the World (for I did
"nothing to provoke her), hit me a great Slap in the Face, and made my
"Tooth ache; The Pain *did* make me angry; and then, indeed, I hit her a
"little Tap; but it was on her Back; and I am sure it was the smallest Tap
"in the World; and could not possibly hurt her half so much as her great
"Blow did me."

"Law, Miss! replied Miss *Jennett*, How can you say so? when you
"know that you struck me first, and that yours was the great Blow, and
"mine the little Tap; for I only went to defend myself from your mon-
"strous Blows."

Such like Defences they would all have made for themselves, each insisting on not being in Fault, and throwing the Blame on her Companion: But Mrs *Teachum* silenced them by a positive Command; and told
them, that she saw they were all equally guilty, and as such would treat
them.

Mrs *Teachum's* Method of punishing I never could find out. But this is
certain, the most severe Punishment she had ever inflicted on any
Misses, since she had kept a School, was now laid on these wicked
Girls, who had been thus fighting, and pulling one another to Pieces, for
a sorry Apple.

The first thing she did, was to take away all the Apples; telling them,
that before they had any more Instances of like Kindness from her, they
should give her Proofs of better deserving them. And when she had
punished them as much as she thought proper, she made them all embrace one another, and promise to be Friends for the future; which, in
Obedience to her Commands, they were forced to comply with, tho'
there remained a Grudge and Ill-will in their Bosoms; every one thinking she was punished most, altho she would have it, that she deserved
to be punished least; and they contrived all the sly Tricks they could
think on to vex and teaze each other.

A Dialogue between Miss Jenny Peace, *and Miss* Sukey Jennett; *wherein the
latter is at last convinced of her own Folly in being so quarrelsome; and, by her
Example, all her companions are brought to see and confess their Fault.*

The next Morning Miss *Jenny Peace* used her utmost Endeavours to bring
her School-fellows to be heartily reconciled; but in vain: For they all insisted on it, that they were not to blame; but that the whole Quarrel
arose from the Faults of others. At last ensued the following Dialogue
between Miss *Jenny Peace* and Miss *Sukey Jennett*, which brought about
Miss *Jenny's* Designs; and which we recommend to the Consideration of
all our young Readers.

Miss Jenny. Now pray, Miss *Sukey*, tell me. What did you get by your
Contention and Quarrel about that foolish Apple?

Miss Sukey. Indeed, Ma'am, I shall not answer you. I know that you
only want to prove, that you are wiser than me, because you are older.
But I don't know but some People may understand as much at Eleven

Years old, as others at Thirteen: But, because you are the oldest in the School, you always want to be tutoring and governing. I don't like to have more than one Governess; and if I obey my Mistress, I think that is enough.

Miss Jenny. Indeed, my dear, I don't want to govern you, nor to prove myself wiser than you: I only want, that, instead of quarrelling, and making yourself miserable, you should live at peace, and be happy. Therefore, pray do answer my Question. Whether you got any-thing by your Quarrel?

Miss Sukey. No! I cannot say I got anything by it: For my Mistress was angry, and punished me; and my Hair was pulled off, and my Cloaths torn in the Scuffle: Neither did I value the Apple: But yet I have too much Spirit to be imposed on. I am sure I had as good a Right to it, as any of the others: And I would not give up my Right to any one.

Miss Jenny. But don't you know, Miss *Sukey*, it would have shewn much more Spirit to have yielded the Apple to another, then to have fought about it? Then, indeed, you would have proved your Sense; for you would have shewn, that you had too much Understanding to fight about a Trifle. Then your Cloaths had been whole, your Hair not torn from your Head, your Mistress had not been angry, nor had your Fruit been taken away from you.

Miss Sukey. And so, Miss, you would fain prove, that it is wisest to submit to every-body that would impose upon one? But I will not believe it, say what you will.

Miss Jenny. But is not what I say true? If you had not been in the Battle, would not your Cloaths have been whole, your Hair not torn, your Mistress pleased with you, and your Apples your own?

Here Miss *Sukey* paused for some time: For as Miss *Jenny* was in the Right, and had Truth on her Side, it was difficult for Miss *Sukey* to know what to answer. For it is impossible, without being very silly, to contradict Truth: And yet Miss *Sukey* was so foolish, that she did not care to own herself in the Wrong; tho' nothing could have been so great a Sign of her Understanding.

When Miss *Jenny* saw her thus at a Loss for an Answer, she was in Hopes she should make her Companion happy; for, as she had as much Good-nature as Understanding, that was her Design. She therefore pursued her Discourse in the following Manner:

Miss Jenny. Pray, Miss *Sukey*, do, answer me one Question more. Don't you lie awake at Nights, and fret and vex yourself, because you are angry with your School-fellows? Are not you restless and uneasy because you cannot find a safe Method to be revenged on them, without being punished yourself? Do, tell me truly, Is not this your Case?

Miss Sukey. Yes, it is. For if I could but hurt my Enemies, without being hurt myself, it would be the greatest Pleasure I could have in the World.

Miss Jenny. Oh fy, Miss *Sukey*! What you have now said is wicked. Don't you consider what you say every Day in your Prayers? And this

Way of thinking will make you lead a very uneasy Life. If you would hearken to me, I could put you into a Method of being very happy, and making all those Misses you call your Enemies become your Friends.

Miss Sukey. You could tell me a Method, Miss! Do you think I don't know as well as you what is fit to be done? I believe I am as capable of finding the Way to be happy, as you are of teaching me.

Here Miss *Sukey* burst into Tears, that any-body should presume to tell her the Way to be happy.

Miss Jenny. Upon my Word, my Dear, I don't mean to vex you; but only, instead of tormenting yourself all Night in laying Plots to revenge yourself, I would have you employ this one Night in thinking of what I have said. Nothing will shew your Sense so much, as to own that you have been in the Wrong: Nor will any-thing prove a right Spirit so much, as to confess your Fault. All the Misses will be your Friends, and perhaps follow your Example. Then you will have the Pleasure of having caused the Quiet of the whole School; your Governess will love you; and you will be at Peace in your Mind, and never have any more foolish Quarrels, in which you all get nothing but Blows and Uneasiness.

Miss *Sukey* began now to find, that Miss *Jenny* was in the Right, and she herself in the Wrong; but yet she was so proud she would not own it. Nothing could be so foolish as this Pride; because it would have been both good and wise in her to confess the Truth the Moment she saw it. However, Miss *Jenny* was so discreet, as not to press her any farther that Night; but begged her to consider seriously on what she had said, and to let her know her Thoughts the next Morning. And then left her.

When Miss *Sukey* was alone, she stood some time in great Confusion. She could not help feeling how much hitherto she had been in the Wrong; and that Thought stung her to the Heart. She cried, stamped, and was in as great an Agony as if some sad Misfortune had befallen her. At last, when she had somewhat vented her Passion by Tears, she burst forth into the following Speech:

'It is very true what Miss *Jenny Peace* says; for I am always uneasy. I "don't sleep in Quiet; because I am always thinking, either that I have "not my Share of what is given us, or that I cannot be revenged on any "of the Girls that offend me. And when I quarrel with them, I am "scratched and bruised, or reproached. And what do I get by all this? "Why, I scratch, bruise, and reproach them in my Turn. Is not that Gain "enough? I warrant I hurt them as much as they hurt me. But then in- "deed, as Miss *Jenny* says, if I could make these Girls my Friends, "and did not wish to hurt them, I certainly might live a quieter, and "perhaps a happier Life.—But what, then, have I been always in the "Wrong all my Life-time? for I always quarrelled and hated everyone "who had offended me.—Oh! I cannot bear that Thought! It is "enough to make me mad! when I imagined myself so wise and so "sensible, to find out that I have been always a Fool. If I think a "Moment longer about it, I shall die with Grief and Shame. I must "think myself in the Right; and I will too.—But, as Miss *Jenny* says, I

"really am unhappy; for I hate all my School-fellows: And yet I dare
"not do them any Mischief; for my Mistress will punish me severely if
"I do. I should not so much mind that neither: But then those I intend
"to hurt will triumph over me, to see me punished for their sakes. In
"short, the more I reflect, the more I am afraid Miss *Jenny* is in the
"Right; and yet it breaks my Heart to think so.'

Here the poor Girl wept so bitterly, and was so heartily grieved, that
she could not utter one Word more; but sat herself down, reclining her
Head upon her Hand, in the most melancholy Posture that could be:
Nor could she close her Eyes all Night; but lay tossing and raving with
the Thought how she should act, and what she should say to Miss *Jenny*
the next Day.

When the Morning came, Miss *Sukey* dreaded every Moment, as the
Time drew nearer when she must meet Miss *Jenny*. She knew it would
not be possible to resist her Arguments; and yet Shame for having been
in Fault overcame her.

As soon as Miss *Jenny* saw Miss *Sukey* with her Eyes cast down, and
confessing, by a Look of Sorrow, that she would take her Advice, she
embraced her kindly; and, without giving her the Trouble to speak, took
it for granted, that she would leave off quarrelling, be reconciled to her
School-fellows and make herself happy.

Miss *Sukey* did indeed stammer out some Words, which implied a
Confession of her Fault; but they were spoke so low they could hardly
be heard: Only Miss *Jenny*, who always chose to look at the fairest Side
of her Companions Actions, by Miss *Sukey's* Look and Manner, guessed
her Meaning.

In the same manner did this good Girl, *Jenny*, persuade, one by one,
all her School-fellows to be reconciled to each other with Sincerity and
Love.

Miss *Dolly Friendly*, who had too much Sense to engage in the Battle
for the sake of an Apple, and who only was provoked to strike a Blow
for Friendship's Cause, easily saw the Truth of what Miss *Jenny* said;
and was therefore presently convinced that the best Part she could have
acted for her Friend, would have been to have withdrawn her from the
Scuffle.

THOMAS DAY (1748-1789)
From *The History of Sandford and Merton* (1783)

Although admitted to the Middle Temple and called to the bar, Day was interested more in experimental farming than in law. A fervent promoter of Rousseau and a disciple of his primitivism, he tailored his two works for children—*The History of Sandford and Merton* (three volumes, 1783, 1786, 1789) and *The History of Little Jack* (1788)—to conform to the philosophy of his master. Harry Sandford, a farmer's son, is a sensible, informed little boy (although to the modern reader he is an insufferable, priggish know-it-all); Tommy Merton, from a wealthy family, is coddled, illiterate, and high-handed. After Harry rescues Tommy from a snake, the two boys become friends

and fellow-pupils of the sententious Mr Barlow. Harry is docile, receptive and entirely agreeable to his tutor, whereas Master Merton presents a frequently uproarious challenge to Mr Barlow's attempts to improve him. Throughout his book Day never misses an opportunity to use the contrasts between the boys to praise the industrious poor and denigrate the idle rich.

The narrative line of *Sandford and Merton* is almost non-existent, since much of the book is an array of uplifting stories recounted by each of the protagonists. In the extract that follows, Tommy tells a story that is borrowed from LaFontaine ("Education", viii. 24).

TOMMY LEARNS TO READ

From this time forward Mr Barlow and his two young pupils used constantly to work in their garden every morning; and when they were fatigued they retired to the summerhouse, where little Harry, who improved every day in reading, used to entertain them with some pleasant story or other, which Tommy always listened to with the greatest pleasure. But Harry going home for a week, Tommy and Mr Barlow were left alone.

The next day, after they had done work, and had retired to the summerhouse as usual, Tommy expected Mr Barlow would read to him, but, to his great disappointment, found that he was busy, and could not. The next day the same accident was renewed, and the day after that. At this Tommy lost all patience and said to himself—"Now, if I could but read like Harry Sandford, I should not need to ask anybody to do it for me, and then I could divert myself: and why (thinks he) may not I do what another has done? To be sure little Harry is very clever; but he could not have read if he had not been taught; and if I am taught, I daresay I shall learn to read as well as he. Well, as soon as ever he comes home, I am determined to ask him about it."

The next day Harry returned; and as soon as Tommy had an opportunity of being alone with him—"Pray, Harry," said Tommy, "how came you to be able to read?"

Harry. Why, Mr Barlow taught me my letters, and then spelling; and then, by putting syllables together, I learned to read.

Tommy. And could not you show me my letters?

Harry. Yes, very willingly.

Harry then took up a book; and Tommy was so eager and attentive, that at the very first lesson he learned the whole alphabet. He was infinitely pleased with his first experiment, and could scarcely forbear running to Mr Barlow to let him know the improvement he had made; but he thought he should surprise him more if he said nothing about the matter till he was able to read a whole story. He therefore applied himself with such diligence, and little Harry, who spared no pains to assist his friend, was so good a master, that in about two months he determined to surprise Mr Barlow with a display of his talents. Accordingly one day, when they were all assembled in the summerhouse, and the book was given to Harry, Tommy stood and said that, if Mr Barlow pleased, he would try to read.—"Oh, very willingly," said Mr Barlow; "but I should as soon expect you to fly as to read!" Tommy smiled with a consciousness of his own proficiency, and, taking up the book, read with fluency—

THE HISTORY OF THE TWO DOGS

In a part of the world, where there are many strong and fierce wild beasts, a poor man happened to bring up two puppies of that kind which is most valued for size and courage. As they appeared to possess more than common strength and agility, he thought that he should make an acceptable present to his landlord, who was a rich man living in a great city, by giving him one of them, called Jowler; while he brought up the other, named Keeper, to guard his own flocks.

From this time the manner of living was entirely altered between the brother whelps. Jowler was sent into a plentiful kitchen, where he quickly became the favourite of all the servants, who diverted themselves with his little tricks and wanton gambols, and rewarded him with great quantities of pot-liquor and broken victuals; by which means, as he was stuffing from morning till night, he increased considerably in size, and grew sleek and comely. He was, indeed, rather unwieldy, and so cowardly that he would run away from a dog only half as big as himself. He was also much addicted to gluttony, and was often beaten for the thefts he committed in the pantry; but as he had learned to fawn upon the footmen, and would stand upon his hind legs to beg when he was ordered, and besides this, would fetch and carry, he was much caressed by all the neighbourhood.

Keeper, in the meantime, who lived at a cottage in the country, neither fared so well, looked so plump, nor had learned all these pretty little tricks to recommend him: but as his master was too poor to maintain anything that was not useful, and was obliged to be always in the air, subject to all sorts of weather, and labouring hard for a livelihood, Keeper grew hardy, active, and diligent. He was also exposed to incessant danger from the wolves, from whom he had received many a severe bite while guarding the flocks. These continual combats gave him such intrepidity, that no enemy could make him turn his back. His care and assiduity so well defended the sheep of his master, that not one had ever been missing since they were placed under his protection. His honesty too was so great, that no temptation could overpower it; and though he was left alone in the kitchen while the meat was roasting, he never attempted to taste it, but received with thankfulness whatever his master chose to give him. From living always in the air he had become so hardy, that no tempest could drive him to shelter when he ought to be employed in watching the flocks; and he would plunge into the most rapid river in the coldest weather of the winter at the slightest sign from his master.

About this time it happened that the landlord of the poor man went to examine his estate in the country, and brought Jowler with him to the place of his birth. On his arrival there, he could not help viewing with great contempt the rough, ragged appearance of Keeper, and his awkward look, which discovered nothing of the address he so much admired in Jowler. This opinion, however, was altered by means of an accident which happened to him. As he was one day walking in a thick wood, with no other company than the two dogs, a hungry wolf, with eyes that sparkled like fire, bristling hair, and a horrid snarl that made the gentleman tremble, rushed out of a neighbouring thicket, and seemed ready to devour him. The unfortunate man gave himself over for lost, especially when he saw that his faithful Jowler, instead of coming to his assistance, ran sneaking away, with his tail between his legs, howling with fear. But in this moment of despair the undaunted Keeper, who had followed him humbly and unobserved at a distance, flew to his assistance, and attacked the wolf with so much courage and skill, that he was compelled to exert all his strength in his own defence. The battle was long and bloody; but in the end Keeper laid the wolf dead at his feet, though not without receiving several severe wounds himself, and presenting a bloody and mangled spectacle to the eyes of his master, who came up at that instant. The gentleman was filled with joy for his escape, and gratitude to his valiant deliverer; having learned by his own experience that appearances are not always to be trusted, and that great virtues and good dispositions may sometimes be found in cottages, while they may be totally wanting among the great.

"Very well, indeed," said Mr Barlow; "I find that when young gentlemen choose to take pains, they can do things almost, perhaps quite, as well as other people. But what do you say to the story you have been reading, Tommy? Would you rather have owned the genteel dog that left his master to be devoured, or the poor, rough, ragged, meagre, neglected cur, that exposed his own life in his defence?"—"Indeed, sir," said Tommy, "I would rather have had Keeper; but then I would have fed him, and washed him, and combed him, till he had looked as well as Jowler."—"But, then, perhaps, he would have grown idle, and fat, and cowardly, like him," said Mr Barlow: "but here is some more of it; let us read to the end of the story." Tommy then went on thus:—

The gentleman was so pleased with the noble behaviour of Keeper, that he requested the poor man to make him a present of the dog. With this request, though with some reluctance, the farmer complied. Keeper was therefore taken to the city, where he was caressed and fed by everybody; and the disgraced Jowler was left at the cottage, with strict injunctions to the man to hang him up as a worthless, unprofitable cur.

As soon as the gentleman had departed, the poor man was going to execute his commission; but considering the noble size and comely look of the dog, and, above all, being moved with pity for the poor animal, who wagged his tail and licked his new master's feet just as he was putting the cord about his neck, he determined to spare his life, and see whether a different treatment might not produce different manners. From this day Jowler was in every respect treated as his brother Keeper had been before. He was fed but scantily; and, from this spare diet, he soon grew more active and fond of exercise. The first shower he was in he ran away, as he had been accustomed to do, and sneaked to the fireside; but the farmer's wife soon drove him out of doors, and compelled him to bear the rigour of the weather. In consequence of this, he daily became more vigorous and hardy, and in a few months regarded cold and rain no more than though he had been brought up in the country.

Changed as he already was in many respects for the better, he still retained an insurmountable dread of wild beasts; till one day, as he was wandering through a wood alone, he was attacked by a large and fierce wolf, who, jumping out of a thicket, seized him by the neck with fury. Jowler would fain have run, but his enemy was too swift and violent to suffer him to escape. Necessity makes even cowards brave. Jowler, being thus stopped in his retreat, turned upon his enemy, and, very luckily seizing him by the throat, strangled him in an instant. His master then coming up, and having witnessed his exploit, praised him, and stroked him with a degree of fondness he had never done before. Animated by this victory, and by the approbation of his master, Jowler, from that time, became as brave as he had before been pusillanimous; and there was very soon no dog in the country who was so great a terror to beasts of prey.

In the meantime, Keeper, instead of hunting wild beasts or looking after sheep, did nothing but eat and sleep, which he was permitted to do from a remembrance of his past services. As all qualities both of mind and body are lost, if not continually exercised, he soon ceased to be that hardy, courageous animal he was before; and he acquired all the faults which are the consequences of idleness and gluttony.

About this time the gentleman went again into the country, and taking his dog with him, was willing that he should exercise his prowess once more against his ancient enemies the wolves. Accordingly, the country-people having quickly found one in a neighbouring wood, the gentleman went thither with Keeper, expecting to see him behave as he had done the year before. But how great was his surprise when, at the first onset, he saw his beloved dog run away with every mark of timidity! At this moment another dog sprang forward, and seizing the wolf with the greatest intrepidity, after a bloody contest left him dead upon the ground. The gentleman could not help lamenting the cowardice of his favourite, and admiring the noble spirit of the other dog, whom, to his infinite surprise, he found to be the same Jowler that he had discarded the year before. "I now see," said he to the farmer, "that it is vain to expect courage in those who live a life of indolence and repose; and that constant exercise and proper discipline are frequently able to change contemptible characters into good ones."

"Indeed," said Mr Barlow, when the story was ended, "I am sincerely glad to find that Tommy has made this acquisition. He will now depend upon nobody, but be able to divert himself whenever he pleases. All that has ever been written in our own language will be from this time in his power; whether he may choose to read little entertaining stories such as we have heard today, or to learn the actions of great and good men in history, or to make himself acquainted with the nature of wild beasts and birds which are found in other countries, and have been described in books. In short, I hardly know of anything that from this moment will not be in his power; and I do not despair of one day seeing him a very sensible man, capable of teaching and instructing others."

"Yes," said Tommy, something elated by all this praise, "I am determined now to make myself as clever as anybody; and I don't doubt, though I am such a little fellow, that I know more already than many grown-up people; and I am sure, though there are now fewer than six blacks in our house, there is not one of them who can read a story as I can." Mr Barlow looked a little grave at this sudden display of vanity; and said rather coolly, "Pray, who has attempted to teach them anything?"—"Nobody, I believe," said Tommy. "Where is the great wonder, then, if they are ignorant?" replied Mr Barlow; "you would probably have never known anything had you not been assisted; and even now, you know very little."

In this manner did Mr Barlow begin the education of Tommy Merton, who had naturally very good dispositions, although he had been suffered to acquire many bad habits, which sometimes prevented them from appearing.

LADY ELEANOR FENN (1743-1813)

From *Cobwebs to Catch Flies; or, Dialogues in Short Sentences, Adapted to Children From the Age of Three to Eight Years* (Two volumes, *c.* 1783)

Lady Fenn's dialogues are "in words of three, four, five and six letters" for "children from three to five years of age" in volume one, and "in words of one, two, three and four syllables" for children from five to eight in volume two. In the Dedication Lady Fenn described herself as "mistress of the infantine language", and as one who did not "blush to supply prattle for infants". She dedicated her book to "fond mothers", and hoped that "the mother who herself watches the dawn of reason in her babe, who teaches him the first rudiments of knowledge, who infuses the first ideas in his mind, will approve my *Cobwebs*". Although Lady Fenn and her antiquarian husband, the first editor of the *Paston Letters*, were childless, she wrote grammars and miscellanies for the young, in addition to this gently instructive reader.

THE TOILET (Volume I)
In Words of Four Letters

Girl. I like this cap, but it will not keep on. Why will it not keep on?
Maid. It is too big for you, miss.
Girl. It is off; it will fall off.
Maid. You had best lay it down, miss.
Girl. I like to have it; I will put it on.
Mamma. My dear! lay it down when you are bid to do so; do not wait to be made to do well.
Girl. I will not, mamma. Smith, I will be good. Pray, may I look in this box?
Mamma. You see it is shut now; you may see it by-and-by.
Girl. I will not hurt the lock.

Mamma. You must not try.

Girl. May I play with your muff.

Mamma. You may.

Girl. What is this made of?

Mamma. Fur; and fur is skin with the hair on.

Girl. It is like puss; how soft it is. How warm it is when I hold it to my nose! it is like wool.

Mamma. Now come and kiss me: I am sure you will be good to John; go and play with him.

Girl. Do you stay all day? do you stay till John is in bed?

Mamma. Yes; till you are both in bed. Now go.

Girl. Pray let me get my work bag first. May I get my work bag?

Mamma. Why do you want it?

Girl. I want some silk out of it; that I may work a ball for John.

THE STUBBORN CHILD (Volume II)

Mr Steady was walking with his little son, when he met a boy with a satchel on his shoulder crying and sobbing dismally. Mr Steady accosted him, kindly inquiring what was the matter.

Mr Steady. Why do you cry?

Boy. They send me to school, and I do not like it.

Mr Steady. You are a silly boy; what! would you play all day?

Boy. Yes, I would.

Mr Steady. None but babies do that; your friends are very kind to you. If they have not time to teach you themselves, then it is their duty to send you where you may be taught, but you must take pains yourself, else you will be a dunce.

Little Steady. Pray, may I give him my book of fables out of my pocket?

Mr Steady. Do, my dear.

Little Steady. Here it is—it will teach you to do as you are bid—I am never happy when I have been naughty; are you happy?

Boy. I cannot be happy; no person loves me.

Little Steady. Why?

Mr Steady. I can tell you why; because he is not good.

Boy. I wish I was good.

Mr Steady. Then try to be so; it is easy; you have only to do as your parents and friends desire you.

Boy. But why should I go to school?

Mr Steady. Good children ask for no reasons—a wise child knows that his parents can best judge what is proper; and unless they choose to explain the reason of their orders, he trusts that they have a good one; and he obeys without inquiry.

Little Steady. I will not say Why, again, when I am told what to do; but I will always do as I am bid directly.—Pray, sir, tell the story of Miss Wilful.

Mr Steady. Miss Wilful came to stay a few days with me. Now she knew that I always would have children obey me; so she did as I bade her; but she did not always do a thing as soon as she was spoken to, but would often whine out, Why? That always seems to me like saying, I think I am as wise as you are; and I would disobey you if I durst.

One day I saw Miss Wilful going to play with a dog, with which I knew it was not proper for her to meddle: and I said, Let that dog alone. Why? said Miss. I play with Wag, and I play with Phillis, and why may I not play with Pompey?

I made her no answer; but thought she might feel the reason soon.

Now the dog had been ill-used by a girl who was so naughty as to make a sport of holding meat to his mouth, and snatching it away again: which made him take meat roughly, and always be surly to girls.

Soon after, Miss stole to the dog, held out her hand as if she had meat for him, and then snatched it away again. The creature resented this treatment, and snapped at her fingers.—When I met her crying, with her hand wrapped in a napkin, So, said I, you have been meddling with the dog. Now you know why I bade you let Pompey alone.

Little Steady. Did she not think you were unkind not to pity her? I thought (do not be displeased, papa) but I thought it was strange that you did not comfort her.

Mr Steady. You know that her hand was not very much hurt, and the wound had been dressed when I met her.

Little Steady. Yes, papa, but she was so sorry.

Mr Steady. She was not so sorry for her fault as for its consequences.

Little Steady. Papa!

Mr Steady. Her concern was for the pain which she felt in her fingers not for the fault which had occasioned it.

Little Steady. She was very naughty, I know, for she said that she would get a pair of thick gloves, and then she would tease Pompey.

Mr Steady. Naughty girl! how ill-disposed! Then my lecture was lost upon her. I bade her, whilst she felt the smart, resolve to profit by Pompey's lesson; and learn to believe, that her friends might have good reason for their orders, though they did not think it proper always to acquaint her with them.

Little Steady. I once cut myself with a knife which I had not leave to take, and when I see the scar, I always consider that I ought not to have taken the knife.

Mr Steady. That, I think, is the school-house; now go in, and be good.

THE
RATIONAL
EXHIBITION

FOR CHILDREN

London. Printed by Darton and Harvey,
Grace Church Street. 1800.

MARY WOLLSTONECRAFT (1759-1797)
From *Original Stories from Real Life* (1788)

In the same year as the publication of Wollstonecraft's *Mary: A Fiction* her publisher, Joseph Johnson, issued the book for children he had commissioned her to write: *Original Stories from Real Life*. This was two years before the appearance of her *Vindication of the Rights of Men* (1790), and four years earlier than her famous feminist document, *A Vindication of the Rights of Woman* (1792). Wollstonecraft, even at this early stage of her writing, made a compelling and lucid case for the exercise of reason in the upbringing of children. As the Preface to the *Stories* says, "the author attempts to cure those faults by reason which ought never to have taken root in the infant mind". The influences of Locke and Rousseau are evident in Wollstonecraft's belief that "knowledge should be gradually imparted, and flow more from example than teaching: example directly addresses the senses, the first inlet to the heart, the object

education should have constantly in view and over which we have most power". Her aim in *Original Stories*—"to fix principles of truth and humanity on a solid and simple foundation"—is carried out by the icily rational Mrs Mason, whose charges are Caroline and Mary. The assiduous tutor never misses a chance to make every incident informative. Coming upon two wounded birds, she promptly draws the girls' attention to the fact that these animals are suffering more than her charges did when they had small-pox, decides that one bird can be helped, and abruptly turns her heel on the other bird's head to "put it out of pain". Later in her life, as the mother of two daughters (one of them the future Mary Shelley), Wollstonecraft may have relaxed her strict principles, though her adult books suggest that, like Mrs Mason, she always adhered to the pre-eminence of virtue in the moral hierarchy.

CHAPTER VII

Virtue the Soul of Beauty—The Tulip and the Rose—The Nightingale—External Ornaments—Characters.

The next morning Mrs Mason met them first in the garden; and she desired Caroline to look at a bed of tulips, that were then in their highest state of perfection. I, added she, choose to have every kind of flower in my garden, as the succession enables me to vary my daily prospect, and gives it the charm of variety; yet these tulips afford me less pleasure than most others I cultivate—and I will tell you why—they are only beautiful. Listen to my distinctions;—good features, and a fine complexion, I term *bodily* beauty. Like the streaks of the tulips they please the eye for a moment; but this uniformity soon tires, and the active mind flies off to something else. The soul of beauty, my dear children, consists in the body gracefully exhibiting the emotions and variations of the informing mind. If truth, humanity, and knowledge inhabit the breast, the eyes will beam with a mild lustre, modesty will suffuse the cheeks; and smiles of innocent joy play over all the features. At first sight regularity and color will attract, and have the advantage; because the hidden springs are not directly set in motion; but when internal goodness is reflected, every other kind of beauty, the shadow of it, withers away before it—as the sun obscures a lamp.

You are certainly handsome, Caroline; I mean, have good features;

but you must improve your mind to give them a pleasing expression, or they will only serve to lead your understanding astray. I have seen some foolish people take great pains to decorate the outside of their houses, to attract the notice of strangers, who gazed, and passed on; while the inside, where they were to receive their friends, was dark and inconvenient. Apply this observation to mere personal attractions; they may, for a few years, charm the superficial part of your acquaintance, whose notions of beauty are not built on any principles. Such persons might look at you, as they would glance their eye over these tulips, and feel for a moment, the same pleasure that a view of the variegated rays of light would convey to an uninformed mind. The lower class of mankind, and children, are fond of finery; gaudy, dazzling appearances catch their attention; but the discriminating judgment of a person of sense, requires, besides color, order, proportion, grace and usefulness, to render the idea of beauty complete.

Observe the rose, it has all the perfections I speak of; color, grace, and sweetness—and even when the fine tints fade, the smell is grateful to those who have before contemplated its beauties. I have only one bed of tulips, though my garden is large, but, in every part of it, roses catch your sight.

You have seen Mrs B. and think her a very fine woman; yet her complexion has only the clearness that temperance gives; and her features, strictly speaking, are not regular: Betty, the house-maid, has, in both these respects, much the superiority over her. But, though you cannot at once define in what her beauty consists, your eye follows her whenever she moves; and every person of taste listens for the modulated sounds which proceed out of her mouth, to be improved and pleased. It is conscious worth, *truth*, that gives dignity to her walk, and simple elegance to her conversation. She has, indeed, a most excellent understanding, and a feeling heart; sagacity and tenderness, the result of both, are happily blended in her countenance; and taste is the polish, which makes them appear to the best advantage. She *is* really beautiful; and you see her varied excellencies again and again, with increasing pleasure. They are not obtruded on you, for knowledge has taught her true humility: she is not like the flaunting tulip, that forces itself forward into notice; but resembles the modest rose, you see yonder, retiring under its elegant foliage.

I have mentioned flowers—the same order is observed in the higher departments of nature. Think of the birds; those that sing best, have not the finest plumage; indeed just the contrary; God divides His gifts, and amongst the feathered race the nightingale (sweetest of warblers, who pours forth her varied strain when sober eve comes on) you would seek in vain in the morning, if you expected that beautiful feathers should point out the songstress: many who incessantly chatter, and are only tolerable in the general concert, would surpass her, and attract your attention.

I knew, some time before you were born, a very fine, a very handsome girl; I saw she had abilities, and I saw with pain that she attended to the most obvious, but least valuable gift of heaven. Her ingenuity slept, while she tried to render her person more alluring. At last she caught the smallpox—her beauty vanished, and she was for a time miserable; but the natural vivacity of youth overcame her unpleasant feelings. In consequence of the disorder, her eyes became so weak that she was obliged to sit in a dark room; to beguile the tedious day she applied to music, and made a surprising proficiency. She even began to think, in her retirement, and when she recovered her sight grew fond of reading.

Large companies did not amuse her, she was no longer the object of admiration, or if she was taken notice of, it was to be pitied, to hear her former self praised, and to hear them lament the depredation that dreadful disease had made in a fine face. Not expecting or wishing to be observed, she lost her affected airs, and attended to the conversation, in which she was soon able to bear a part. In short, the desire of pleasing took a different turn, and as she improved her mind, she discovered that virtue, internal beauty, was valuable on its own account, and not like that of the person, which resembles a toy, that pleases the observer, but does not make the possessor happy.

She found, that in acquiring knowledge, her mind grew tranquil, and the noble desire of acting conformably to the will of God succeeded, and drove out the immoderate vanity which before actuated her, when her equals were the objects she thought most of, and whose approbation she sought with such eagerness. And what had she sought? to be stared at and called handsome. Her beauty, the sight of it did not make others good, or comfort the afflicted; but after she had lost it, she was comfortable herself, and set her friends the most useful example.

The money that formerly she appropriated to ornament her person, now clothed the naked; yet she really appeared better dressed, as she had acquired the habit of employing her time to the best advantage, and could make many things herself. Besides, she did not implicitly follow the reigning fashion, for she had learned to distinguish, and in the most trivial matters acted according to the dictates of good sense.

The children made some comments on this story, but the entrance of a visitor interrupted the conversation, and they ran about the garden, comparing the roses and tulips.

MARIA EDGEWORTH (1767-1849)
"The Purple Jar" from *Early Lessons* (1801)

The dutiful daughter in a large family, the Irish novelist Maria Edgeworth knew the habits, likes, and dislikes of children at first hand. While she endorsed with enthusiasm such reading for children as Mrs Barbauld's *Lessons*, she objected strenuously to fairy and giant stories as impractical and misleading. In the Preface to an early collection of her stories, *The Parent's Assistant* (1796), she drew the line separating the fantastic and the useful in this question: "why should the mind be filled with fantastic visions instead of useful knowledge?" (p. xi). However, she was not unaware of the need to enliven moral precepts by making "the stories in which they are introduced in some measure dramatic" (p. x). *Early Lessons*—originally published the year after Edgeworth's famous novel

Castle Rackrent—is a collection of short stories (whose number increased in later editions) that have clearly distinguished "good" and "bad" young characters and a concluding moral. A skilful raconteur, Edgeworth often revealed features of her own personality as a child in the characters of her stories; it is comforting to think that she herself might have been as impulsive as Rosamond. She pleased her young readers so much that she wrote several sequels to the "lessons" provided by her successful characters Rosamond, Harry, Lucy, and Frank.

On this general theme Maria Edgeworth also wrote *Practical Education* (1798), a collaborative effort with her father; *A Rational Primer* (1799); and *Moral Tales For Young People* (1801).

THE PURPLE JAR

Rosamond, a little girl about seven years old, was walking with her mother in the streets of London. As she passed along, she looked in at the windows of several shops, and saw a great variety of different sorts of things, of which she did not know the use, or even the names. She wished to stop to look at them, but there was a great number of people in the streets, and a great many carts, carriages, and wheelbarrows, and she was afraid to let go her mother's hand.

"O, mother; how happy I should be," she said as she passed a toyshop, "if I had all these pretty things!"

"What, all! Do you wish for them all, Rosamond?"

"Yes, mamma, all."

As she spoke, they came to a milliner's shop, the windows of which were decorated with ribands and lace, and festoons of artificial flowers.

"Oh mamma, what beautiful roses! Won't you buy some of them?"

"No, my dear."

"Why?"

"Because I don't want them, my dear."

They went a little further, and came to another shop, which caught Rosamond's eye. It was a jeweller's shop, and in it were a great many pretty baubles, ranged in drawers behind glass.

"Mamma, will you buy some of these?"

"Which of them, Rosamond?"

"Which? I don't know which; any of them will do, for they are all pretty."

"Yes, they are all pretty; but of what use would they be to me?"

"Use! Oh, I'm sure you could find some use or other for them if you would only buy them first."

"But I would rather find out the use first."

"Well, then, mamma, there are buckles; you know that buckles are useful things, very useful things."

"I have a pair of buckles, I don't want another pair," said her mother, and walked on. Rosamond was very sorry that her mother wanted nothing. Presently, however, they came to a shop which appeared to her far more beautiful than the rest. It was a chemist's shop, but she did not know that.

"Oh, mother, oh!" cried she, pulling her mother's hand, "look, look! blue, green, red, yellow, and purple! Oh, mamma, what beautiful things! Won't you buy some of these?"

Still her mother answered as before, "Of what use would they be to me, Rosamond?'

"You might put flowers in them, mamma, and they would look so pretty on the chimney-piece. I wish I had one of them."

"You have a flower-pot," said her mother, "and that is not a flower-pot."

"But I could use it for a flower-pot, mamma, you know."

"Perhaps, if you were to see it nearer, if you were to examine it, you might be disappointed."

"No, indeed, I'm sure I should not; I should like it exceedingly."

Rosamond kept her head turned to look at the purple vase, till she could see it no longer.

"Then, mother," said she, after a pause, "perhaps you have no money."

"Yes, I have."

"Dear me, if I had money I would buy roses, and boxes, and buckles, and purple flower-pots, and everything." Rosamond was obliged to pause in the midst of her speech.

"O mamma, would you stop a minute for me? I have got a stone in my shoe, it hurts me very much."

"How comes there to be a stone in your shoe?"

"Because of this great hole, mamma—it comes in there: my shoes are quite worn out. I wish you would be so very good as to give me another pair."

"Nay, Rosamond, but I have not money enough to buy shoes, and flower-pots, and buckles, and boxes, and everything."

Rosamond thought that was a great pity. But now her foot, which had been hurt by the stone, began to give her so much pain that she was obliged to hop every other step, and she could think of nothing else. They came to a shoemaker's shop soon afterwards.

"There, there! mamma, there are shoes; there are little shoes that would just fit me, and you know shoes would be really of use to me."

"Yes, so they would, Rosamond. Come in." She followed her mother into the shop.

Mr Sole, the shoemaker, had a great many customers, and his shop was full, so they were obliged to wait.

"Well, Rosamond," said her mother, "you don't think this shop so pretty as the rest?"

"No, not nearly; it is black and dark, and there are nothing but shoes all round; and, besides, there's a very disagreeable smell."

"That smell is the smell of new leather."

"Is it? Oh!" said Rosamond, looking round, "there is a pair of little shoes; they'll just fit me, I'm sure."

"Perhaps they might; but you cannot be sure till you have tried them on, any more than you can be quite sure that you should like the purple vase *exceedingly*, till you have examined it more attentively."

"Why, I don't know about the shoes, certainly, till I have tried; but, mamma, I am quite sure that I should like the flower-pot."

"Well, which would you rather have, that jar, or a pair of shoes? I will buy either for you."

"Dear mamma, thank you—but if you could buy both?"

"No, not both."

"Then the jar, if you please."

"But I should tell you, that in that case I shall not give you another pair of shoes this month."

"This month! that's a very long time indeed! You can't think how these hurt me; I believe I'd better have the new shoes. Yet, that purple flower-pot. Oh, indeed, mamma, these shoes are not so very, very bad! I think I might wear them a little longer, and the month will soon be over. I can make them last till the end of the month, can't I? Don't you think so, mamma?"

"Nay, my dear, I want you to think for yourself; you will have time enough to consider the matter, whilst I speak to Mr Sole about my clogs."

Mr Sole was by this time at leisure, and whilst her mother was speaking to him, Rosamond stood in profound meditation, with one shoe on, and the other in her hand.

"Well, my dear, have you decided?"

"Mamma!—yes,—I believe I have. If you please, I should like to have the flower-pot; that is, if you won't think me very silly, mamma."

"Why, as to that, I can't promise you, Rosamond; but, when you have to judge for yourself, you should choose what will make you happy, and then it would not signify who thought you silly."

"Then, mamma, if that's all, I'm sure the flower-pot would make me happy," said she, putting on her old shoe again; "so I choose the flower-pot."

"Very well, you shall have it; clasp your shoe and come home."

Rosamond clasped her shoe, and ran after her mother. It was not long before the shoe came down at the heel, and many times she was obliged to stop to take the stones out of it, and she often limped with pain; but still the thoughts of the purple flower-pot prevailed, and she persisted in her choice.

When they came to the shop with the large window, Rosamond felt much pleasure upon hearing her mother desire the servant, who was with them, to buy the purple jar, and bring it home. He had other commissions, so he did not return with them. Rosamond, as soon as she got it, ran to gather all her own flowers, which she kept in a corner of her mother's garden.

"I am afraid they'll be dead before the flower-pot comes, Rosamond," said her mother to her, as she came in with the flowers in her lap.

"No, indeed, mamma, it will come home very soon, I dare say. I shall be very happy putting them into the purple flower-pot."

"I hope so, my dear."

The servant was much longer returning home than Rosamond had expected; but at length he came, and brought with him the long-wished for jar. The moment it was set down upon the table, Rosamond ran up to it with an exclamation of joy: "I may have it now, mamma?" "Yes, my dear, it is yours." Rosamond poured the flowers from her lap upon the carpet, and seized the purple flower-pot.

"Oh, dear mother!" cried she, as soon as she had taken off the top, "But there's something dark in it which smells very disagreeably. What is it? I didn't want this black stuff."

"Nor I, my dear."

"But what shall I do with it, mamma?"

"That I cannot tell."

"It will be of no use to me, mamma."

"That I cannot help."

"But I must pour it out, and fill the flower-pot with water."

"As you please, my dear."

"Will you lend me a bowl to pour it into, mamma?"

"That was more than I promised you, my dear; but I will lend you a bowl."

The bowl was produced, and Rosamond proceeded to empty the purple vase. But she experienced much surprise and disappointment on finding, when it was entirely empty, that it was no longer a *purple* vase. It was a plain white glass jar, which had appeared to have that beautiful colour merely from the liquor with which it had been filled.

Little Rosamond burst into tears.

"Why should you cry, my dear?" said her mother; "it will be of as much use to you now as ever, for a flower-pot."

"But it won't look so pretty on the chimney-piece. I am sure, if I had known that it was not really purple, I should not have wished to have it so much."

"But didn't I tell you that you had not examined it; and that perhaps you would be disappointed?"

"And so I am disappointed, indeed. I wish I had believed you at once. Now I had much rather have the shoes for I shall not be able to walk all this month; even walking home that little way hurt me exceedingly. Mamma, I will give you the flower-pot back again, and that purple stuff and all, if you'll only give me the shoes."

"No, Rosamond, you must abide by your own choice, and now the best thing you can possibly do is to bear your disappointment with good humour."

"I will bear it as well as I can," said Rosamond, wiping her eyes, and she began slowly and sorrowfully to fill the vase with flowers.

But Rosamond's disappointment did not end here. Many were the difficulties and distresses into which her imprudent choice brought her, before the end of the month. Every day her shoes grew worse and worse, till at last she could neither run, dance, jump, or walk in them. Whenever Rosamond was called to see anything, she was detained pulling her shoes up at the heels, and was sure to be too late. Whenever her mother was going out to walk, she could not take Rosamond with her, for Rosamond had no soles to her shoes, and at length, on the very last day of the month, it happened that her father proposed to take her with her brother to a glasshouse, which she had long wished to see. She was very happy; but, when she was quite ready, had her hat and gloves on, and was making haste down stairs to her brother and father, who were waiting for her at the hall door, the shoe dropped off. She put it on again in a great hurry, but as she was going across the hall, her father turned round. "Why are you walking slipshod? no one must walk slip-shod with me. Why, Rosamond," said he, looking at her shoes with disgust, "I thought that you were always neat; go, I cannot take you with me."

Rosamond coloured and retired. "O mamma," said she, as she took off her hat, "how I wish that I had chosen the shoes! They would have been of so much more use to me than that jar: however, I am sure—no not quite sure, but I hope I shall be wiser another time."

CATHARINE PARR TRAILL (1802-1899)
From *The Young Emigrants; or, Pictures of Canada* (1826)

Six years before her marriage to Lieutenant Traill and their emigration to Upper Canada, Catharine Strickland wrote this unique Canadian travelogue for children. It was based on accounts like John Howison's *Sketches of Upper Canada* (1821), and on letters received from friends who had already arrived in Canada. Although the author herself had not yet experienced the new land, *The Young Emigrants* foreshadows her later and famous *Backwoods of Canada* (1836) in its use of the epistolary form, and in its wealth of naturalist's lore.

Because of financial ruin in England, the fictitious Clarence family emigrates to the much-feared "wild woods of Canada". They settle close to Lake Ontario, in a farming community about thirty-six miles from York (Toronto). Richard and Agnes Clarence write to their sister, Ellen, who, because of ill health, has remained in Eng-

land; their letters show that the Clarences, while transplanting names and customs from home, learn to appreciate a rich newness. (So too did Catharine Traill, her brother Samuel Strickland, and her sister Susanna Moodie adjust successfully to unaccustomed hardships in Canada.) As pioneers the Clarence children turn out to be sensible and hardy, informed and observant; their story is unusual as an example of informational children's fiction in which children act as the instructors.

Traill's next and more vigorous book for children, *Canadian Crusoes* (1852), combined first-hand knowledge of landscape, vegetation, and her own children with the borrowed theme of the stranded but self-reliant journeyer. About some children who must look after themselves after they are lost in the bush, it is the first distinctly Canadian Robinsonnade.

LETTER V
AGNES TO ELLEN

Roselands, June 22

After a silence of some months, I again sit down to write to my beloved sister, assured that a letter from her absent Agnes will be welcomed with delight. With what joy should I hail the day that made us once more inmates of the same dwelling. I think I should then be quite happy, and not have a thought or wish beyond the home I now inhabit, which is becoming dearer to me every day.

It is true, I find a great deal more to employ my hands than I have ever been accustomed to; but my labours are light. My health is good, and as my exertions conduce to the general comfort and happiness of my family, I endeavour to perform them with cheerfulness, and with a grateful heart; for how much better am I off, than many who are far more deserving than myself. Ah! dear Ellen, how thankful we ought to be, to that merciful God who has kindly watched over and preserved us from the dangers of crossing the great Atlantic, and has bestowed so many blessings on us; more, indeed, than we could possibly expect. Should we not be most ungrateful to Him, were we at any time to indulge ourselves in discontent and repining, because we cannot possess all those luxuries and enjoyments which I *once* thought so indispensable, but which I find, by experience, are not necessary for our happiness, and can very well be dispensed with.

I remember, I used once to place the utmost importance on the smartness of my dress, the fashion of my bonnet, and the shape of my gown; but now my dress is cut to the most convenient shape; and my chief study in choosing a hat, is to suit it to the different seasons of the year. And, indeed, I am quite as well pleased with my dark stuff and blue cotton gowns, and with my checked or linseywoolsey apron, as I was formerly in wearing the finest muslin or richest silk. I think I see my sister smile at my change of ideas, and hear her exclaim, "A blue cotton gown and checked apron!" Yes, dearest Ellen, this is my winter's attire, and I am quite reconciled to wearing it. Indeed, were I to do otherwise, I should be laughed at for affecting a singularity of dress. Nor need I be ashamed of appearing in such homely apparel, when I see my neighbours, Jane and Charlotte Hamilton, who have received as good an education as myself, wearing the same. It is a general thing in this country to dress according to your circumstances, and to suit the fashion to the seasons and to your own convenience. The ladies all wear a thick, warm stuff gown, trimmed with fur, for the winter, with a blue or grey cotton for morning. Cloth pelisses are worn only by rich people, and then only in towns or cities. We, who are more humbly situated, are contented with plaids, lined with green, purple, or red baize. We have fur bonnets, tied close to the face; and fur or feather muffs and tippets. Our shoes are also lined with fur or flannel; as, when we travel during the cold season, the warmest clothing is requisite. In spring and summer we cast off our furs and wrappings, and dress as light and thin as possible; the heat being at times insupportable, during the months of July and August.

Among other useful arts, I have learned to make very pretty muffs and tippets, with feathers sewed together: they are greatly admired, and they look quite as handsome as some of the expensive furs. Flora Gordon has taught me to plat straw, and I shall try my skill in platting a cottage-bonnet for little Annie: if I succeed, I shall make a bonnet for mamma, and one for myself, as they will prove very useful to us, every article of dress being very expensive in this country. Even needles are so dear, that I am obliged to be quite miserly over my small stock: you cannot purchase one under a copper (a half-penny.) Every thing else is proportionably dear.

We have had a very pleasant winter. The snow lay, for eight weeks, to the depth of many feet. The fields, the woods, the lakes, every outward object presented the unvaried livery of nature. But though the frost was intense, I felt much less inconvenience from the cold than I had expected: thirty degrees below zero was frequently the temperature of the atmosphere. But, in spite of this cold, it is the most healthful and agreeable season of the year: no colds, no coughs. The air is clear and bracing; and the sky, for many days, continues bright and cloudless. The sun is very powerful, even when the frost is the most intense. We have had a favourable season for sleighing, which is most delightful: you seem actually to glide along over the frozen surface. The bells which are attached to the necks of the horses (to the number of eighteen each) make a pretty jingling noise; and, when accustomed to the sound, you do not like to travel without them. The roads at this season present a lively, bustling scene. You cannot go a mile from home without meeting or passing twenty or thirty sleighs or cutters; parties of gentlemen and ladies skating; and children sliding, with cheeks glowing with exercise and health. The farmers take this opportunity of carrying their corn to the mill, to be ground into flour; and to procure such articles from the more distant towns and settlements, as they cannot meet with near the homesteads (or farm-houses.) You may travel sixty or seventy miles in a sleigh, with one pair of horses, without suffering any fatigue from your journey, or any inconvenience, unless from the cold; but we wrap up so closely in our plaids and furs, leaving only a sufficient part of our faces uncovered to enable us to look about and breathe freely, that we suffer comparatively little to what might be expected.

Andrew and Flora have made many comfortable additions to our travelling attire, by knitting warm mittens and comforters, which we find very useful; for, indeed, you cannot dress too close and thick during the cold weather.

Our fireside presents a scene of equal cheerfulness to that I have described abroad. The hearth is piled with blazing faggots of pine and hickory wood, which fill the room with a delightful warmth, and seem to enliven every face as we gather round the fire. Sometimes we have an agreeable addition to our family-party in the Hamiltons: the evening is then passed in social chat or innocent gaiety. Frank Hamilton plays on the flute to us, or else we sing duets; or one of the party reads aloud, while the rest work, or play at chess, or draw. When the hour of supper arrives, Flora and I lay the cloth, and prepare our frugal meal, which consists of the finest white bread, dried venison, butter, honey, apples, and cranberry-tarts; with birch-wine, warmed in an earthen pipkin over the fire, and sweetened with maple-sugar. Such is our supper, and who would wish for greater delicacies?

In this manner passes our time till the hour of prayer, and then we summon all the household, while papa takes down the great Bible and reads a passage from the Old and New Testament, and explains the subject to us. Do you remember, dear Ellen, Burns's poem of the "Cotter's Saturday Night?" I always think of those beautiful lines, when I see our dear papa open the sacred volume, and look round upon us with that benevolent and amiable expression that so well becomes his mild and placid features: he seems to regard us all as his children and his equals, though he is superior to us in every respect. At such times, the spirit of peace and truth seems to rest upon us, and every face beams with piety and gratitude to the Almighty, "who has given us grace, with one accord, to make our common supplications unto him," and who has assured us, that where two or three are gathered together in His name, there is He in the midst of them. Nor are you, my beloved sister, absent from our prayers. You are *never* forgotten by your parents, or by your own Agnes and Richard; and we never rise from our devotions without first having implored the blessing and protection of the Almighty for our own dear Ellen. Such are the amusements and employments of our winter evenings; but they are varied according to circumstances. Sometimes I spend an hour or two in instructing Flora, and I have already taught little Annie some of her letters: she is quite a pet, and is as lively and playful as a kitten. I love the little creature as though she were my younger sister. She runs after me, repeating my name in her infantine accents, calling me Miss *Annice*, for she cannot say Agnes. Flora takes great pride in her, and already talks of teaching her the use of the knitting-needles, though Annie is little more than two years old; but Flora is very notable, and says, "Annie must not be idle."

We are very fortunate in having such faithful and industrious domestics: both father and children seem to vie with each other in attention to our comforts, and endeavour, by every possible means, to show their gratitude for the kindness they received at our hands, when they were in sickness and distress, and without friends or any one to pity and relieve them.

Our spring commences in March; but the early part of this season is far from agreeable, and frequently unhealthy, being cold, rainy, and tempestuous. The melting of the snow is very unpleasant: the roads are then quite impassable, being very slippery and swampy. The air is overcharged with fogs and damps, owing to the exhalations which are drawn up from the earth by the rays of the sun. Towards the end of April, the ground becomes once more firm and dry: the fields begin to wear the livery of spring, though the air is still cold and damp. In May there is little vestige of ice or snow left, excepting in the hollows of the dells and dingles, where it has been sheltered from the effects of the thaw and sun. Towards the middle of May, the air becomes soft and warm; vegetation proceeds with astonishing rapidity; the fields, woods, and banks are covered with an emerald verdure; flowers and buds, of a thousand lovely hues, which have been nourished by the snow, spring up among the turf; the forest-leaves expand, and all nature seems to hail the return of spring.

It is now June, and every thing above, below, and around us, presents a scene of exquisite beauty and freshness to the eye. The fruit-trees are loaded with blossoms, and the woods are waving with an endless variety of green. Cloudless skies and continual sunshine prevail. I wish my dear Ellen were here, to enjoy with me the beauties of this most delightful season of the year.

The wild flowers here are remarkably beautiful: I send you a few sketches from nature, of my chief favourites. I have also commenced a *hortus siccus*,* which will be an amusing study for us at some future time.

---

* *Hortus siccus*, (or dried garden,) an appellation given to a collection of specimens of plants, carefully dried and preserved.

Gather handsome specimens of flowers, grasses, or mosses, and spread the leaves and petals of the flowers quite flat between sheets of blotting-paper, laying a flat board over

Perhaps it will amuse my dear Ellen to hear how I pass my time, and what are my employments.

I rise in general at five o'clock, and, while Flora is milking the cows, I am in the dairy taking the cream off the milk, and making the cheese; which useful art I learned while staying at Woodley Grange, with my good friend Mrs Hartley; and I have now a dozen specimens of my skill in my cheese-room, which will soon be fit for use. Twice a week we churn, and Flora assists me in making the butter. As soon as the business of the dairy is over, I fill my apron with dross corn, and, attended by my little maid Flora, bearing a pitcher of clear water in her hand, I go to my poultry-yard, where I am greeted by fowls of all sorts and sizes, which run and fly to meet me, eager to receive their breakfasts from my hand. I have some favourites among my fowls, especially one chicken with a *cross-bill*, which attracted my attention on account of the slow progress she made in picking; so I took her under my protection, and now she is so fond of me, she flies into my lap and picks out of my hand, and seems, by her caresses, to be quite sensible of my regard for her. The foxes abound so in the woods, that it is with difficulty I can preserve any of my fowls from their depredations. Last week I had four young broods of nice little chickens, thirty-eight in the whole; and now I have only two little ones left out of that number, those wicked foxes having eaten all the rest. My best old brood-goose hatched twelve little goslings, and I was quite proud of the addition to my poultry-yard; but the foxes came last night, and robbed me of all but four.

Richard found me lamenting over the loss of my poor goslings. He consoled me with his usual kindness, promising he would contrive some means of securing my fowls from any further depredations. He instantly set to work, and, with Andrew for his assistant, began to rail my poultry-yard all round. I watch their progress with much interest, and shall be rejoiced when it is completed; for I cannot bear to see my nice little chickens devoured by those disagreeable foxes; and the wild cats from the woods are quite as bad as the foxes.

Richard has promised to make me some coops for my young broods, some pens for my fatting fowls; and to build a nice house for the accommodation of my old hens, ducks, and geese.

As soon as I have attended to the wants of my poultry, and Flora has collected all the eggs she can find, I give my two weanling calves, Blackberry and Strawberry, their breakfast of warmed milk, which they receive with gratitude from our hands. We then return to the house, and prepare breakfast; for in Canada, my dear Ellen, it is not sufficient to

---

each sheet containing your specimens, on which place a heavy weight; taking care to shift your flowers into fresh sheets of paper, at least once a day. When thoroughly dried and flattened, wash the backs of the leaves, flowers &c. over with a camel's hair pencil, dipped in a solution of gum-tragacanth and spirits of wine; and arrange them, according to class, on the pages of a blank book. If this is carefully done, you will have a good *hortus siccus*, which, if the specimens are scarce and well chosen, will be of considerable value to those young persons who take pleasure in the study of botany.

give orders, and look on while the servants work: you must also lend your assistance, and help to do some of the labours of the house.

Once a week we bake. This is my busy day, and I find enough to employ me. The household-bread is made with a mixture of rye and maize-flour, with new milk; and it is far nicer, and more delicate, than the best English bread I ever tasted. My cakes and puddings gain me great credit. I also make all the pastry. I intend preserving a great deal of fruit this summer, such as cranberries, raspberries, and strawberries. This we can do with very little expense, as we have a plentiful store of maple-sugar, having made nearly six hundred weight this spring.

Papa engaged a party of Indians to make the sugar for us, as they far excel the settlers in the art of refining it. The method practised round us, is to top the maples when the sap rises, and place a trough under them; but this is very wasteful, as it kills the tree. The Indian plan is much better: with a hollow knife they scoop out a piece from the trunk of the tree, at a certain distance from the ground; into this incision they insert a spout or tube of elderwood, through which the sap flows into the troughs below. Every day the liquor is collected into one great vessel. A fire is lighted round it, and the sap is kept boiling till the watery particles have evaporated: it is then purified with eggs, and kept stirred with an iron ladle. Two gallons of sap are reckoned to produce one pound of sugar. From two hundred and sixty maple-trees, the Indians produced six hundred weight of sugar, and a quantity of molasses: a goodly stock you will say, for such a small household as ours.

I used often to walk with papa and mamma into the woods, to visit the Indians, while they were making the sugar. Their picturesque figures, dresses, attitudes, and employments, contrasted with the ruddy glare of the fires, and the dark trees of the forest above them, would have formed a subject worthy of the pencil of a West or a Salvator Rosa.

Some of the men were tending the fires stirring the liquor in the boiling kettles, or purifying it: others collecting the fresh sap, tapping the trees, or binding up the wounds in those that had ceased to flow. Here a group of Indian children were seated on their fathers' blankets, round the fires, weaving baskets or mats, or scooping the tubes of elder-wood: there a party were dancing the Indian dance, or singing, in wild, irregular cadence, the songs of their native tribes; while some, more industrious, were employed in collecting wood and supplying the fires with fuel.

Among the Indians there was one old man, for whom I contracted quite a friendship. He used to lift me over the fallen timbers, and place me near the fire at which he was at work, spreading his blanket on a block or trunk of wood, for my accommodation. This old Indian told me he was called Hawk-head by his own people, but that he had been baptized into the Christian church by a white missionary, who came from a distant country and preached the word of God in their village. But this was many years ago, when he was in the pride of his strength; and he had forgotten much of his duty since that time. He said, in excuse for it, "Young lady! the Hawk-head has grown old, and his memory has faded, and his eyes have waxed dim, since he heard the words of missionary John. He has seen his children, to the third generation, rise up before him, ready to fill his place; and he expects soon to be called away to the land of spirits."

I was much interested by the conversation of this venerable man, and hoped to improve the good seed that the missionary had sown in his heart. I explained to him many points of faith, of which he was anxious to be informed; and I also mentioned to him my intention of opening an evening school, for the instruction of the children of his tribe in the knowledge of God and of their Saviour. The old man said, "Hawk-head would be glad to see his children taught that which is right and good;" and he promised to speak to his children on the subject. I found my Indian proselyte a powerful auxiliary, as he possessed great influence over the minds of the tribe of which he was the chief. I have now fourteen Indian children under my tuition, who are making great improvement in their moral conduct. Several Indian mothers came to our school, a short time since, and entreated that they also might be taught what was good, as well as their children.

At first our school opened under very unpromising auspices: few of the labourers would allow their children to attend it, and we had but four little Indians, who had been prevailed upon by my friend the Hawk-head to attend. But, in spite of this disappointment, we resolved not to be discouraged; and in the course of another month we had gained ten more Indians, and several of the children of the Irish peasants. The school has only been established since the beginning of last March, and we have now twenty-five regular scholars; and I am happy to say that a considerable alteration has already taken place in the manners and behaviour of the inhabitants of the village, which, when we first settled here, was a sad, wicked, disorderly place.

Besides our constant attendance at the school, we have some who only come occasionally; (perhaps once a week); but these are idle, and of irregular habits, and do not like to observe the necessary restraints which we are forced to exact. Some few come from motives of curiosity, or to pass away a dull hour; but we do not exclude any. And I trust that not unfrequently it happens, that

"Those who came to scoff remain'd to pray."

You do not know, my dear Ellen, what real and heartfelt pleasure we feel in instructing these children in their moral duties, and teaching them the knowledge of God and the advantages of religion.

Jane and Charlotte Hamilton are my assistants in the business of the school. Charlotte returned home last Christmas, to Oakdale. She is as near my own age as possible. I like her much, she is so sprightly and amusing; but I love her sister Jane best, partly because I have known her longer, and partly because I fancy there is a resemblance between her and my own dear Ellen. Charlotte declares she shall love you, and is delighted when I talk to her of you, or read a portion of your letters to her, which I always do when I am so fortunate as to receive one from my Ellen. How happy should I be, could I welcome the beloved writer of those letters to our dwelling; and I trust the time may not be very distant when I shall enjoy that pleasure.

Our garden already begins to look very pretty. I work in it every day, when the weather is not too warm. I have several parterres of beautiful native flowers, besides those plants which we brought from Roselands; and the seeds which you sent to us in the winter have now become strong plants. Every root we put into the ground flourishes, and increases in a wonderful manner, owing to the richness and fertility of the soil. The labours of our hands are repaid in a fourfold degree; and in the course of another year or two, the garden will become a lovely spot. At present all our fruits are confined to the wild sorts, excepting such as we are supplied with by our kind neighbour, whose garden having been under cultivation some years, is now become very productive. The fence which Richard made round the garden last year, has taken root, and is thriving nicely, presenting to the eye a wall of lively green.

We have just finished getting our seed-corn into the ground. The wheat-crops are up, and look beautifully green and fresh. Spring is the busy time of the year, both on the farm and within-doors. Papa has astonished our Canadian neighbours by some of his English improvements; such as building corn-stands, making five-barred gates, English hay-stacks, and sheep-pens.

Our stock has increased considerably since last year. We have a flock of ten young lambs, as white as snow, which feed on the lawn before our door with the old ewes; these are under Andrew's care, and he is very proud of his flock. Flora has a cosset-lamb, which she doats on: it was a very weakly twin when she first took it under her protection. She fed it for a whole fortnight with warm milk out of a teapot, till it grew strong, and learned to drink by itself. It is now so tame, that it runs after her all over the fields. We have also three calves, two of which are weanlings. We have bought another yoke of oxen. We have also fifteen head of swine, which get their living during one half the year in the fields and woods, feeding on the wild nuts and esculent roots, which they find, in vast profusion, under the trees in the forest.

The Canadian farmers live entirely on their own produce. Their chief subsistence consists in pork, mutton, venison, poultry, game, fish, the best bread, cakes of Indian corn, milk, eggs, and sugar. Besides this, they manufacture their own malt, candles, and soap; for which articles they pay no duties. Thus you see, my dear sister, that if we have not the luxuries and superfluities of life, the real, substantial comforts may be easily obtained by industry and forethought.

Taxes are very low; *viz.* for every acre of cultivated land, the settler pays one penny; waste land, one farthing. Live stock pays a tax of one penny in the pound. Besides this, we have highway-rates to pay, or so many days in the year to labour on the roads, which is very necessary;

and it is certainly the interest of every person to improve them as much as possible.

Papa intends making potash this year; likewise building a saw-mill, which can be worked by the little stream of water that flows through our grounds. He will then ship timber for Montreal, which he hopes will answer well.

The settlers who make potash, clear the land by firing the woods, or setting fire to the timber, after they are piled in heaps. You will see twenty or thirty acres, chopped into lengths and heaped together, all blazing at once. Of a night, the effect is very grand. But it is a dangerous practice; for if the weather is dry and warm, there is a great chance of the flames communicating from the woods to the cornfields and fences, and from thence to the out-buildings and the homesteads.

Last summer, the woods near us caught fire, owing to the extreme dryness of the season, and occasioned considerable damage to the farmer on whose land it commenced, scorching up one hundred and twenty acres of meadow land. We had one acre of wheat in the ear destroyed; and we were beginning to entertain great fears for the safety of our corn and cattle, when a very heavy shower of rain falling, (which seemed as if by the interposition of the Almighty himself,) extinguished the flames.

When the forests take fire, which not unfrequently happens, they present a most awful and imposing spectacle. The flames rush to the tops of the trees, roaring, crackling, crashing, and filling the air with glowing sparkles and burning splinters, as the trees sink beneath the wasting effects of the devouring element; wreaths of red and yellow smoke hover and wave above the burning woods, while the surrounding atmosphere becomes tinged with a lurid and angry redness. When the flames are extinguished, the scene presents an appearance of desolation, dreary beyond description. Instead of waving woods of green, once so charming to the eye, you behold only the trunks of black and branchless trees: white ashes (beneath which the fire still lingers) strew the once-verdant and flowery ground: all is dark and dismal, that was lately so fresh and lovely. Such, my dear Ellen, is the appearance of a Canadian forest on fire. But even this (which in many respects might be considered as a calamity) is not without its benefits; the earth being freed, in the course of a few hours, from a superfluity of timber, which would take the settler at least many weeks, or even months, to accomplish; and the wood-ashes which strew his land, render it fruitful to a most astonishing degree. Thus, in nature, we often see that which we at first rashly accounted an evil, become, through the superintending providence of an all-wise and merciful God, a positive blessing and benefit to mankind.

Our kind parents have promised to indulge Richard and me by a view of the falls of the Niagara, (if the winter should prove favourable for travelling,) and also a tour along the coast of the lake Erie; and we anticipate much pleasure from our excursion, especially as our neighbour, Mr

Hamilton, has consented to let his son and daughters accompany us in the journey. But as some months must necessarily intervene, we must not permit ourselves to be too sanguine, lest disappointment should follow; for, as the wise writer of the book of Ecclesiastes says, "There is no new thing under the sun;" so, from our own experience, we may add, "There is no certain thing under the sun."

Were it not for the society of the Hamiltons, we should find this place quite a solitude, as our other neighbours consist chiefly of mechanics or labourers, (I mean those in our immediate vicinity,) whose education has unfitted them for the pleasures of intellectual conversation, and we cannot take interest in theirs. But we practise a mutual kindness towards each other, and there is no lack of friendship on either part; each acting on the law of obligation, which forms a great bond of unity between the inhabitants of this country.

Sometimes we are enlivened by an occasional visit from travellers, such as the Canadian merchants, timber-merchants, overseer of the roads, tax-gatherer, or our Indian hunters or fowlers. According to the custom of this country, we entertain all strangers, setting before them the best food the house affords, and taking care of their horses; giving them accommodation for as long a time as our hospitality is required. We then speed them on their journey, wishing them health and prosperity.

Sometimes we chance to meet with an agreeable, sensible person among these wayfaring men; but in general they are very talkative, and inquisitive about the concerns of their neighbours, and very silent and reserved respecting their own.

At this time we are entertaining a very amiable lady, with her son, a young man about five and twenty. They are travelling home, from York (where the lady has a daughter, who is married and settled in that place) to the city of New York; and she has kindly offered to forward any packet we might wish to send to England, by the first packet that sails for Liverpool.

They arrived yesterday morning, and will leave us again this afternoon; so I must hasten to draw this already long letter to a speedy conclusion, as it will take me some little time to pack the flower-sketches I have prepared for you; also, a few Indian toys, which were presented to me by one of my little scholars; and a specimen of my feather-work, which I shall have great pleasure in forwarding to my dear Ellen; assured that a trifle from her Agnes, however insignificant in *real* value, will be prized by her as a remembrance, from her fondly-attached friend and sister,

AGNES CLARENCE

HENRY SHARPE HORSLEY
From *The Affectionate Parent's Gift, and the Good Child's Reward* (1828)

Writing in what he called "the plain garb of honest sincerity", this versifier, about whom little is known, made liberal and unrestricted use of maudlin, pathetic exempla to further his practical and pious design: "to lead the tender Mind of Youth in the early Practice of Virtue and Piety, and thereby promote temporal Prosperity and eternal Happiness". A collection of poems and essays, *The Affectionate Parent's Gift* was also intended to satisfy children's "thirst after novelty"; which, however, Horsley thought "ought to be kept within the restricted limits of prudence by those who have the control over them, and the culture of their minds entrusted to their care".

SCHOOL

Children are sent to school to learn,
    And diligent should be;
Then their improvement will shine forth,
    And all will plainly see,

That they are good, and friends will praise;
    Their parents will caress
The child who diligently tries
    Sound learning to possess.

Abundant cause for gratitude
    Have children, who are taught
At School to read, to spell, and write,
    And are from ign'rance brought.

What is a child, unlearnt, untaught,
    His mind is wild and vague;
A book is seal'd—his vacant time
    Is irksome and a plague.

What better than poor Afric's son,
    Or savage of the wood,
Who wildly run thro' deserts, moors,
    To join the chase of blood?

But learning curbs the wand'ring mind,
    It chases nature's night;
Affords a mental feast, and gives
    A soul-reviving light.

Prize, children, prize your book while young,
    Anticipate your school;
When you've a chance to learn, and not,
    You ought to die a fool.

Children who neglect to learn,
  Give evidence they're bad;
What must a tender parent feel,
  Whose son is such a lad!

Such children must be whipt and scourg'd,
  They don't deserve to eat;
For 'tis the diligent alone
  Are worthy of their meat.

Contrast a child that's good, with one
  Who hates his book and school;
What picture does the blockhead give,
  But that he is a fool?

Then view the diligent and good,
  The child whose willing mind
Is bent on learning—ever tries
  To seek, the prize—he'll find.

A VISIT TO NEWGATE

The Father of two little boys,
   Resolved one day to take
A walk through Newgate with the lads,
   Just for example's sake:

One of these boys was very good,
   The other the reverse;
A pilfering little petty thief,
   Was stubborn and perverse.

The father's fears would oft pourtray
   The little rascal's end;
If he was not reclaim'd, and soon,
   And did his conduct mend.

Come, Jack, the father said, you'll see
   What thieving does my lad;
This prison's built thus strong to keep
   The wicked and the bad.

The outer door turns on its hinge,
   The massive bars between;

And through the gratings of the cells,
    The inmates faintly seen.

'Twas here the voice of sorrow struck
    Th' affrighted ear of all;
The clinking chains, the frenzied yell,
    The harden'd culprit's bawl.

Confin'd within a grated cell,
    A little boy they spy'd,
With nothing but a crust to eat,
    All other food denied.

For why this little boy put here?
    For thieving you must know;
And there are many more beside,
    In lock-ups down below.

The little urchin's meagre face
    Was moisten'd with his tears;
The dread of punishment had rous'd
    His keen foreboding fears.

His parents he at first would rob,
    Then after bolder grew;
Stole trifles first, then grasp'd at all,
    Or any thing in view.

Exploring still the vaulted maze,
    Some dismal sobs assail'd
Their nerve-drawn ears—'twas grief, alas!
    Repentance unavail'd.

The sighs were shuddering exiles' cast
    To echo 'long the walls,
Repeating chill'd responses hoarse,
    And mock'd the victim's calls.

'Twas some poor men, who, doom'd to die
    Upon the coming day,
Were venting frantic tears of grief,
    And kneeling down to pray.

This was matur'd full-grown crime,
    Its end, and its reward;
Reproaches in full stature stood,
    And death to fainting aw'd.

Come, Children, view the march of crime,
    Exploring shun the road;
"Steal not at all," your Maker says,
    Such is the law of God.

A VISIT TO THE LUNATIC ASYLUM

Come child with me, a father said,
I often have a visit paid
To yon receptacle of woe,
For Lunatics.—Come, child, and know,
And prize the blessing you possess,
And prove the feeling you profess.
Come, shed a tear o'er those devoid
Of what you have through life enjoy'd:
See, in this mansion of distress,
The throngs of those who don't possess
Their reason; but with constant moan
Cast ashes on her vacant throne;
Her sceptre cankering in the dust,
Fair reason weeping o'er the rust;
Her seat deserted, fallen, decay,
And midnight horrors shade fair day.
Reason, thy grateful cheering light
Entomb'd 'neath ashes, clad in night,

Lays prostrate—where thy being's ceas'd,
Thy sons are levell'd with the beast.

What means that horrid dreadful yell,
Those screeches from yon grated cell;
The frightful clinking of the chain,
And wild effusions of the brain?

How madly now he tears his hair,
What wildness mixes with his stare;
With rage he rends his tatter'd clothes,
More vicious and still stronger grows.
What awful wreathings vent in rage,
With eye-balls starting, dread presage;
My God! can creature man thus sink,
Plung'd headlong down th' appalling brink.

Point out the man who grateful shows
That he the worth of reason knows;
That he his reason holds from God,
And stays by gratitude the rod
That might afflict—that might chastise—
The man who does the gift despise.

Were reason's channels choak'd and dried,
You of her benefits denied;
Read here what you would surely be,
Your picture in these inmates see.

Who could withhold a grateful heart,
For the possession of that part
Which lifts the mortal from the beast?
Yes, gratitude it claims at least.

But, oh! possessor ever know,
If gratitude you'd truly show,
Let every reasoning power be given
Up to the service of kind Heav'n.

THE DEATH OF A MOTHER

Supported by the yielding pillow,
   The tender Mother sat in bed,
With her children weeping round her,
   With list'ning ears at what she said.

She faintly utter'd—"My children,
   "Soon I must leave you, little dears;
"Now I feel death's hand upon me,
   "But don't distress me with your tears.

"The mandate's issued, I must leave you,
   "You feel the summons cruel, dears;
"Death with hasty strides approaches,
   "Life's curtain draws—a new world appears.

"Soon your mother will be lifeless,
   "For you I'd wish but to be spar'd;
"Ah, why this wish, I ne'er shall have it,
   "Never see my children rear'd.

"Submit then nobly, what's appointed,
　"'Tis the unerring will of Heaven;
"'Tis God who summons up your Mother,
　"'Tis He who has the mandate given.

"May God protect you, infant darlings,
　"Take my blessing from my heart;
"Oh! I feel death's arrow piercing,
　"I fall the victim of his dart."

Thus sunk the tender dying mother,
　While her children wept around,
And survey'd her pallid visage,
　While life's yielding cords unbound.

Life had fled—her frame was cooling,
　Oh! the sobs, the infants' sigh;
Weeping statues—breaking silence,
　Weeping, asks the question, why?

Why, oh, death! select our Mother,
　When we needed most her care;
Could not thy cruel hand have spar'd her—
　Could'st thou not our Mother spare?

Oh! this day—a day of sorrow,
　Clad in sable mourning's dress;
Now the cruel monarch's emblems
　Feeds on infantine distress.

Tears moisten the mould that covers
　Her dear remains from our eye,
While her happy spirit hovers
　Round her children, ever nigh.

Who could bear to see them weeping,
　And not mingle one soft tear?
Could you witness infants' crying
　O'er a loving mother's bier?

Where's the child who thus refuses?
　Or, while weeping—grateful prove,
That their Mother lives to succour,
　And are worthy Parents' love.

JANE MARCET (1769-1858)
From *Mary's Grammar Interspersed With Stories and Intended For The Use of Children* (1835)

A devoted pedagogue, Mrs Marcet made it clear in her Preface that she had introduced stories in the grammar "with the view of amusing children during the prosecution of so dry a study". Amusement, however, plays a secondary role: the stories in *Mary's* *Grammar* are largely exercises in identifying parts of speech. Thanks to these, to tests, and to the constant dinning of grammatical rules, young Mary proceeds to triumph over the mysteries of parsing, participles, and pronouns.

NOUNS. LESSON I

A little girl was sitting one day with a book in her hand, which she was studying with a woe-begone countenance, when her mother came into the room. "Why, Mary!" said she, "what is the matter? Your book is not very entertaining, I fear."

"No, indeed it is not," replied the child, who could scarcely help crying; "I never read such a stupid book; and look," added she, pointing to the pencil marks on the page, "what a long hard lesson I have to learn! Miss Thompson says, that now I am seven years old, I ought to begin to learn grammar: but I do not want to learn grammar; it is all nonsense; only see what a number of hard words that I cannot understand!"

Her mother took up the book, and observed that the lesson marked out for her to learn was not the beginning of the Grammar.

"No, mamma, the beginning is all about the letters of the alphabet, and spelling; but I am sure I know my letters, vowels, and consonants too, and I can spell pretty well: so Miss Thompson said I might begin here," and she pointed out the place to her mother, who read as follows:—" 'There are in the English language nine sorts of words, or parts of speech: article, noun, pronoun, adjective, verb, adverb, preposition, conjunction, and interjection.' "

When she had finished, Mary said, "Well, mamma, is not all that nonsense?"

"No, my dear; but it is difficult for you to understand, so you may skip over that. Let us see what follows." Mary seemed much pleased; and her mother continued reading. " 'An article is a word prefixed to nouns to point them out, and show how far their signification extends.' "

"Well, mamma, that is as bad as the rest; and if it is not real nonsense, it is nonsense to me at least, for I cannot understand it; so pray let us skip over that too."

"Let us see if something easier comes next," said her mother, and she went on reading. " 'A noun is the name of any thing that exists: it is therefore the name of any person, place, or thing.' Now Mary, I think you can understand that: what is your brother's name?"

"Charles," replied Mary.

"Well then, Charles is a noun, because it is a name; it is the name of a person."

"And am I a noun as well as Charles, mamma?"

"I is not your name," replied her mother; "when I call you, I do not say, 'Come here, I.'"

"Oh no; you say, 'Come here, Mary.'"

"Then *Mary* is a noun, because it is your name."

"But sometimes you say, 'Come here, child;' is child a noun as well as Mary?"

"Yes, because you are called child as well as Mary."

"And when I am older, mamma, I shall be called a girl, and not a child; and is a girl a noun too?"

"Yes, every name is a noun."

"Then papa is a noun, and mamma is a noun, and little Sophy is a noun, and baby is her other noun, because it is her other name; and John and George. Oh, what a number of nouns! Well, I think I shall understand nouns at last;" and her countenance began to brighten up.

"There are a number of other nouns," said her mother. "Sheep and horses, cats and dogs, in short, the names of all animals, are just as much nouns as the names of persons."

"But the Grammar does not say so, mamma!"

"It is true," replied her mother, "that it does not mention animals; but when it says that a noun is the name of any thing that exists, animals certainly exist, so they are nouns."

"Well, I think mamma, the Grammar ought to have said persons and animals."

"Or it might have said animals alone: for persons are animals, you know, Mary."

"Oh yes, I know that men, women, and children are all animals; and they are nouns, as well as geese and ducks, woodcocks and turkeys: and oh! my pretty canary bird too; and I suppose the names of ugly animals, such as rats and frogs and toads and spiders are nouns also?"

"Certainly," replied her mother; "but look, Mary, the Grammar says that the name of a place is also a noun."

"What place, mamma?"

"All places whatever. A town is the name of a place that people live in."

"Yes," said Mary, "so London, and Hampstead, and York are nouns; but a house is a place people live in too, mamma."

"Therefore *house* is a noun as well as *town*. What is this place we are now sitting in called, Mary?"

"It is called a room; so *room* is the name of a place to sit in, and *stable* a place to keep horses in, and *dairy* is a place to keep milk and butter in; and they are all nouns. And *cupboard* is a noun, mamma, because it is the name of a place to keep sweetmeats in."

"Certainly," replied her mother.

"Then the *house* and the *garden*, and the *church* and the *fields*, are nouns? What great nouns!" exclaimed Mary; "and are little places nouns?"

"Certainly; this little box is a place to hold sugar plums in, therefore box is a noun; and the key-hole of the door is a place to put the key in, so key-hole is a noun."

"And drawer is a noun, I am quite sure, mamma; for it is a place I keep my toys in. But, mamma, I think the key-hole of the lock, and the box for the sugar plums, are more like things than places?"

"They are both; for things that are made to hold something, such as a drawer and a box, are also places; especially if they are made for the purpose of keeping things safe."

"Oh yes," said Mary; "papa's desk is a place where he keeps his letters and bills so carefully; you know, mamma, I am never allowed to touch any thing in it. Then there is the tea-chest, which is a place and a thing too. It is a very pretty thing and a very safe place; for you know you always keep it locked. Oh, I begin to like nouns, they make me think of so many pretty things."

"I am glad to hear it, my dear," said her mother; "but I think we have had enough of them today. You must not learn too much at once, or you will not be able to remember what you learn. We shall find enough to say on nouns for a second lesson."

JACOB ABBOTT (1803-1879)
"The Reason Why" from *Rollo at School* (1839)

Carefully educated in the classics and religion at Hallowell Academy, Bowdoin College, and at Andover Theological Seminary, Jacob Abbott exerted a strong influence over American children's literature as a New England teacher and minister. One of his earliest works was *The Young Christian* (1832), essays on prayer, the Bible, confession, and self-improvement. The books most frequently associated with his name are the Rollo series, begun in 1834, with a second series, beginning in 1853, cataloguing Rollo's European travels. Some of the titles in the first series—*Rollo Learning to Talk, Rollo Learning to Read, Rollo at Work, Rollo at Play, Rollo at School, Rollo's Vacation,* and *Rollo's Experiments*—convey Abbott's intention to provide a descriptive account of growing up. Rollo lives on a New England farm with a kind father, gentle mother, older sister, and troublesome younger brother. Abbott announced, in the Preface to *Rollo at Work* (1837), that he was concerned not merely with advancing "thinking powers" and "promoting the progress of children in reading and . . . language", but also with "cultivating the amiable and gentle qualities of the heart." That cultivation seems quaintly formal today; without embarrassment, it defers to propriety and authority—as in this account of how and when explanations are dispensed.

THE REASON WHY

One afternoon, in the recess, Henry was playing with some stones in the walk, near the gate, and Rollo and Dovey and some other children were sitting by, on the grass. Henry was making a well. He had dug a small hole in the walk, and had put little stones all round it inside, as men stone up a well, and then he asked Dovey if she would not go in and get some water to pour into his well.

"No," said Dovey. "I can't go very well now; I am tired."

"Well, Rollo, you go, won't you?"

"Why—no—," said Rollo. "I can't go—very well."

He then asked one or two other children, but nobody seemed inclined to go.

"Oh dear me," said Henry, with a sigh, "I wish somebody would go; or else I wish water would come in my well of itself, as it does in men's wells. I don't see why it won't."

"It is because your well is not deep enough," said one of the children.

"Then I will dig it deeper," said Henry; and he took out the stones and began to dig it deeper, with a pointed stick, which served him for a shovel. But after digging until he was tired, his well was as dry as ever.

"I don't see why the water won't come," said he. "I mean to ask Miss Mary."

"No you mustn't ask Miss Mary," said a little round-faced boy standing there, with a paper windmill in his hand.

"Yes, I shall," said Henry.

"No, you mustn't; it is wrong to ask why."

"No, it isn't."

"Yes, it is," said George, "my mother said so."

"It is not wrong to ask why," said Rollo; "my father said it wasn't. It is very right."

George insisted that it was wrong. His mother knew, he said, as well as anybody, and she said it was wrong. Rollo was, however, not convinced; and the other children took sides, some with George, and some with Rollo; and, finally, after considerable dispute, they all arose, and went off in search of Miss Mary, to refer the question to her.

They entered the school-room, and all crowded up around Miss Mary's desk, Rollo and George at the head.

"Is it wrong, Miss Mary," said Rollo, "to ask why?"

"Isn't it, Miss Mary?" said George.

"That depends upon circumstances," said Miss Mary.

The children did not know what she meant by "depends upon circumstances," and they were silent. At length one of the children said.

"George says that his mother told him it was wrong; but Rollo's father said it was right."

"It is a very important question," said Miss Mary. "I will answer it by and by, to the whole school. So you may go out and play for the rest of the recess, but do not talk about it any more among yourselves."

So the children went out to play until the bell rang to call them in.

At the close of the school, or rather just before the hour of closing it, Miss Mary, having asked the children to put their books away, addressed them as follows:

"Two of the scholars came to me with this question today: whether it was proper for children to ask their parents or teachers the reasons of things. One thought it was, and the other thought it was not. I told them I would consider the question when all the school could hear, and we will accordingly take it up now. George, you may tell us why you thought it was not."

George was quite a little boy, and he was at first rather intimidated at being called upon before the whole school to state his opinion. So he only answered faintly that his mother told him so.

"When was it, George?"

"Yesterday."

"Do you recollect what you were doing when she told you, and what she said? Tell us all about it."

"Why, I was playing with some blocks, and mother said I must go to bed, and I asked her why; she said I was always asking why, and it was wrong to ask her why."

"Well, Rollo, now let us hear your story."

"Why, one day I was playing in a tub of water by the pump, and I had a little cake-tin which I was sailing about for a ship, and I had another flat piece of tin for my raft. My ship would sail about very well, but my raft would not sail at all; it would sink directly to the bottom. I could not make it stay up. And so I went in to my father, and I asked why one would sail and the other would not, when they were both tin. And he said he was very glad that I asked him, and that it was right for children to ask why."

"Very well," said Miss Mary, as soon as Rollo had finished. "You have both told your stories very well.

"For children to ask their parents the reason for anything they see or hear, is sometimes right and sometimes wrong. It depends upon circumstances. In George's case, now, the circumstances were very different from those of Rollo's. Rollo's motive was a desire of knowledge. He wanted to have a difficulty explained, and so he went to his father, at a proper time and under proper circumstances, and asked him. In such cases as this, it is very right to ask the reason why.

"But in George's case it was different. He asked why he must go to bed, not from a desire to learn and understand, but only because he did not want to go. He knew well enough why he must go. It was time. He only asked for the purpose of making delay, and perhaps getting leave to sit up longer.

"This now is a very common case of boys' asking why. They are told to do something, and instead of obeying promptly and at once, they ask why they must do it. It is one kind of disobedience, and it is, of course, always wrong.

"Then it is always wrong," said Lucy, "to ask our father and mother the reason for what they tell us to do?"

"No," said Miss Mary; "not unless you make it an excuse for putting off obeying. For instance, if George had gone to bed directly and good humouredly when his mother told him to go, and then, the next day, when he saw that she was at leisure, if he had gone and said to her, 'Mother, what is the reason that children are generally sent to bed earlier than grown persons?' I don't think she would have considered it wrong. If he had asked the question in that way, it would have shewn that he really wanted to know; but in the other way he stops to ask about the reason of the command, at the time when he ought to have gone off and obeyed it."

"My father never lets me ask him the reason for what he tells me to do," said Henry.

"You mean, I rather think, that he never lets you stop to ask him the reason at the time when you ought to be doing it."

"No,' said Henry. "I don't think he would let me ask him at all."

"Suppose you try the experiment. Next time he gives you any command which you do not understand, go and obey it at once, with alacrity, and then, afterwards, when he is at leisure, go and ask him pleasantly if he will tell you the reason."

"I will," said Henry, "but I know he won't tell me."

"Well," said Miss Mary, "we will now close the school; and I want you all to remember what I have told you. It is right for you to want to understand what you see and hear; and it is even right for you to wish to know the reasons for the commands your parents give you. But you must always do it at a proper time, and with proper motives, and you must never stop to ask why, when the command is given and you ought to be obeying it. And above all, you must never stop to say, 'Why must I?' in a repining tone, when you don't really wish to know why, but only to show your unwillingness to obey."

That night, when Henry went home from school, he had an opportunity to put Miss Mary's opinions to the test, sooner than he had expected. He walked along with Rollo as far as their roads went together, and then he turned down a green lane, which led, after some time, to a pleasant-looking house, with a fine large martin-house upon a tall pole near it. This was where Henry lived. He heard his father at work in the barn, and he went and looked in. His father and a boy were grinding some scythes. He looked at them a few minutes, and then went into the house.

His mother was at work in the kitchen, getting supper. A small table was set in the middle of the room with two plates upon it, for Henry's father and mother. At another table, by the window, there was a large pan of milk, and a bowl full by the side of it.

"Is this my bowl of milk?" said Henry.

"Yes," said his mother.

So Henry took up his bowl of milk, and carried it carefully out to the door, and put it down on a large stone which was in the back yard, and which made a sort of seat, where he often went to eat his bread and milk. Then he went in and got a spoon and a large piece of bread, and came out and sat down upon the stone and ate his supper. After this his mother told him it was time to go after the cows, and so he put on his cap and walked along.

Henry went through a pair of bars which led to a lane by the side of the barn. He went down this lane for some distance, until he reached the place where the path entered among the trees and bushes. He was just disappearing in the thicket, when his father saw him through the back barn door. He called aloud.

"Henry."

Henry turned round, saw his father, and answered,

"What, sir?" in a loud voice.

"Are you going after the cows?"

"Yes, sir," said Henry.

"Well,—don't go over the bridge,—but go round by the stepping-stones,—going and coming."

Henry was so far off that his father had to call in a loud voice, and to speak very slowly and distinctly, in order to make him hear. After he had done speaking, he paused a moment, in order to observe whether Henry appeared to understand him.

"*Why* mustn't I go over the bridge?"

His father, in reply to this question, only said, "Obey!"

Henry understood by this that he did not think it proper for him to ask the reason.

"There, said he to himself, "I told Miss Mary so. My father never lets me ask why."

The bridge which his father meant, was only a couple of old logs laid across a brook in the woods, so that they could get over. The cows could not walk upon it, and so they usually came across through the water. They had thus worn a deep place in the brook, both above and below the bridge, and here Henry used to love to stop and play, sailing boats, watching little fishes, skippers, &c. There was another way of going in the pasture, by turning off just before you come to the bridge, through some cedar bushes, until you come to the brook at another place below; and there, there were stepping-stones. The path beyond led on to the pasture, though it came out into a little different part of it.

Now Henry preferred to go by the bridge, and he asked his father why he mustn't, not because he really wished to know the reason, but only as a way of begging his father to let him go that way.

Henry, however, obeyed. He left the path which led to the bridge, at the proper place, and went through among the cedars and other trees which grew near the brook, until he came to the stepping-stones. He then went on to the pasture and found the cows. He drove them along towards home, and tried to make them go by the path his father had directed him to take; but they liked the other road better, as well as he, and, notwithstanding all his efforts, they would go into the woods by the path which led to the bridge.

"Now I *must* go by the bridge," said Henry.

On second thoughts, however, he concluded to obey his orders at all hazards. So he went to the entrance of the woods, where the cows had gone in, and shouted to them some time to make them go on, and then he went himself round the other way.

The cows stopped a few minutes to drink at the brook and accordingly they and Henry came out at the junction of the two paths very nearly together. Henry then drove them along the lane towards the house.

He wondered what the reason could be why his father would not let him take the usual path; and just then he happened to think of the experiment which Miss Mary had advised him to try.

"Here is a fine chance," said he to himself. "I will ask my father, but *I know* he won't tell me."

Accordingly, when he reached the yard, he went to the barn to find his father. It was almost dark, and he was just shutting the great doors. Henry pushed the doors to, for him, and his father fastened them. Then he took hold of his father's hand, and they walked towards the house.

"Father," said he, in a good natured tone, "will you be good enough to tell me what the reason was why you were not willing to have me go over the bridge?"

"Oh yes," said his father. "We found a great hornet's nest close by the bridge today, and I don't want you to go that way until we destroy it, for fear you will get stung."

"A hornet's nest?" said Henry.

"Yes" said his father, "a monstrous one."

"How big?" said Henry.

"Oh, as big as your head."

"As big as my head?" said Henry, with astonishment.

"Yes, cap and all."

"Do you think the hornets would have stung me?" asked Henry again, after a moment's pause.

"No, I don't think they would."

"Then why didn't you let me go?"

"Because they *might* have stung you, though probably they would not have done it, if you had let them alone."

"When are you going to destroy the nest?" said Henry.

"Early to-morrow morning,"

Here they reached the house, and Henry's father went in to his supper. Henry himself sat down upon the door step, saying to himself.

"Well, Miss Mary was right, it seems, after all."

The next day, when Henry came to school, he went to Miss Mary's table, and told her he had tried the plan of asking his father the reason at the proper time.

"And did he tell you?" said Miss Mary.

"Yes," said Henry smiling; "he did."

"I thought he would. Parents are generally willing to give their children reasons, if they ask at a proper time and in a proper manner."

Miss Mary then asked Henry what it was that he asked his father the reason for, and he told her the whole story. She then asked him if he was willing that she should tell the story to all the scholars, and he said yes; and she accordingly did so.

BARBARA HOFLAND (1770-1844)
"Janetta and her Jujubes"
from *Farewell Tales Founded on Facts* (1840)

A widow who chose a gifted but improvident landscape painter as her second husband, Mrs Hofland wrote not only to instruct the young but to support her family. Necessarily a prolific writer, she used in many of her stories her own domestic experiences, and those involving the school she established at Harrogate. "Janetta and her Jujubes" illustrates Mrs Hofland's belief that every action should be submitted to prolonged and intense scrutiny. Janetta learns that selfless generosity can be "foolish and imprudent".

JANETTA AND HER JUJUBES

"Oh, Mamma, what a very large bag of jujubes! I never saw so many together before."

"Perhaps not, my dear, but they are things that will keep; and you are not the only person in the house that is troubled with a cough: take them, my love, and give them to those who have colds; I am afraid I may want jujubes for myself before long."

Away went Janetta, happiest of the happy, though a bad cold somewhat depressed her spirits; but she knew some whom she thought worse than herself, and she was eager to administer to their relief; besides, there was some pleasure in exhibiting so large a paper of such very pretty-looking things; for although jujubes are nearly tasteless, they look as if they were delicious, and are more tempting than many much sweeter confections.

Janetta was the only daughter of a lady who had an establishment for twenty little girls, whom she educated with all the tenderness of maternal love, and the wisdom gained by knowledge and experience; being assisted in communicating the accomplishments called for by their rank in life, by her excellent husband, and several judicious teachers. In this situation, it will readily occur to every thinking person, the only daughter of the governess ran no little risk of being spoiled, especially if she was a clever and pretty child, as it was the interest of every person around her, to exhibit her acquirements, and contribute to her attainments—to engage her affections and indulge her wishes, in order that her influence might, in some shape or other, prove beneficial to them, during their residence with her mamma. Perhaps few situations in early life can be found, where a child may be equally important, and, of course, equally surrounded by those temptations likely to injure her temper, awaken her pride, and destroy that simplicity and ingenuousness, which are the best characteristics of her age: her faculties are likely to be prematurely nurtured, but her virtues to be blighted, by that consciousness of power which is so generally injurious to all, even when time and trouble should have taught better things.

Happily for Janetta, the parents she was blest with, influenced by a deep sense of religion, sound understandings, and that actual knowledge of her predicament necessary for her real welfare, guarded her in every point; and whatever might be, and indeed *must* be, their gratification in her progress, never suffered her superiority to induce vanity, much less exultation, over others. She was a child with the rest, subject to the same discipline, instructed with the same kindness; and although the real sweetness of her temper, and her constant industry in improvement, might have rendered her valuable as a peace-maker to the quarrelsome, or an assistant to the indolent, neither, in general, sought her interference, because they held her to be governed by the same rules which bound themselves, and referred all matters of moment to their governess.

But wherever a proper favour was to be obtained, a childish error to be forgiven, an indulgence desired, Janetta was always applied to, less on account of her supposed powers of persuasion, than in order to confer on her the pleasure she evidently felt; so far from being a selfish child (the great error of only children) she might be said to live *in* and *for others*, to the utter exclusion of that usually most interesting person, *self*; and the circumstance of being surrounded by so large a family circle, of course offered abundant means for the exercise of that kindness and generosity which was inherent by nature, fostered by education, and become habitual from situation.

Such was Janetta, when she walked off with her prize of jujubes, recalling to mind all who had colds, or were likely to have them, yet coming to the very false conclusion, that so large a supply could not, by possibility, be wanted; but it furnished a proof of her mamma's great kindness to every body, and elicited a hope, that "surely that dear mamma would not have occasion for them herself."

It did however so happen, that when Mrs Alston was retiring for the night, she thought it prudent to have a few jujubes under her pillow, and entered her daughter's room which joined her own, for the purpose of taking them, but she did not find any; and not liking to disturb her, retired without them; and having an indifferent night, had the pain of hearing her daughter cough very frequently, without, as she thought, taking the means of relief she had so abundantly provided.

On Janetta entering her room in the morning, as was her custom, the first inquiry was—"Where did you put the jujubes, my dear?" and next, "Why did you not take them yourself, in the night?"

"Dear mamma, I had not one left; therefore, I could not put any under my pillow, as you directed."

"What could you possibly have done with them, Janetta? I insist upon knowing."

"I think jujubes are very odd things, for they really went in the strangest way imaginable: but I will tell you exactly all I know."

Of this, Mrs Alston could have no doubt, for Janetta's integrity was always able to bear examination, and she listened with a calm but somewhat serious air, to the explanation which followed.

"When I left you, I recalled to mind who amongst the young ladies were troubled with colds like myself, and I counted seven; so I got seven pieces of paper, mamma, and made up seven parcels—*good, handsome* parcels, and gave one to each of them. I thought I did very right, and was taking proper care of the young ladies."

"So you were, Janetta; go on with your account."

"Then I got two little papers, and put a few into each, for the two little ones, mamma, because I thought it would please them; and I made a package for Miss Jessop, because she was a stranger; and then I handed them about to the rest, and laid them open on the table, and though nobody seemed to like them, or care for them, when I returned from practising, I found there was not half a dozen left; but I wrapt those up for myself, remembering also you had said, it was possible you might want some, but, in the course of the evening, somebody asked for them, and so *all* were gone before bed-time."

"You are the most imprudent girl, I have ever known, Janetta. Had the jujubes been husbanded as they ought, for those who required them, they would have lasted several days, for I bought all the confectioner had; and, living so far from the town, I shall be some time before I can get more. Go down immediately, and see if you can beg a few for me. I hope I shall find some person in the house who will have more thought for my wants than my own daughter has had."

Poor Janetta burst into tears; her heart was so full of love to every creature around her, and so especially fond of her parents, that she had never, in her short life, received before a reproach on the score of deficient affection; nor could she acknowledge its justice, though she was agonized with the sense of its severity. With lingering footsteps she, however, sought to obey the command she had received, and had some consolation in soon returning with a plentiful supply of jujubes from those she had dealt them to so freely, and who were happy in offering them to the governess they loved.

Janetta found her papa in the dressing-room when she returned, and she laid them down on the table, with an eager anxious air.

"I am much obliged to my young friends, and glad to see that they have used my gift wisely." said Mrs Alston.

"But, mamma, dear—*dear* mamma, do not think they love you better than I do, or that they think more about you than *me*; pray, *pray* do not say such words to me again; punish me any other way. I am naughty—I am foolish; but surely I always love *you*? Oh, papa, speak, pray for me!"

Mrs Alston had risen and turned away, too much affected to reply, yet desirous to make a deep impression on the mind and memory of her beloved daughter, whom it was really necessary to wound for her future benefit.

"My dear Janetta," said the fond and anxious father, "be assured your mamma cannot say one severe word to you, that does not wound herself much more. Judge, therefore, how much she feels at this very moment, and then you will see the necessity, for her sake and mine, of—I will not say conquering a fault, but attaining a virtue."

"I did not think the jujubes were so very, *very* valuable," said poor Janetta, sobbing; "I did not remember they were to cure dear mamma; and, for myself, I did not mind my cough."

"No, my child, in that consists your error, an *uncommon* one; but it is one, nevertheless. You cannot suppose, my love, that we think the loss of a pound of jujubes material; on the contrary, I shall sincerely rejoice if I can impress upon your mind a lesson I have long desired to teach you, Janetta. You have, my dear, contracted a love for *giving*, which, to a certain point, you must conquer; because, otherwise you will always keep yourself *poor*, and by that means be incapable of fulfilling your duties. Do you understand me?"

Janetta shook the curls from her brow, and gazed through her tears with something like returning confidence, in her father's face, as she answered—"I know very well, papa, that every body must be *just*, before they are generous; and mamma I am sure will say for me, that I never borrowed the least thing in my life, to a needleful of sewing silk, that I didn't pay it again as soon as possible; but I did think one might give away their own. I now see the jujubes were not my own; they were given, as it were, in trust for the sick, and I was a careless girl to do as I did; yet I meant to be careful and prudent, and every thing—indeed I did."

"I believe you, my child, but with all these good intentions, you did a very unjust thing, Janetta—unjust to me."

"You mean to dear mamma; I will never forgive myself for forgetting she might want them."

"No, I mean to us both, by entirely omitting due and proper care to *our daughter*, who really required care, and whose cough the whole night through, has made our hearts ache in a manner those only who are parents themselves can sympathize with."

Janetta appeared equally puzzled and distressed. Naturally acute as her mind was, she did not, at first, comprehend who was the person alluded to; but the moment she did, darting into her father's arms, she cried—"*your* daughter! dear *mamma's* daughter! I did not think, I did not consider—oh! I had no right to forget you loved me," and again the poor child wept.

"This want of due consideration for yourself, my love is what I complain of," said Mrs Alston, sitting down, and drawing her tenderly towards her; "in your extreme kindness to others, you forget your own rights and wants so entirely, that if this disposition is not checked, or I ought rather to say *regulated*, in early life, my love, when the time comes for us to be taken from you, we shall have every reason to fear that you will give away all we have laboured to procure for you, and our old age will be oppressed with the dread of our only child being impoverished, aged, infirm, and friendless.

It is not easy for the very young to conceive it possible they can become old and infirm. Janetta was excessively shocked at the idea of her dear parents being grieved on her account; but the latter part of the picture did not come home to her feelings, save in the last word, which absolutely astonished her; for as the whole wealth of her situation consisted in her daily exercise of her affections, and the grand business of her life was promoting the happiness of others, she had no idea of the possibility of losing kindness under circumstances when it would be most valuable and she eagerly exclaimed—"Friendless! surely, mamma, I can never be friendless! people would not forsake me because I had done my best to serve them."

"Not *because* you had done your best to serve them; but, my love, the friends of your youth will, as you already know, be soon scattered abroad in the world, and, depend upon it, *other* people will be more likely to blame you for extravagance than commend you for generosity. You may say, perhaps truly, 'I spend nothing on myself.' They will answer—'No matter, you spent more than you could afford; you have forfeited the situation in life to which you were born, and which your education fitted you to enjoy. We will give you alms, but cannot admit you to our society.' Do you not see the possibility of all this Janetta? nay, its extreme probability, unless you correct yourself?"

Janetta sat seriously a long time, and then said—"I meant to do right, but I dare say I have been wrong. I should not like to be poor myself, though I like poor people, and pity them very much; for I should be obliged to feel all along the same sort of misery I had just now, when I went from one to another, begging jujubes—so ashamed! so distressed!"

"Only much *more* ashamed—much *more* distressed."

"The catechism says—'I must do my duty in that state of life unto which it shall please God to call me.' From what you say, mamma, it means also, that I must *preserve* myself in that state or situation of life in which it has pleased God to place me?"

"I do, my love, and for that reason recommend you to be prudent, and to remember, that there are cares and duties belonging to yourself, as well as to your fellow creatures, and that if they are not performed, others must suffer from your self-neglect—indeed, with whom you are connected."

"But you must not conclude, from any thing your mamma now says, that you are to run into an opposite extreme, Janetta," said her papa; "for that would be much the greater error of the two."

"There is no fear of that dear papa; for I shall have a good deal to do to cure myself of giving away every thing I have given to me, because it is so pleasant, and comes so natural as it were; but indeed I *will* reason upon it—I will *think* about it, and remember, for your sakes, not to strip *your* little girl of *every* thing, as I used to do."

Away went Janetta, with the light step and the light heart of childhood, to water every one's garden, and cherish every one's flowers, without, as heretofore, neglecting her own. She was at that period of life when the lessons and impressions of religion are received with the warmest sensibility, and excite the purest gratitude, but do not therefore check (for any length of time) that happy buoyancy of spirit which seems granted to every young creature, as the especial boon of its early existence. Her father praised her labours, more especially as they regarded the improvements in her own garden, repeating, as he had often done before, "that her kind attentions to others, her consideration for them, and her generosity to them, had his warmest approval, except in its *excess*, which was, as she well knew, a daily increasing evil, until her mamma took up the affair of the jujubes, as the foundation of a very needful remonstrance."

"Needful, indeed, dear papa; for when I look back, I see clearly how foolish and imprudent I have been in my generosity, even destroying my power of charity; yet one is only a pleasure, and the other a positive duty; but I hope to be a great deal better before I am a woman; for I am determined strictly to imitate you and mamma, whom every body knows to be liberal and kind, and then cakes, fruit, and pocket-money, will be much more wisely distributed than the jujubes were."

SAMUEL GRISEWOLD GOODRICH (1793-1860), PETER PARLEY (pseudonym)

From *Make the Best of It; or Cheerful Cherry, and Other Tales* (1843)

A prolific publisher, Samuel Goodrich was the most successful Connecticut Yankee in the field of juvenile literature during the mid-nineteenth century. The son of a Congregational minister, he was born in the small farming community of Ridgefield; after a short education and a period of clerking in a country store, he bounded into the publishing trade at the ripe age of eighteen. His numerous books all purported to be factual not fantastic, realistic not romantic. His campaign against make-believe was very spirited—whether mounted by such creations as Gilbert Goahead and Robert Merry, or presented in the textbook chatter of his most famous persona, Peter Parley. This old white-haired fund of information—leaning on his wooden cane to support a bandaged, gouty foot—enjoyed a loyal following on both sides of the Atlantic. The short tales in *Parley's Magazine* (1833-44), collections of stories like *Make the Best of It*, and countless little textbooks on subjects ranging from history and geography to arithmetic and spelling, were all eagerly awaited—and even imitated by several spurious "Parleys". The children's writer Goodrich most admired was Hannah More (q.v.); he visited her at Barley Wood when she was in her eighties. (He may have dimly remembered More's story about "Parley the Porter" when he settled on the alliterative Peter Parley, which was both a pseudonym and an aptly named fictional character of great loquacity.) A good-natured go-getter himself, Goodrich observed in the Conclusion to *Make the Best of It*, that "it has been my chief object . . . to set forth the excellence of good temper and cheerfulness, united with energy and perseverance; to show that sources of proper enjoyment will be found all around us if we but look for them in a right spirit." Each of his stories has a clear-cut moral having to do with such things as obedience to parents, caution, and material success, but they are not over-serious; they are energetic and, like the author himself, cheerful.

THE PLEASURE BOAT:
or,
THE BROKEN PROMISE

A Gentleman, who lived in a fine house upon the banks of a beautiful lake, had five children, the two youngest of whom were twins—a boy and girl: these were four years old; while the others, a brother and two sisters, were much older.

The father of this family had a very pretty boat, and it was one of the greatest pleasures that the children could enjoy, to sail in it upon the lake. It was delightful to glide over the blue water; to see the fishes playing down deep in its bosom; to see the birds shooting over its surface, and often dipping their wings in the wave; and above all—it was delightful to visit a little island in the lake, upon which a pair of swans had hatched a brood of young ones, and which were now able to swim with their parents over the water.

One fine summer day these children begged their parents to let them go to the lake, and sail upon it in the boat; but the parents were afraid that they would get drowned, and refused their consent. The children then requested permission to go and walk along the border of the lake, saying that they would not go out in the boat. Upon this promise, the parents consented to the request, and accordingly the children started for their ramble.

They strolled along the edge of the water for some time, picking flowers upon the banks, or gathering shells and pebbles on the beach. By and by they saw the swans near the island, at a little distance, and they looked so quiet, beautiful and happy, that the children longed to get into the boat, and go out and see them. At last Thomas, the eldest of the group, proposed that they should do so, saying that the water was so smooth, no doubt their parents would be willing to let them go.

Now as Thomas was the eldest, he had influence over the others, and as he promised to be very careful, they consented. Having all got into the boat, Thomas took the paddle, placed it at the stern, and shoved the little vessel briskly through the water.

Directing its course at the same time that he urged it forward, he took the party from place to place, and at last they came to the island of the swans. Close by its margin they found the flock, consisting of the two parent birds, and their three young ones.

The swans were well acquainted with the children, and seemed to regard them as friends; so that when the boat approached, they arched their long necks, and came up close to it. The old ones even put their heads forward and ate some corn out of the hands of the twins, which they had brought for the purpose. The young ones ate the pieces of bread which were given to them in the water, and dived down to seize the grains of corn that were thrown out.

The twins, who were named Frank and Fanny, were greatly charmed with all this, but they seemed to enjoy it in different ways. Fanny was mild and gentle in her feelings, and her happiness seemed to partake of her general character. She regarded the swans with a pleased but tranquil look, and spoke to them in soft and tender tones.

But Frank was more ardent in his temper. He could not conduct himself with much order. He threw up his arms, and clapped his hands, and shouted till the borders of the lake echoed with his merry cries. Nor was all this enough. He was very anxious to take hold of one of the little swans. His sisters both warned him against this, and told him that in stooping over as he had done several times, he was in danger of falling into the water.

But most children are thoughtless, and seldom fear danger, till they have had some experience of evil. So it was with our joyous little boy of the boat. He heeded not the caution of his sisters, but continued his pranks, and at last, reaching forward to seize one of the young swans, fell headlong into the water!

There was a wild shriek from all the children as their little brother plunged into the lake and disappeared beneath the water. In a few seconds the poor boy came to the surface, and being very near the boat, the two sisters reached suddenly forward to take hold of him; this turned the boat on its side, and in an instant it was upset and all the party were thrown into the water.

Fortunately the water at this place was not deep, and Thomas soon succeeded in getting his sisters, including little Fanny, to the island, which was close at hand. But Frank, who was the cause of the accident, was still in the water, and had disappeared beneath its surface.

I cannot tell you with what agony Thomas searched about in the water for his dear little brother. I cannot tell you how his older sisters, standing on the shore, wrung their hands in anxiety and grief. I cannot tell you how little Fanny too cried out to Thomas to bring brother Frank out of the water.

Already Frank had been two or three minutes in the lake, and Thomas knew that if he was not very soon taken out he would never breathe again. It was, therefore, with a degree of distress which I cannot describe, that he plunged into the water, and searched along the bottom for his little brother. At last he felt something upon the sand, and, laying hold of it, he drew it forth, and lo! it was little Frank. Thomas brought him to the land, but how pale and deathlike was the face of the child!

One of the sisters took him in her arms, and held him to her bosom, seeking to bring back the colour and warmth to his cold cheek. She sat down with him in her lap, and they all knelt around, and while they wept they took his little cold hands in theirs, and with streaming eyes kissed him over and over again.

It was heart-rending to see little Fanny, looking into his face with terror at seeing it so white and so still. It seemed to her like sleep, but oh, how fearful seemed that strange, cold sleep, in one, but a few minutes before, the very image and impress of love and life and joy.

With timid and trembling fingers, Fanny at length took the hand of her brother, and lifting it to her lips, kissed it tenderly; and then she kissed his cheek; and then she spoke gently to him, saying, "Dear Frank, do you not know little Fanny? will you not speak to Fanny? will you not open your eyes, and look at me?" There was no answer, and the child burst into a gush of tears. But at this moment there was a slight movement in the little boy's frame, and he opened his eyes.

These signs of life gave inexpressible joy to the children. They even sobbed aloud, and clapped their hands, and wept, and jumped up and down, all in the same moment. After some minutes, and symptoms of great distress, Frank recovered, and looking round, seemed to know his sisters, and to become conscious of his situation. Soon after this, Thomas swam to the boat, and having pushed it to the shore and baled out the water, the little party returned towards their home.

Now these children loved their parents very much, but they were afraid to meet them, and really did not wish to go home. The reason was that they were conscious of their error, and saw that their disobedience had put to risk the life of their little brother. It was proposed by one of the unhappy party to conceal the fact, and account for the condition of Frank by saying that he had slipped into the water while walking along the bank. Thus it is that one fault begets another. Disobedience brings about accident, and this leads to falsehood: nay, it makes children, who before loved father and mother, dread their presence, seek to avoid them, and at last to deceive them.

But I am glad to say, that in this instance the little party did not act thus: they went straight to their mother, told the truth, confessed their faults, and begged forgiveness. This was granted, and then the father knelt down, and they all knelt with him, and they thanked God that the life of the little boy had been saved, and prayed that the erring boys and girls might be kept from further disobedience.

Come Walk with Me.

WORDS AND MUSIC COMPOSED FOR MERRY'S MUSEUM.

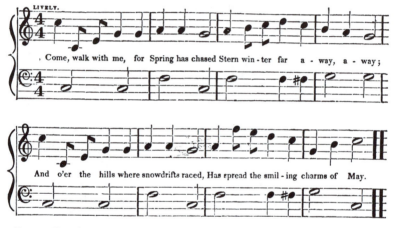

, Come, walk with me, for Spring has chased Stern win-ter far a-way, a-way;

And o'er the hills where snowdrifts raced, Has spread the smil-ing charms of May.

Come walk with me, for now 'tis morn,
And birds and flowers are every where ;
The dewdrop trembles on the thorn,
And love and music fill the air.

Come walk with me in yonder dell,
Where wild flowers dally with the rill ;
And where the wood-thrush sings so well,
When all around seems hushed and still.

Come walk with me, and let us go
To yonder peak by lightnings riven,
And mark the scene that spreads below,
And seems to mingle earth with heaven.

Come walk with me, and let our feet,
With careless saunter, choose the way,
For all above, below, is sweet,
And pleasure cannot go astray.

Come walk with me, and let us leave
Dull care, with all its load, behind,
And with our hearts and fingers weave
Fresh chaplets for the brow and mind.

Come walk with us, and if we seem
Like rainbow-chasing youth to-day,
O, let us not disdain the beam
That lights the heart — for now 'tis May '

From *Merry's Museum For Boys and Girls* (1846)

Having edited *Parley's Magazine* for eleven years (1833-44), Goodrich assumed editorship of its sequel, *Merry's Museum for Boys and Girls* (1844-72), until 1854. Published in semi-annual issues, these generously illustrated magazines contained stories of information and morality, puzzles, conundrums and anagrams, and specially written songs.

THE TRAP

"Hist, Jane! There he comes, the sparrow! Whew! he's on the very top of the cage! Keep still!"

Yes—there he stands, peering about, to see if there is any harm near. Pretty, innocent bird, how little do you know the danger that threatens you! You think these two children cannot mean you any mischief; and, as to puss, you imagine that she has too soft and gentle a look to harbor evil designs. And so you will jump down and pick up the little bits of meal that are spread in the box; and when you are least thinking of it, down will go the lid, and then you will be snug and fast in the trap! Poor little sparrow, how your heart will beat then, and how you will struggle and scream when James puts his hand into the cage and takes you out, and makes you a prisoner!

Now this, no doubt, is very good sport to you, James and Jane; but it is quite otherwise with the little bird. Pray do not harm him, after you have had the pleasure of success in your scheme, and showed that you *really can catch a bird*. I beg you to let him go again, and I am sure you will be the happier for it.

But we must not leave this story without some improvement of it. Gentle reader, you see that the boy and girl have a very innocent look and that there is some nice meal around the trap. The innocent looks are to make the bird think there is no harm near, and the meal is to entice him into the trap. In your experience of life, you will often find things to remind you of this scene. When cunning people wish to make a dupe of you, and use you for their own purposes, they will have soft looks, and will entice you by flattering speeches, till the time is ready, and then the trap will be sprung. I would not have you unduly suspicious; but when a person flatters you, and looks very winningly in your face, pray think of the sparrow and the Indian meal, and the trap and the picture in Merry's Museum!

ANAGRAM

This is a word or sentence, the letters of which may be transposed so as to form a new word or sentence. The following are among the best:—

Radical reform,	*Rare, mad frolic.*
James Stuart,	*A just matter.*
Gallantries,	*All great sin.*
Telegraph,	*Great help.*
Astronomers,	*Moon-starers.*
Lawyers,	*Sly ware.*
Old England,	*Golden Land.*

MILITARY SPIRIT

"Hold up your head, Caesar. There! that's right. Now look up: a soldier should never look down. Hold up your stick,—steady,—steady! Now, Caesar, you'll do. We shall march for Mexico to-morrow. Bravo! We'll beat the usurper Paredes and his ragamuffins.

"Rub-a-dub—rub-a-dub—dub! dub! It'll be good fun, Caesar, won't it? Now, suppose General Taylor says, Fire! Fire! Fire! So we all blaze away. Then the enemy run like a flock of sheep. On, boys, on! Hurrah for the stars and stripes! We've beat 'em—haven't we, Caesar?

"It's real fun! How I should like to be a soldier, and have a real sword, and a fine horse, and gold epaulets, and black moustaches; and have every body say, 'How fine he looks!' And when I come home from the wars, it will be so nice to have every body say, I have got a heap of glory; and they must make me president of the United States! They may say what they please about its being wicked to kill folks,when the surest way to be a great man is to fight a great battle. The more a man kills, the greater he is! Don't you think so, Caesar? Poor dog! you don't understand what I say—but you'll do for a private soldier, whose business is to be shot down. The real fun of war, after all, is only meant for the officers. They get the highest pay, the least work, and all the glory. The common soldiers take the hard knocks; and nobody cares what becomes of them. So I'll be an officer, to be sure. Forward! March!"

7. SUNDAY SCHOOL MORALISTS

Even Geography, Writing and Arithmetic may be made, in some measure, subservient to religious instruction, by proper observations on the form and division of the earth among the different nations which inhabit it; by a judicious use of copies; and by quotations relative to Scripture History. —Mrs Trimmer, Guardian of Education *(1803)*

Although the Rational Moralists had at least a tacit respect for religion, they were primarily concerned to dispense information to their child readers on the understanding that this—along with reason, natural piety, and the discreet guidance of their elders—would groom them to enjoy a vague and ideal state called "happiness". Side by side with these writers (though often in opposition to them) there existed another group of writer-educators who made religion the touchstone of their educational philosophies and for whom happiness did not denote the temporal, as with the Rational Moralists, but the spiritual. Involved in the establishment of Britain's first Sunday Schools, active participants in the vanguard of the Evangelical movement, and supporters of charitable endeavours at home and of missionary outreach, these writers produced a vast amount of literature designed, as Hannah More put it, "to persuade children of the absolute claim of religion". Much of it belongs to an enormous body of literary ephemera—religious tracts and minor tales—that is now chiefly of interest in revealing social attitudes. (It has been expertly described by Margaret Cutt in *Ministering Angels*, 1979.) The best is represented by the work of four well-known female writers: Anna Laetitia Barbauld, Sarah Trimmer, Hannah More, and Mary Sherwood.

Foremost among the influences on these writers was Evangelicalism. Beginning within the established churches—of both high and low degree—this movement of the masses believed in the experience of conversion and in salvation by faith, and sought to restore the authority of the Bible and to encourage evangelization at home and abroad. The movement most closely associated with the spread of Evangelicalism is Methodism. Under the practical direction of John Wesley (1703-91) Methodism made a strong appeal to religious sentiment, which found its most conspicuous expression in camp-meetings and revivals.

Evangelicals were fervent believers, and their enthusiasm was expressed in active ways. They practised self-discipline and self-improvement and performed good works among the poor in the ever-growing industrial districts of England. They endeavoured to help landless labourers dispossessed by the enclosure movement as well as mill and mine workers whose children had little hope of grammar schooling or tuition at a private academy. Their concern for social problems resulted in the foundation of several charitable and reform agencies—for example, The National Society for the Promoting of Education of the Children of the Poor—and in the establishment of England's first Sunday Schools under the urging of the wealthy Evangelical layman Robert Raikes. At York in 1786 a Church of England Sunday School Society was formed, and on the opening Sunday more than five hundred children attended programs in the ten schools.

The High Church principles of Sarah Trimmer, therefore, were not in the least compromised when she endorsed the Sunday School movement in *The Oeconomy of Charity* (1787). Dedicating her treatise to Queen Charlotte and fixing her gaze on her own sex, Mrs Trimmer outlined the benefits of the Sunday School in general and of her own successful experiment with a "sabbath school" in the town of Brentford. Though her concern for the poor was genuine, her literary manner was self-righteous and she was not above giving expression to some good old High Church snobbery. "God only knows," she warned, "what the lower classes of people will become if Sunday-Schools are suffered to drop, and something farther is not done for their reformation." Her Sunday School was open from 8 a.m. to 6 p.m., during which time the children read, spelled, recited, sang, and played outdoors. Mrs Trimmer's chief objectives were "the reformation of manners, the implanting of religious knowledge, and the proper observance of the Sabbath-Day".

These same objectives were pursued in varying degrees by all the Sunday School Moralists, with an additional emphasis on the importance of the family. Of the writers represented here, Mrs Barbauld wrote comforting hymns of praise, in prose, for children to memorize rather than sing, adapting the tone and message of Isaac Watts to her own day. Mrs Trimmer, in her most famous book for children, used a family of robins to teach obedience and to show the benefits of a mutually supportive family. Hannah More invented a personification of virtue and hope in adversity in the impoverished Shepherd of Salisbury-Plain. The best writer of this group is Mrs Sherwood, whose uplifting stories about the Fairchild family—each one containing, besides the narrative, a prayer and a hymn— were immensely popular. The importance of a religious education is the underlying theme of all Mrs Sherwood's stories, as in the one about the unfortunate Augusta Noble, whose last hours are described with chilling urgency as a gruesome lesson about the dual importance of obedience to parents and firm religious principles. The American Susan Bogert Warner resorted to tearful sentimental fiction, which in its own way was quite effective—it was very popular until early in this century—to teach perseverance and other virtues. Not represented here because they published after 1850 are even more popular Evangelical writers: Maria Charlesworth, Charlotte Tucker, and Sarah Smith ("Hesba Stretton").

All these writers wrote stories and verses that were accessible, emotionally satisfying, and highly approved of—they were often given as gifts to the poor or as prizes to the well behaved. The Evangelical books and tracts throbbed with an active, felt religion and found an eager audience. Furthermore they had a widespread influence. They helped shape the attitudes of English and North American society throughout the nineteenth century, and in advocating such social reforms as abolitionism and child-labour legislation, became a voice that was gradually heeded in Victorian England.

ANNA LAETITIA BARBAULD (1743-1825)
From *Hymns in Prose for Children* (1781)

A Presbyterian poet and teacher, Mrs Barbauld set high standards for her writing and did not consider it proper to lower poetry "to the capacities of children", as the "deservedly honoured" Dr Watts had done. Nevertheless her twelve hymns were "intended to be committed to memory, and recited". At the dawn of the industrial age, when farmers were being displaced and children were working long hours, she expressed in soothing word-pictures her apparent conviction that all was for the best in the best of all possible worlds. As the twelfth hymn declared, "the earth is pleasant, for it is God's earth, and it is filled with many delightful things". In the hymn below she uses a picturesque bucolic scene to explain the sensible hierarchy of the world.

HYMN VIII

See where stands the cottage of the labourer, covered with warm thatch; the mother is spinning at the door; the young children sport before her on the grass; the elder ones learn to labour, and are obedient; the father worketh to provide them food: either he tilleth the ground, or he gathereth in the corn, or shaketh his ripe apples from the tree: his children run to meet him when he cometh home, and his wife prepareth the wholesome meal.

The father, the mother, and the children, make a family; the father is the master thereof. If the family is numerous, and the grounds large, there are servants to help to do the work: all these dwell in one house; they sleep beneath one roof; they eat of the same bread; they kneel down together and praise God every night and every morning with one voice; they are very closely united, and are dearer to each other than any strangers. If one is sick, they mourn together; and if one is happy, they rejoice together.

Many houses are built together; many families live near one another; they meet together on the green, and in pleasant walks, and to buy and sell, and in the house of justice; and the sound of the bell calleth them to the house of God, in company. If one is poor, his neighbour helpeth him; if he is sad, he comforteth him. This is a village; see where it stands enclosed in a green shade, and the tall spire peeps above the trees. If there be very many houses, it is a town—it is governed by a magistrate.

Many towns, and a large extent of country, make a kingdom: it is enclosed by mountains; it is divided by rivers; it is washed by seas; the inhabitants thereof are countrymen; they speak the same language; they make war and peace together—a king is the ruler thereof.

Many kingdoms, and countries full of people, and islands, and large continents, and different climates, make up this whole world—God governeth it. The people swarm upon the face of it like ants upon a hillock: some are black with the hot sun; some cover themselves with furs against the sharp cold; some drink of the fruit of the vine; some the pleasant milk of the cocoanut; and others quench their thirst with the running stream.

All are God's family; he knoweth every one of them, as a shepherd knoweth his flock; they pray to him in different languages, but he understandeth them all; he heareth them all; he taketh care of all; none are so great, that he cannot punish them; none are so mean, that he will not protect them.

Negro woman, who sittest pining in captivity, and weepest over thy sick child; though no one seeth thee, God seeth thee; though no one pitieth thee, God pitieth thee: raise thy voice, forlorn and abandoned one; call upon him from amidst thy bonds, for assuredly he will hear thee.

Monarch, that rulest over an hundred states; whose frown is terrible as death, and whose armies cover the land, boast not thyself as though there were none above thee:—God is above thee; his powerful arm is always over thee; and if thou doest ill, assuredly he will punish thee.

Nations of the earth, fear the Lord; families of men, call upon the name of your God.

Is there any one whom God hath not made? let him not worship him: is there any one whom he hath not blessed? let him not praise him.

SARAH TRIMMER (1741-1810)
From *Fabulous Histories, designed for the Instruction of Children, respecting their treatment of animals* (1786)

Mother of twelve children, Mrs Trimmer was also an energetic writer of religious and instructional literature. Her first juvenile book, *An Easy Introduction to the Knowledge of Nature, and Reading the Holy Scriptures* (1780), set the tone for her subsequent work. Although she commended the establishment of Sunday Schools and Schools of Industry, she also endorsed parental instruction as natural and paramount. In *Fabulous Histories*, published frequently in the next century under the title *The History of the Robins*, Mrs Trimmer presented a series of fables using a robin family to teach about a human family. The conscientious and sympathetic Mrs Benson leads her two children, eleven-year-old Harriet and six-year-old Frederick, to an understanding of the compassionate care of these birds for their offspring as a paradigm of parents' benevolent concern for their children.

CHAPTER XXIV

For three successive days nothing remarkable happened, either at Mr Benson's or the Redbreast's nest. The little family came daily to the breakfast-table, and Robin daily recovered from his accident, though not sufficiently to fly well; but Dicky, Flapsy, and Pecksy, continued so healthy, and improved so fast, that they required no further care; and the third morning after their tour to the grove, &c. they did not commit the least error. When they retired from the parlour into the court-yard, to which Robin accompanied them, the father expressed great delight, that they were at length able to shift for themselves. And now a wonderful change took place in his own heart. That ardent affection for his young, which had hitherto made him, for their sakes, patient of toil, and fearless of danger, was on a sudden quenched; but, from the goodness of his disposition, he still felt a kind solicitude for their future welfare; therefore called them around him, and thus addressed them.

"You must be sensible, my dear young ones, that from the time you left the egg-shell, till the present instant, both your mother and I have nourished you with the tenderest love. We have taught you all the arts of life which are necessary to procure you subsistence, and preserve you from danger. We have shewn you a variety of characters in the different classes of birds; and pointed out those which are to be imitated, and those which are to be shunned. You must now shift for yourselves; but before we part, let me repeat my admonition, to use industry, avoid contention, cultivate peace, and be contented with your condition. Let none of your own species excel you in any amiable quality, for want of your endeavours to equal the best; and do your duty in every relation of life, as we have done ours by you. Prefer a calm retirement to the gay scenes of levity and dissipation, for there is the greatest degree of happiness to be found. You, Robin, I would advise, on account of your infirmity, to attach yourself to Mr Benson's family, where you have been so kindly cherished."

Whilst he thus spake, his mate stood by, who finding the same change beginning to take place in her own breast, she viewed her family with tender regret; and when he ceased, cried out: "Adieu, ye dear objects of my late cares and solicitude! may ye never more stand in need of a mother's assistance! Though nature now dismisses me from the arduous task, which I have long daily performed, I rejoice not, but would gladly continue my toil, for the sake of its attendant pleasures. Oh! delightful sentiments of maternal love, how can I part with you? Let me, my nestlings, give you a last embrace." Then spreading her wings, she folded them successively to her bosom, and instantly recovered her tranquillity. Each young one expressed its grateful thanks to both father and mother, and with these acknowledgments filial affection expired in their breasts; instead of which, a respectful friendship succeeded. Thus was that tender tie dissolved, which had hitherto bound this little family together; for the parents had performed their duty, and the young ones had no need of farther assistance.

The old Redbreasts having now only themselves to provide for, resolved to be no longer burthensome to their benefactors, and after pouring forth their gratitude in the most lively strains, they took their flight together, resolving never to separate. Every care now vanished, and their little hearts felt no sentiments but those of cheerfulness and joy. They ranged the fields and gardens, sipped at the coolest springs, and indulged themselves in the pleasures of society, joining their cheerful notes with those of other gay choristers, who animate and heighten the delightful scenes of rural life.

The first morning that the old Redbreasts were missing from Mrs Benson's breakfast-table, Frederick and his sister were greatly alarmed for their safety; but their mamma said, she was of opinion that they had left their nestlings; as it was the nature of animals in general to dismiss their young, as soon as they were able to provide for themselves. That is very strange, replied Miss Harriet; I wonder what would become of my brother and me, were you and papa to serve us so? And is a boy of six, or a girl of eleven years old, capable of shifting for themselves? said her mamma. No, my dear child, you have need of a much longer continuance of our care than birds and other animals; and therefore God has ordained that parental affection, when once awakened, should always remain in the human breast, unless extinguished by the undutiful behaviour of the child.

And shall we see the old Redbreasts no more? cried Frederick. I do not know that you will, replied Mrs Benson, though it is not unlikely that they may visit us again in the winter; but let not their absence grieve you, my love, for I dare say they are very safe and happy.

At that instant the young ones arrived, and met with a very joyful reception. The amusement they afforded to Master Benson, reconciled him to the loss of their parents; but Harriet declared, she could not help being sorry that they were gone. I shall, for the future, mamma, said she, take a great deal of notice of animals; for I have had much entertainment in observing the ways of these Robins. I highly approve your resolution, my dear, said Mrs Benson, and hope the occasional instruction I have at different times given you, has furnished you with general ideas respecting the proper treatment of animals. I will now inform you, upon what principles the rules of conduct I prescribe to myself on this subject are founded.

I consider, that the same almighty and good God, who created mankind, made all other living creatures likewise; and appointed them their different ranks in the creation, that they might form together a community, receiving and conferring reciprocal benefits.

There is no doubt that the Almighty designed all beings for happiness, proportionable to the faculties he endued them with; therefore, whoever wantonly destroys that happiness, acts contrary to the will of his Maker.

The world we live in seems to have been principally designed for the use and comfort of mankind, who, by the divine appointment, have dominion over the inferior creatures; in the exercise of which, it is certainly their duty to imitate the *supreme Lord of the Universe*, by being merciful to the utmost of their power. They are endued with Reason, which enables them to discover the different natures of brutes, the faculties they possess, and how they may be made serviceable in the world; and as beasts cannot apply these faculties to their own use in so extensive a way, and numbers of them (being unable to provide for their own sustenance) are indebted to men for many of the necessaries of life, men have an undoubted right to their labour in return.

Several other kinds of animals, which are sustained at the expense of mankind, cannot labour for them; from such they have a natural claim to whatever they can supply towards the food and raiment of their benefactors; and therefore, when we take the wool and milk of the flocks and herds, we take no more than our due, and what they can very well spare; as they seem to have an over-abundance given them, that they may be able to return their obligations to us.

Some creatures have nothing to give us but their own bodies: these have been expressly destined, by the *supreme Governor*, as food for mankind, and he has appointed an extraordinary increase of them for this very purpose; such an increase, as would be very injurious to us if all were suffered to live. These we have an undoubted right to kill; but we should make their short lives as comfortable as possible.

Other creatures seem to be of no particular use to mankind, but as they serve to furnish our minds with contemplations on the wisdom, power, and goodness of God, and to exhilarate our spirits by their cheerfulness. These should not be wantonly killed, nor treated with the least degree of cruelty, but should be at full liberty to enjoy the blessings assigned them; unless they abound to such a degree, as to become injurious, by devouring the food which is designed for man, or for animals more immediately beneficial to him, whom it is his duty to protect.

Some animals, such as wild beasts, serpents, &c. are in their nature ferocious, noxious, or venemous, and capable of injuring the health, or even of destroying the lives of men, and other creatures of a higher rank than themselves: these, if they leave the secret abodes which are allotted them, and become offensive, certainly may with justice be killed.

In a word, my dear, we should endeavour to regulate our regards according to the utility and necessities of every living creature with which we are any ways connected; and consequently should prefer the happiness of *mankind* to that of any *animal* whatever. Next to these (who being partakers of the same nature with ourselves, are more properly our *fellow-creatures*) we should consider our cattle and domestick animals, and take care to supply every creature that is dependent on us with proper food, and keep it in its proper place: after their wants are supplied, we should extend our benevolence and compassion as far as possible to the inferior ranks of beings; and if nothing farther is in our power, should at least refrain from exercising cruelties on them. For my own part, I never willingly put to death, or cause to be put to death, any creature but when there is a real necessity for it; and have my food dressed in a plain manner, that no more lives may be sacrificed for me, than nature requires for my subsistence in that way which God has allotted me. But I fear I have tired you with my long lecture, so will now dismiss you.

Whilst Mrs Benson was giving these instructions to her daughter, Frederick diverted himself with the young Robins, who having no kind parents now to admonish them, made a longer visit than usual; so that Mrs Benson would have been obliged to drive them away, had not Pecksy, on seeing her move from her seat, recollected that she and her brother and sister had been guilty of an impropriety; she therefore reminded them that they should no longer intrude, and led the way out at the window; the others followed her, and Mrs Benson gave permission to her children to take their morning's walk before they began their lessons.

HANNAH MORE (1745-1833)
The Shepherd of Salisbury-Plain, Part I (1795)

The Cheap Repository Tracts, with which Hannah More's name was associated as instigator and regular writer, were early attempts to offer moral edification in the short inexpensive format of the chapbook. The Cheap Repositories were intended for wide distribution. Shopkeepers and hawkers bought them in bulk at reduced rates, while the gentry bought them in quantities to distribute to the poor. Hannah More, a spinster who supported herself by her writing, was a prolific contributor to the tracts; titles such as *Dan and Jan; or Faith and Works, The Good Militiaman, The Market Woman, a true tale; or Honesty Is the Best Policy,* and *Patient Joe; or, The Newcastle Collier* indicate the purport of her staunchly moral tales, which urged a patient and virtuous acceptance of the way things were. Her most famous tract was the two-part story of the Shepherd of Salisbury-Plain. A living model of the Beatitudes (Matt., 3.5-11), the poor Shepherd recounts how, through the sustenance of the Scriptures and the sharpening of his wits, he and his wife and eight children were able to endure.

THE SHEPHERD OF SALISBURY-PLAIN

Mr Johnson, a very worthy, charitable Gentleman, was travelling sometime ago across one of those vast Plains which are well known in Wiltshire. It was a fine summer's evening, and he rode slowly that he might have leisure to admire God in the works of his creation. For, this Gentleman was of opinion, that a walk, or a ride, was as proper a time as any to think about good things, for which reason, on such occasions he seldom thought so much about his money, or his trade, or public news, as at other times, that he might with more ease and satisfaction enjoy the pious thoughts which the visible works of the great Maker of heaven and earth are intended to raise in the mind.

His attention was all of a sudden called off by the barking of a Shepherd's dog, and looking up, he spied one of those little huts which are here and there to be seen on those great Downs; and near it was the Shepherd himself, busily employed with his dog in collecting together his vast flock of sheep. As he drew nearer, he perceived him to be a clean, well looking, poor man, near fifty years of age. His coat, though at first it had probably been of one dark colour, had been in a long course of years so often patched with different sorts of cloth, that it was now become hard to say which had been the original colour. But this, while it gave a plain proof of the Shepherd's poverty, equally proved the exceeding neatness, industry, and good management of his wife. His stockings no less proved her good housewifery, for they were intirely covered with darns of different coloured worsted, but had not a hole in them; and his shirt, though nearly as coarse as the sails of a ship, was as white as the drifted snow, and neatly mended where time had either made a rent, or worn it thin. This is a rule of judging, by which one shall seldom be deceived. If I meet with a labourer, hedging, ditching, or mending the highways with his stockings and shirt tight and whole however mean and bad his other garments are, I have seldom failed, in visiting his cottage to find that also clean and well-ordered, and his wife notable, and worthy of encouragement. Whereas a poor woman, who will be lying a-bed, or gossipping with her neighbours when she ought to be fitting out her husband in a cleanly manner, will seldom be found to be very good in other respects.

This was not the case with our Shepherd: And Mr Johnson was not more struck with the decency of his mean and frugal dress, than with his open honest countenance, which bore strong marks of health, cheerfulness, and spirit.

Mr Johnson, who was on a journey, and somewhat fearful from the appearance of the sky, that rain was at no great distance, accosted the Shepherd with asking what sort of weather he thought it would be on the morrow.—"It will be such weather as pleases me," answered the Shepherd. Though the answer was delivered in the mildest, and civillest tone that could be imagined, the Gentleman thought the words themselves rather rude and surly, and asked him how that could be, "Because," replied the Shepherd, "it will be such weather as shall please God, and whatever pleases him always pleases me."

Mr Johnson, who delighted in good men and good things, was very well satisfied with his reply. For he justly thought that though an hypocrite may easily contrive to appear better than he really is to a stranger; and that no one should be too soon trusted, merely for having a few good words in his mouth: yet as he knew that "out of the abundance of the heart the mouth speaketh;" he always accustomed himself to judge favourably of those who had a serious deportment and solid manner of speaking. "It looks as if it proceeded from a good habit," said he, "and though I may now and then be deceived by it, yet it has not often happened to me to be so.—Whereas if a man accosts me with an idle, dissolute, vulgar, indecent, or prophane expression, I have never been deceived in *him*, but have generally on inquiry found his character to be as bad as his language gave me room to expect."

He entered into conversation with the Shepherd in the following manner. Yours is a troublesome life, honest friend, said he. To be sure, Sir, replied the Shepherd, 'tis not a very lazy life; but 'tis not near so toilsome as that which my GREAT MASTER led for my sake, and he had every state and condition of life at his choice, and *chose* a hard one— while I only submit to a lot that is appointed me.—You are exposed to great cold and heat, said the Gentleman;—true, Sir, said the Shepherd; but then I am not exposed to great temptations; and so throwing one thing against another, God is pleased to contrive to make things more equal than we poor, ignorant, short-sighted creatures, are apt to think. David was happier when he kept his father's sheep on such a plain as this, and singing some of his own Psalms perhaps, than ever he was when he became king of Israel and Judah. And I dare say we should never have had some of the most beautiful texts in all those fine Psalms, if he had not been a Shepherd, which enabled him to make so many fine comparisons and similitudes, as one may say, from country life, flocks of sheep, hills, and vallies, and fountains of water.

You think then, said the Gentleman, that a laborious life is a happy one. I do, Sir, and more so especially, as it exposes a man to fewer sins. If king Saul had continued a poor laborious man to the end of his days, he might have lived happy and honest, and died a natural death in his bed at last, which you know, Sir, was more than he did. But I speak with reverence, for it was divine Providence over-ruled all that, you know, Sir, and I do not presume to make comparisons.—Besides, Sir, my employment has been particularly honoured—Moses was a Shepherd in the plains of Midian.—It was to "Shepherds keeping their flocks by night" that the angels appeared in Bethlehem, to tell the best news, the gladdest tidings, that ever were revealed to poor sinful men: often, and often has the thought warmed my poor heart in the coldest night, and filled me with more joy and thankfulness than the best supper could have done.

Here the Shepherd stopped, for he began to feel that he had made too free, and had talked too long. But Mr Johnson was so well pleased with what he said, and with the cheerful, contented manner in which he said it, that he desired him to go on freely, for that it was a pleasure to him to meet with a plain man, who, without any kind of learning but what he had got from the Bible, was able to talk so well on a subject in which all men, high and low, rich and poor, are equally concerned.

Indeed I am afraid I make too bold, Sir, for it better becomes me to listen to such a Gentleman as you seem to be, than to talk in my poor way; but as I was saying, Sir, I wonder all working men do not derive as great joy and delight as I do, from thinking how God has honoured poverty! Oh! Sir, what great, or rich, or mighty men have had such honour put on them, or their condition, as Shepherds, Tent-makers, Fishermen, and Carpenters have had?

My honest friend, said the Gentleman, I perceive you are well acquainted with scripture. Yes, Sir, pretty well, blessed be God! through his mercy I learnt to read when I was a little boy; though reading was not so common when I was a child, as, I am told, through the goodness of Providence and the generosity of the rich, it is likely to become now-a-days. I believe there is no day for the last thirty years, that I have not peeped at my Bible.—If we can't find time to read a chapter, I defy any man to say he can't find time to read a verse; and a single text, Sir, well followed and put in practice every day, would make no bad figure at the year's end: three hundred and sixty-five texts, without the loss of a moment's time, would make a pretty stock, a little golden treasury, as one may say, from new year's day to new year's day; and if children were brought up to it, they would look for their text, as naturally as they do for their breakfast. No labouring man, 'tis true, has so much leisure as a Shepherd, for while the flock is feeding, I am obliged to be still, and at such times I can now and then tap a shoe for my children or myself, which is a great saving to us, and while I am doing that I repeat a bit of a chapter, which makes the time pass pleasantly in this wild, solitary place. I can say the best part of the Bible by heart—I believe I should not say the *best* part, for every part is good, but I mean the *greatest* part. I have led but a lonely life, and have often had but little to eat, but my Bible has been meat, drink and company to me, as I may say—and when want and trouble have come upon me, I don't know what I should have done indeed, Sir, if I had not had the promises of this book for my stay and support.

You have had great difficulties then? said Mr Johnson. Why, as to that, Sir, not more than neighbours fare, I have but little cause to complain, and much to be thankful; but I have had some little struggles, as I will leave you to judge. I have a wife and eight children, whom I bred up in that little cottage which you see under the hill about half a mile off. What, that with the smoke coming out of the chimney, said the Gentleman. O no, Sir, replied the Shepherd smiling, we have seldom smoke in the evening, for we have little to cook, and firing is very dear in these parts. 'Tis that cottage which you see on the left hand of the Church, near that little tuft of hawthorns. What, that hovel with only one room above and one below with scarcely any chimney, how is it possible you can live there with such a family? O! it is very possible, and very certain too, cried the Shepherd. How many better men have been worse lodged! how many good christians have perished in prisons and dungeons, in comparison of which my cottage is a palace. The house is very well, Sir, and if the rain did not sometimes beat down upon us through the thatch when we are a-bed, I should not desire a better; for I have health, peace, and liberty, and no man maketh me afraid.

Well, I will certainly call on you before it be long: But how can you contrive to lodge so many children? We do the best we can, Sir. My poor wife is a very sickly woman, or we should always have done tolerably well. There are no gentry in the parish, so that she has not met with any great assistance in her sickness. The good curate of the parish who lives in that pretty parsonage in the valley, is very willing, but not very able to assist us on these trying occasions, for he has little enough for himself and a large family into the bargain. Yet he does what he can, and more than many richer men do, and more than he can well afford. Besides that, his prayers and good advice we are always sure of, and we are truly thankful for that, for a man must give, you know, Sir, according to what he hath, and not according to what he hath not.

Are you in any distress at present? said Mr Johnson. No, Sir, thank God, replied the Shepherd. I get my shilling a day, and most of my children will soon be able to earn something; for we have only three under five years old. Only! said the Gentleman, that is a heavy burden. Not at all; God fits the back to it. Though my wife is not able to do any out-of-door work, yet she breeds up our children to such habits of industry that our little maids, before they are six years old can first get a halfpenny, and then a penny a day, by knitting. The boys who are too little to do hard work, get a trifle by keeping the birds off the corn; for this the farmers will give them a penny or two-pence, and now and then a bit of bread and cheese into the bargain. When the season of crow-keeping is over, then they glean or pick stones: any thing is better than idleness, Sir, and if they did not get a farthing by it, I would make them do it just the same, for the sake of giving them early habits of labour.

So you see, Sir, I am not so badly off as many are; nay, if it were not that it costs me so much in 'Potecary's stuff for my poor wife, I should reckon myself well off. Nay, I do reckon myself well off; for, blessed be God, he has granted her life to my prayers, and I would work myself to a 'natomy, and live on one meal a day to add any comfort to her valuable life; indeed I have often done the last, and thought it no great matter neither.

While they were in this part of their discourse, a fine plump cherry-cheek little girl ran up out of breath, with a smile on her young happy face, and without taking any notice of the Gentleman, cried out with joy—Look here, father, only see how much I have got to-day! Mr Johnson was much struck with her simplicity, but puzzled to know what was the occasion of this great joy. On looking at her, he perceived a small quantity of coarse wool, some of which had found its way through the holes of her clean, but scanty and ragged woollen apron. The father said, this has been a successful day indeed, Molly; but don't you see the gentleman? Molly now made a curtsey down to the very ground; while Mr Johnson inquired into the cause of the mutual satisfaction which both father and daughter had expressed, at the unusual good fortune of the day.

Sir, said the Shepherd, poverty is a great sharpener of the wits.—My wife and I cannot endure to see our children (poor as they are) without shoes and stockings, not only on account of the pinching cold which cramps their poor little limbs, but because it degrades and debases them; and poor people, who have but little regard to appearances will seldom be found to have any great regard for honesty and goodness: I don't say this is always the case; but I am sure it is so too often. Now shoes and stockings being very dear we could never afford to get them without a little contrivance. I must shew you how I manage about the shoes when you condescend to call at our cottage, Sir; as to stockings, this is one way we take to help get them. My young ones, who are too little to do much work, some times wander at odd hours over the hills for the chance of finding what little wool of sheep may drop when they rub themselves, as they are apt to do in the bushes.* These scattered bits of wool the children pick out of the brambles, which I see, have torn sad holes in Molly's apron to day; they carry this wool home, and when they have got a pretty parcel together, their mother cards it, for she can sit and card in the chimney corner, when she is not able to wash, or work about house. The biggest girl then spins it; it does very well for us without dying, for poor people must not stand for the colours of their stockings. After this our little boys knit it for themselves, while they are employed in keeping crows in the fields, and after they get home at night. As for

* This piece of frugal industry is not imaginary, but a real fact, as is the character of the Shepherd, and his uncommon knowledge of the scriptures. [Author's note.]

the knitting the girls and their mother do, that is chiefly for sale, which helps to pay our rent.

Mr Johnson lifted up his eyes in silent astonishment at the shifts which honest poverty can make rather than beg or steal; and was surprised to think how many ways of subsisting there are which those who live at their ease little suspect. He secretly resolved to be more attentive to his own petty expences than he had hitherto been: and to be more watchful that nothing was wasted in his family.

But to return to the Shepherd. Mr Johnson told him that as he must needs be at his friend's house, who lived many miles off, that night, he could not, as he wished to do, make a visit to his cottage at present. But I will certainly do it, said he, on my return, for I long to see your wife and her nice little family, and to be an eye witness of her neatness and good management. The poor man's tears started into his eyes on hearing the commendation bestowed on his wife: and wiping them off with the sleeve of his coat, for he was not worth a handkerchief in the world, he said—Oh Sir, you just now, I am afraid, called me an humble man, but indeed, I am a very proud one. Proud! exclaimed Mr Johnson, I hoped not—Pride is a great sin, and as the poor are liable to it as well as the rich, so good a man as you seem to be, ought to guard against it. Sir, said he, you are right, but I am not proud of myself, God knows, I have nothing to be proud of. I am a poor sinner—but indeed, Sir, I am proud of my wife. She is not only the most tidy, notable woman on the Plain, but she is the kindest wife and mother, and the most contented, thankful christian that I know. Last year I thought I should have lost her in a violent fit of rheumatism, caught by going to work too soon after her lying in, I fear; for tis but a bleak, coldish place, as you may see, Sir, in winter, and sometimes, the snow lies so long under the hill, that I can hardly make myself a path to get out and buy a few necessities in the next village; and we are afraid to send out the children, for fear they should be lost when the snow is deep. So, as I was saying, the poor soul was very bad indeed, and for several weeks lost the use of all her limbs except her hands: a merciful Providence spared her the use of these, so that when she could not turn in her bed she could contrive to patch a rag or two for her family. She was always saying, had it not been for the great goodness of God, she might have had the palsy instead of the rheumatism and then she could have done nothing—but no body had so many mercies as she had.

I will not tell you what we suffered during that bitter weather, Sir, but my wife's faith and patience during that trying time, were as good a lesson to me as any Sermon I could hear, and yet Mr Jenkins gave us very comfortable ones too, that helped to keep up my spirits.

One Sunday afternoon when my wife was at the worst, as I was coming out of Church, for I went one part of the day, and my eldest daughter the other, so my poor wife was never left alone.—As I was coming out of Church, I say, Mr Jenkins, the minister, called out to me, and asked me how my wife did, saying he had been kept from coming to see her by the deep fall of snow, and indeed from the parsonage-house to my hovel it was quite impassable. I gave him all the particulars he asked, and I am afraid a good many more; for my heart was quite full. He kindly gave me a shilling, and said he would certainly try to pick out his way and come and see her in a day or two.

While he was talking to me, a plain farmer-looking Gentleman in boots, who stood by, listened to all I said, but seemed to take no notice. It was Mr Jenkins's wife's father, who was come to pass the Christmas holidays at the parsonage-house: I had always heard him spoken of as a plain frugal man, who lived close himself, but was remarked to give away more than any of his show-away neighbours.

Well! I went home with great spirits at this seasonable and unexpected supply; for we had tapped our last six-pence, and there was little work to be had on account of the weather. I told my wife I was not come back empty-handed. No, I dare say not, says she; you have been serving a master "who filleth the hungry with good things, though he sendeth the rich empty away." True, Mary says I; we seldom fail to get good spiritual food from Mr Jenkins, but to-day he has kindly supplied our bodily wants. She was more thankful when I shewed her the shilling, than, I dare say, some of your great people are when they get a hundred pounds.

Mr Johnson's heart smote him when he heard such a value set upon a shilling: surely, said he to himself, I will never waste another; but he said nothing to the Shepherd, who thus pursued his story.

Next morning before I went out, I sent part of the money to buy a little ale and brown sugar to put into her water gruel: which you know Sir, made it nice and nourishing. I went out to cleave wood in a farm-yard, for there was no standing out on the plain, after such snow as had fallen in the night. I went with a lighter heart than usual, because I had left my poor wife a little better; and comfortably supplied for this day, and I now resolved more than ever to trust God for the supplies of the next. When I came back at night, my wife fell a crying as soon as she saw me. This, I own I thought but a bad return for the blessings she had so lately received, and so I told her. O, said she, it is too much—we are too rich—I am now frightened, not lest we should have no portion in this world, but for fear we should have our whole portion in it.—Look here, John! So saying she uncovered the bed whereon she lay, and shewed me two warm, thick, new blankets. I could not believe my own eyes, Sir, because when I went out in the morning, I had left her with no other covering than our little old, thin, blue rug. I was still more amazed when she put half a crown into my hand, telling me she had had a visit from Mr Jenkins and Mr Jones, the latter of whom had bestowed all these good things upon us. Thus, Sir, have our lives been crowned with mercies. My wife got about again; and I do believe, under Providence, it was owing to these comforts: for the rheumatism, Sir, without blankets by night and flannel by day is but a baddish job, especially to people who have little or no fire. She will always be a weakly body; but thank God her soul prospers and is in health. But I beg your pardon Sir, for talking on at this rate. Not at all, not at all, said Mr Johnson; I am much pleased with your story—you shall certainly see me in a few days.—Good night. So saying, he slipped a crown into his hand and rode off. Surely said the Shepherd, *goodness and mercy have followed me all the days of my life*, as he gave the money to his wife when he got home at night.

As to Mr Johnson, he found abundant matter for his thoughts during the rest of his journey. On the whole he was more disposed to envy than to pity the Shepherd. I have seldom seen, said he, so happy a man. It is a sort of happiness which the world could not give, and which, I plainly see, it has not been able to take away. This must be the true spirit of RELIGION. I see more and more that true goodness is not merely a thing of words and opinions, but a LIVING PRINCIPLE brought into every common action of a man's life. What else could have supported this poor Couple under every bitter trial of want and sickness? No, my honest Shepherd, I do not pity, but I respect and even honour thee, and I will visit thy poor hovel on my return to Salisbury with as much pleasure as I am now going to the house of my friend.

If Mr Johnson keeps his word in sending me the account of his visit to the Shepherd's Cottage, I shall be very glad to entertain my readers with it, and shall conclude this first part with

THE SHEPHERD'S HYMN

The Lord my pasture shall prepare,
And feed me with a Shepherd's care;
His presence shall my wants supply,
And guard me with a watchful eye:
My noon-day walks he shall attend,
And all my midnight hours defend.

When in the sultry glebe I faint,
Or on the thirsty mountain pant;
To fertile vales and dewy meads,
My weary, wand'ring steps he leads:
Where peaceful rivers, soft and slow,
Amid the verdant landskip flow.

Though in the paths of death I tread,
With gloomy horrors overspread,
My steadfast heart shall fear no ill;
For thou, O Lord, art with me still;
Thy friendly crook shall give me aid,
And guide me through the dreadful shade.

Though in a bare and rugged way;
Through devious, lonely wilds I stray,
Thy bounty shall my pains beguile,
The barren wilderness shall smile,
With sudden greens and herbage crown'd,
And streams shall murmur all around.

MARY MARTHA SHERWOOD (1775-1851)
From *The History of the Fairchild Family; or, The Child's Manual* (1818)

Born in the same year as Jane Austen, and a clergyman's daughter as well, Mrs Sherwood had a methodically instructive bent that led her to write about governesses such as Caroline Mordaunt, to detail the education of young men such as Henry Milner and John Marten, and to edit a bowdlerized edition (*sans* fairy tales) of Sarah Fielding's *Little Female Academy*. Out of her experience as an officer's wife in India and her missionary zeal she wrote *The History of Little Henry and his Bearer* (1814) and *The Indian Pilgrim* (1817), two books that established her as a strong storyteller who nevertheless gave vent to proselytizing fervour in her adventure-filled narratives. The title page of *The Fairchild Family* announces that this collection

of related stories—each one of which has a prayer and an appropriate hymn—was "calculated to show the importance and effects of a religious education". (Mrs Sherwood borrowed her concluding hymns from several unacknowledged sources; the hymn in the chapter included here, naturally enough, is Dr Watts's twenty-third Divine Song, "Obedience to Parents".) The demise of the foolish and neglectful Augusta Noble underscores the author's solemn purpose—well in advance, incidentally, of the cautionary verse about Pauline who plays with matches in the *Struwwelpeter* (see pp. 299-300). Her book was so popular that in 1842 and 1847 Mrs Sherwood wrote two sunnier volumes under the same title.

FATAL EFFECTS OF DISOBEDIENCE TO PARENTS

When Mr and Mrs Fairchild returned from the old gardener's, they found John ready with the cart; so, wishing Mrs Goodwill a good evening, and thanking her for all her kindness, they returned home.

The next morning Mr Fairchild got up early, and went down to the village. Breakfast was ready, and Mrs Fairchild and the children waiting at the table, when he came back. "Get your breakfast, my dear," said he to Mrs Fairchild; "don't wait for me." So saying, he went into his study, and shut the door. Mrs Fairchild supposing that he had some letters to write, got her breakfast quietly: after which, she sent Lucy to ask her Papa if he would not choose any breakfast. When Mr Fairchild heard Lucy's voice at the study door, he came out, and followed her into the parlour.

When Mrs Fairchild looked at her husband's face, she saw that something had grieved him very much. She was frightened, and said, "My dear, I am sure something is the matter: what is it? Tell me the worst at once: pray do?"

"Indeed, my dear," said Mr Fairchild, "I have heard something this morning which has shocked me dreadfully. I was not willing to tell you before you had breakfast. I know what you will feel when you hear it."

"Do, do, tell it me," said Mrs Fairchild, turning quite white.

"Poor Augusta Noble!" said Mr Fairchild.

"What! Papa?" said Lucy and Emily and Henry.

"She is dead!" said Mr Fairchild.

The children turned as pale as their mother; and poor Mrs Fairchild would have dropped off her chair, if Betty, guessing what was the matter (for she had heard the news too, though she had not chosen to tell it), had not run in, and held her in her arms.

"Oh, poor Lady Noble! poor Lady Noble!" said Mrs Fairchild, as soon as she could speak: "Poor Lady Noble!"

As soon as their mamma spoke, the children all together began to cry and sob, which affected Mr Fairchild so much that he hastened into his study again, and shut the door.

Whilst the children were crying, and Betty holding Mrs Fairchild, for she continued very faint and sick, Mrs Barker came into the parlour. Mrs Barker was a kind woman; and as she lived by herself, was always at liberty to go amongst her neighbours in times of trouble. "Ah, Mrs Fairchild!" she said, "I know what troubles you: we are all in grief, through the whole village."

When Mrs Fairchild saw Mrs Barker, she began to shed tears, which did her much good; after which she was able to ask Mrs Barker what was the cause of the poor child's death, "as," said she, "I never heard that she was ill."

"Ah Mrs Fairchild, the manner of her death is the worst part of the story, and that which must grieve her parent's hearts. You know that poor Miss Augusta was always the darling of her mother, who brought her up in great pride, without fear of God or knowledge of religion: nay, Lady Noble would even mock at religion and religious people in her presence; and she chose a governess for her who had no more of God about her than herself."

"I never thought much of that governess," said Mrs Fairchild.

"As Miss Augusta was brought up without the fear of God," continued Mrs Barker, "she had, of course, no notion of obedience to her parents, farther than just striving to please them in their presence: she lived in the constant practice of disobeying them; and the governess continually concealed her disobedience from Lady Noble. And what is the consequence? The poor child has lost her life, and the governess is turned out of doors in disgrace."

"But," said Mrs Fairchild, "how did she lose her life through disobedience to her parents? Pray tell me, Mrs Barker."

"The story is so shocking I hardly dare tell it you," answered Mrs Barker: "but you must know it.—Miss Augusta had a custom of playing with fire, and carrying candles about, though Lady Noble had often warned her of the danger of this, and had strictly charged the governess to prevent it. But it seems that the governess, being afraid of offending, had suffered her very often to be guilty of this piece of disobedience, without telling Lady Noble. And the night before last, when Lady Noble was playing cards in the drawing-room, with some visitors, Miss Augusta took a candle off the hall table, and carried it up stairs to the governess's room. The governess was not in the room. Miss Augusta went to the closet, and it is supposed was looking in the glass, with the candle in her hand: but this is not known. Lady Noble's maid, who was in a room not far off, was frightened by dreadful screamings: she ran into the governess's room, and there found poor Augusta all in a blaze, from head to foot! The maid burnt herself very much in putting out the fire; and poor Miss Augusta was so dreadfully burnt, that she never spoke afterwards, but died in agonies last night—a warning to all children how they presume to disobey their parents! 'The eye that mocketh at his father, and refuses to obey his mother, the ravens of the valley shall pick it out, and the young eagles shall eat it.' (Prov. xxx, 17)."

When Mrs Fairchild and the children heard this dreadful story, they were very much grieved. Mrs Barker staid with them all day; and it was, indeed, a day of mourning through all the house. This was Wednesday; and on Saturday poor Miss Augusta was to be buried. Mr Fairchild was invited to attend the funeral; and the children also were desired to go, as they had been sometimes the play-fellows of poor Miss Augusta. Mrs Fairchild dressed them in white; and at four o'clock in the afternoon a coach covered with black cloth came to the door of Mr Fairchild's house, to take them to Sir Charles Noble's.

When Lucy and Emily and Henry got into the coach, with their papa, they felt very sorrowful; and not one of them spoke one word all the while the coachman was driving to Sir Charles Noble's. When they came into the park, they saw a hearse, and a great many coaches and other carriages, standing at the door of the house, besides many persons on horseback in black clothes with white scarfs and hat-bands. The hearse was hung with black, and so were several of the coaches; and at the top of the hearse were plumes of white feathers.—Perhaps you may never have seen a hearse: in case you have not, I shall try to describe it to you. It is a long close coach, without windows, used for carrying the dead from their houses to their graves. Sometimes black and sometimes white plumes of feathers are fixed at the top of these hearses, according to the age of the person to be borne. Hearses are always painted or hung with black, and are in general drawn by black horses: so that they make a very dismal appearance.

When the children came near to Sir Charles's house, and saw all the people and carriages waiting to accompany their poor little playmate to her grave, they began to cry afresh, and Mr Fairchild himself looked very sad. "The eye of him that hath seen me shall see me no more: thine eyes are upon me, and I am not." (Job vii.8).

When the coach came to the house-door, a footman came out, dressed in black, and took them into the hall, where white gloves and scarfs were given to them, and they were led into the dining-room. There, upon a large table covered with black cloth, was the coffin of poor Augusta, covered with white velvet, and ornamented with silver. Almost all the gentlemen and ladies of the neighbourhood were in the room; but Sir Charles and Lady Noble were not there. When Emily and Lucy saw the coffin, they began to cry more and more; and little Henry too cried, though he rubbed his eyes, and tried to hide his tears.

When every thing was ready, the coffin was lifted up, and put into the hearse; the company got into the coaches; and they all moved slowly to the parish church, which was close to the village, about two miles distant. As the children passed back through the park in the mourning-coach, they saw many places where they had walked and played with poor Augusta; and this made them the more sorrowful. As for man, "all flesh is grass, and all the goodliness thereof as the flower of the field." (Isa. x1.6.)—When they passed through the park gate, they could hear the church bell tolling very plainly. The carriages moved on very slowly, so that it was between five and six when the funeral reached the church. The churchyard was full of people. The coffin was taken out of the hearse and carried into the church, the clergyman going before and all the people following. The coffin was placed on a bier in the middle of the church whilst the clergyman read the first part of the Funeral Service. Lucy and Emily and Henry stood all the time close to the coffin, crying very bitterly.—Perhaps you have never read the Funeral Service with attention: if you have not, I would advise you to read it immediately, and consider it well; for there are many things in it which may make you wise unto salvation.—Poor Augusta's coffin was then lifted up, and carried, not into the church-yard, but to the door of a vault under the church, which was the burying-place of all the Nobles: and as the people were letting down the coffin into the vault, earth was cast upon it, and the clergyman repeated these words: "Forasmuch as it hath pleased Almighty God of his great mercy to take unto himself the soul of our dear sister here departed, we therefore commit her body to the ground; earth to earth, ashes to ashes, dust to dust; in sure and certain hope of the resurrection to eternal life, through our Lord Jesus Christ; who shall change our vile body, that it may be like his glorious body, according to the mighty working whereby he is able to subdue all things to himself." The coffin then was removed into a dark place in the vault, and Lucy and Emily and Henry saw it no more.

When the service was done, Mr Fairchild returned sorrowfully to the coach, with his children; but before the coachman drove away, the clergyman himself came to the door, and said, "Mr Fairchild, if you are going home, I will take a seat with you in the coach, and drink a dish of tea with Mrs Fairchild this evening; for I feel in want of a little Christian society." Mr Fairchild gladly made room for Mr Somers—for that was the clergyman's name—and the coach drove back to Mr Fairchild's house.

As they were going along, they talked of nothing but poor Miss Augusta and her parents; and Mr Fairchild asked Mr Somers if he knew in what state of mind the poor child died. "Ah, sir!" said Mr Somers, "you have touched upon the very worst part of the whole business. From the time of the accident till the time that the breath left her body, she was insensible: she had not one moment for thought or repentance; and it is well known that Lady Noble never taught her any thing concerning God and her Redeemer, and never would let any body else: nay, she was taught to mock at religion and pious people. She knew nothing of the evil of her own heart, and nothing of the Redeemer, nor of the sin of disobedience to her parents."

"Oh, Mr Somers!" said Mr Fairchild, "what a dreadful story is this! Had this poor child been brought up in the fear of God, she might now have been living, a blessing to her parents and the delight of their eyes. 'Withhold not correction from the child; for if thou beatest him with the rod, he shall not die: thou shalt beat him with the rod, and shalt deliver his soul from hell.' (Prov. xxiii. 13, 14)."

"Poor little Augusta!" said Mr Somers: "Lady Noble would never hearken to me, when I spoke to her on the duty of bringing up her children in the fear of God. I believe she thought me very impertinent, to speak to her upon the subject."

By this time the coach was arrived at Mr Fairchild's door. Mrs Fairchild and Mrs Barker were waiting tea for them: they had both been crying, as might be seen by their eyes. After tea, Mr Somers gave out a hymn, and prayed. I shall put down both the hymn and the prayer in this place; altering only a few words, to suit any little child who wishes to use the prayer by himself.

A PRAYER AGAINST THE SIN OF DISOBEDIENCE TO PARENTS

O Almighty Father! thou who didst command all children to honour their parents, and didst promise to bless those who obeyed this Commandment, give me a heart to keep this law. I know that I ought to do all that my father and mother and masters bid me do, if they do not order me to do any thing wicked; and yet my heart, O Lord God, is so bad, that I do not like to obey them. Sometimes, when they give me an order, I am obstinate and passionate, and refuse to do it even in their sight, and would rather be punished than obey them; and sometimes I try to disobey them slily, when I think that they do not see me: forgetting that thine eye, O Lord God, is always upon me; and though thou, O Lord God, mayest not punish me immediately, yet thou markest all my sins in a book: and I know that the dreadful day will come, when the dead shall be raised, and the books shall be opened; and all I have done, unless I repent and turn unto the Lord, will be read aloud before men and angels, and I shall be cast into hell fire for my sins.

O holy Father! I am sorry for my disobedience. O make me more and more sorry for it; and send thy Holy Spirit to give me a clean heart, that I may obey this thy Commandment. I know that disobedient children, unless they repent, always come to an ill end: there is no blessing on such as do not honour their parents. O then, dear Saviour, hear my prayer! Thou, that diedst for poor sinners, save a wicked child! Give me a new heart; teach me to be obedient to my parents, and to honour and respect them; that I may be blessed in this present life, and may, through the merits of my dying Redeemer, be received into everlasting glory in the world to come.

Now to God the Father, God the Son, and God the Holy Ghost, be all glory and honour, for ever and ever. *Amen* "Our Father," &c.

HYMN XVIII

Let children that would fear the Lord
  Hear what their teachers say,
With rev'rence meet their parents' word,
  And with delight obey.

Have you not heard what dreadful plagues
  Are threat'ned by the Lord
To him that breaks his father's law,
  Or mocks his mother's word?

What heavy guilt upon him lies?
  How cursed is his name?
The ravens shall pick out his eyes,
  And eagles eat the same!

But those who worship God, and give
  Their parents honour due,
Here on this earth they long shall live,
  And live hereafter too.

LUCY LEMAN REDE
From *Flowers That Never Fade* (1838)

These tidy, placid verses, from the pen of a little-known English writer, convey the Sunday School teaching that obedience, service, and perseverance are their own rewards, and portray scenes that are comforting and untroubled.

GOING TO BED

"And so you will not go to bed,
You naughty girl?" her mother said
    To Fanny, who was crying:
"You see how quickly Charles and John,
And baby, too, to bed have gone,
    Without this sobbing, sighing.

Come, kiss mamma, and go up stairs,
And dry your eyes, and say your prayers,
    And don't make all this riot."
Then little Fanny kissed mamma,
And bade good night to her papa,
    And went to bed quite quiet.

THE FISHERMAN

Serene was the morn when the fisherman went
  In his trim little boat out to sea:
His bosom was happy with hope and content,
  As the breast of the good man must be.

He cast out his net, and the fish he soon won,
  And came cheerily home before night:
He hung up his nets to be dried in the sun,
  When it rose in the morn with fresh light.

Then he went to his cot where his supper was spread,
  Rejoiced from his labours to rest;
Thanked God for his blessings; retired to bed,
  With pleasure and peace in his breast.

THE MATCH-WOMAN

Oh! see that poor woman with matches to sell,
  And think how severe is her fate!
She must roam through the streets, although often unwell,
And in heart-rending accents her sad story tell,
  As she lingers in tears at each gate.

Her poor little boy, and the babe at her breast,
  Hunger's craving, I fear, often stings:
Think, then, and be grateful that Heaven has blest
You with parents so good, and by whom you're carest,
  And pray for these poor little things.

THE IDLE BOY

Rise, Edward, rise, the morning sun
Its early race has long begun;
Hark! on ev'ry vernal spray
The little birds sing blithe and gay;
And ev'ry herb that decks the sod,
Breathes forth a morning prayer to God.
And shall you, then, to whom kind Heaven,
Health, strength, and partial friends has given,
Lie, like a sluggard, and forget
To whom you owe so great a debt?
Have you no duties to fulfil?
No tasks on which to try your skill?
Yes, yes, you have, then rise in haste,
And not another moment waste.

SUSAN BOGERT WARNER (1819-1885)
From *The Wide, Wide World* (Three volumes, 1850)

Under the pseudonym Elizabeth Wetherell this American author resorted to "tears and talk" to relate the growth in Christian virtue and sense of her young orphan-heroine, Ellen Montgomery. When her family's fortunes are lost, Ellen must journey alone from the comforting sophistication of New York to the stern household and genteel poverty of her Aunt Fortune in Massachusetts. Although she bears such crosses as having her treasured white stockings dyed a practical but ugly grey (chapter X), Ellen proves to be as spirited and vocal as a later orphan figure, Anne of Green Gables; however, the author frequently subdues her with doses of pacifying morality. This excerpt shows how Sunday School writing could easily lead to sentimental fiction.

CHAPTER XXIII

> *O that I were an Orange tree,*
> *That busy plant!*
> *Then should I always laden be,*
> *And never want*
> *Some fruit for him that dresseth me.*
> —G. Herbert

She was thoroughly roused at last by the slamming of the house-door after her aunt. She and Mr Van Brunt had gone forth on their sleighing expedition, and Ellen waked to find herself quite alone.

She could not long have doubted that her aunt was away, even if she had not caught a glimpse of her bonnet going out of the shed-door—the stillness was so uncommon. No such quiet could be with Miss Fortune anywhere about the premises. The old grandmother must have been abed and asleep too, for a cricket under the hearth, and a wood-fire in the chimney had it all to themselves, and made the only sounds that were heard; the first singing out every now and then in a very contented and cheerful style, and the latter giving occasional little snaps and sparks that just served to make one take notice how very quietly and steadily it was burning.

Miss Fortune had left the room put up in the last extreme of neatness. Not a speck of dust could be supposed to lie on the shining painted floor; the back of every chair was in its place against the wall. The very hearth-stone shone, and the heads of the large iron nails in the floor were polished to steel. Ellen sat a while listening to the soothing chirrup of the cricket and the pleasant crackling of the flames. It was a fine cold winter's day. The two little windows at the far end of the kitchen looked out upon the expanse of snow; and the large lilac bush that grew close by the wall, moved lightly by the wind, drew its icy fingers over the panes of glass. Wintry it was without; but that made the warmth and comfort within seem all the more. Ellen would have enjoyed it very much if she had had any one to talk to; as it was she felt rather lonely and sad. She had begun to learn a hymn; but it had set her off upon a long train of thought; and with her head resting on her hand, her fingers pressed into her cheek, the other hand with the hymn-book lying listlessly in her lap, and eyes staring into the fire, she was sitting the very picture of meditation when the door opened and Alice Humphreys came in. Ellen started up.

"Oh, I'm so glad to see you! I'm all alone."

"Left alone, are you?" said Alice, as Ellen's warm lips were pressed again and again to her cold cheeks.

"Yes, Aunt Fortune's gone out. Come and sit down here in the rocking chair. How cold you are. Oh, do you know she is going to have a great bee here Monday evening. What is a bee?"

Alice smiled. "Why," said she, "when people here in the country have so much of any kind of work to do that their own hands are not enough for it, they send and call in their neighbours to help them— that's a bee. A large party in the course of a long evening can do a great deal."

"But why do they call it a bee?"

"I don't know, unless they mean to be like a hive of bees for the time. 'As busy as a bee,' you know."

"Then they ought to call it a hive and not a bee, I should think. Aunt Fortune is going to ask sixteen people. I wish you were coming."

"How do you know but I am?"

"Oh, I know you aren't. Aunt Fortune isn't going to ask you."

"You are sure of that, are you?

"Yes, I wish I wasn't. Oh, how she vexed me this morning by something she said."

"You musn't get vexed so easily, my child. Don't let every little untoward thing roughen your temper."

"But I couldn't help it, dear Miss Alice; it was about you. I don't know whether I ought to tell you; but I don't think you'll mind it, and I know it isn't true. She said she didn't want you to come because you were one of the proud set."

"And what did you say?"

"Nothing. I had it just on the end of my tongue to say, 'It's no such thing;' but I didn't say it."

"I am glad you were so wise. Dear Ellen, that is nothing to be vexed about. If it were true, indeed, you might be sorry. I trust Miss Fortune is mistaken. I shall try and find some way to make her change her mind. I am glad you told me."

"I am so glad you are come, dear Alice!" said Ellen again. "I wish I could have you always." And the long, very close pressure of her two arms about her friend said as much. There was a long pause. The cheek of Alice rested on Ellen's head which nestled against her; both were busily thinking, but neither spoke; and the cricket chirped and the flames crackled without being listened to.

"Miss Alice," said Ellen, after a long time, "I wish you would talk over a hymn with me."

"How do you mean, my dear?" said Alice, rousing herself.

"I mean, read it over and explain it. Mamma used to do it sometimes. I have been thinking a great deal about her to-day, and I think I'm very different from what I ought to be. I wish you would talk to me and make me better, Miss Alice."

Alice pressed an earnest kiss upon the tearful little face that was uplifted to her, and presently said—

"I am afraid I shall be a poor substitute for your mother, Ellen. What hymn shall we take?"

"Any one—this one if you like. Mamma likes it very much. I was looking it over to-day.

" 'A charge to keep I have—
    A God to glorify;
A never-dying soul to save,
    And fit it for the sky.' "

Alice read the first line and paused.

"There now," said Ellen, "what is a charge?"

"Don't you know that."

"I think I do, but I wish you would tell me."

"Try to tell me first."

"Isn't it something that is given one to do?—I don't know exactly."

"It is something given one in trust, to be done or taken care of. I remember very well once when I was about your age my mother had occasion to go out for half-an-hour, and she left me in charge of my little baby sister; she gave me a charge not to let anything disturb her while she was away, and to keep her asleep if I could. And I remember how I kept my charge too. I was not to take her out of the cradle, but I sat beside her the whole time; I would not suffer a fly to light on her little fair cheek; I scarcely took my eyes from her; I made John keep pussy at a distance; and whenever one of the little round dimpled arms was thrown out upon the coverlet, I carefully drew something over it again."

"Is she dead?" said Ellen timidly, her eyes watering in sympathy with Alice's.

"She is dead, my dear; she died before we left England."

"I understand what a charge is," said Ellen, after a while, "but what is this charge the hymn speaks of? What charge have I to keep?"

"The hymn goes on to tell you. The next line gives you part of it. 'A God to glorify.' "

"To glorify!" said Ellen doubtfully.

"Yes—that is to honour—to give Him all the honour that belongs to Him."

"But can I honour Him?"

"Most certainly; either honour or dishonour; you cannot help doing one."

"I!" said Ellen again.

"Must not your behaviour speak either well or ill for the mother who has brought you up?"

"Yes, I know that."

"Very well; when a child of God lives as he ought to do, people cannot help having high and noble thoughts of that glorious One whom he serves, and of that perfect law he obeys. Little as they may love the ways of religion, in their own secret hearts they cannot help confessing that there is a God, and that they ought to serve Him. But a worldling, and still more an unfaithful Christian, just helps people to forget there is such a Being, and makes them think either that religion is a sham, or that they may safely go on despising it. I have heard it said, Ellen, that Christians are the only Bible some people ever read; and it is true; all they know of religion is what they get from the lives of its professors; and oh, were the world but full of the right kind of example, the kingdom of darkness could not stand. 'Arise, shine!' is a word that every Christian ought to take home."

"But how can I shine?" asked Ellen.

"My dear Ellen!— in the faithful, patient, self-denying performance of every duty as it comes to hand—'whatsoever thy hand findeth to do, do it with thy might.' "

"It is very little that I can do," said Ellen.

"Perhaps more than you think, but never mind that. All are not great stars in the Church; you may be only a little rush-light. See you burn well!"

"I remember," said Ellen, musing, "mamma once told me when I was going somewhere that people would think strangely of her if I didn't behave well."

"Certainly. Why, Ellen I formed an opinion of her very soon after I saw you."

"Did you?" said Ellen, with a wonderfully brightened face; "what was it? Was it good? ah, do tell me!"

"I am not quite sure of the wisdom of that," said Alice, smiling; "you might take home the praise that is justly her right and not yours."

"Oh no, indeed," said Ellen, "I had rather she should have it than I. Please tell me what you thought of her, dear Alice—I know it was good, at any rate."

"Well, I will tell you," said Alice, "at all risks. I thought your mother was a lady, from the honourable notions she had given you; and from your ready obedience to her, which was evidently the obedience of love, I judged she had been a good mother in the true sense of the term. I thought she must be a refined and cultivated person, from the manner of your speech and behaviour; and I was sure she was a Christian, because she had taught you the truth, and evidently had tried to lead you in it."

The quivering face of delight with which Ellen began to listen gave way, long before Alice had done, to a burst of tears.

"It makes me so glad to hear you say that," she said.

"The praise of it is your mother's, you know, Ellen."

"I know it; but you make me so glad!" And hiding her face in Alice's lap, she fairly sobbed.

"You understand now, don't you, how Christians may honour or dishonour their Heavenly Father?"

"Yes, I do; but it makes me afraid to think of it."

"Afraid? It ought rather to make you glad. It is a great honour and happiness for us to be permitted to honour Him—

'A never-dying soul to save,
And fit it for the sky.'

Yes, that is the great duty you owe yourself. Oh, never forget it, dear Ellen! And whatever would hinder you, have nothing to do with it. 'What will it profit a man though he gain the whole world, and lose his own soul?'—

'To serve the present age,
My calling to fulfil—' ''

"What is 'the present age'? said Ellen.

"All the people who are living in the world at this time."

"But, dear Alice, what can I do to the present age?"

"Nothing to the most part of them certainly; and yet, dear Ellen, if your little rushlight shines well there is just so much the less darkness in the world, though perhaps you light only a very little corner. Every Christian is a blessing to the world, another grain of salt to go towards sweetening and saving the mass."

"That is very pleasant to think of," said Ellen, musing.

"Oh, if we were but full of love to our Saviour, how pleasant it would be to do anything for Him! how many ways we should find of honouring Him by doing good."

"I wish you would tell me some of the ways that I can do it," said Ellen.

"You will find them fast enough if you seek them, Ellen. No one is so poor or so young but he has one talent at least to use for God."

"I wish I knew what mine is," said Ellen.

"Is your daily example as perfect as it can be?"

Ellen was silent and shook her head.

"Christ pleased not Himself, and went about doing good; and He said, 'If any man serve Me, let him follow Me.' Remember that. Perhaps your aunt is unreasonable and unkind; see with how much patience and perfect sweetness of temper you can bear and forbear; see if you cannot win her over by untiring gentleness, obedience, and meekness. Is there no improvement to be made here?"

"Oh me, yes!" answered Ellen, with a sigh.

"Then your old grandmother. Can you do nothing to cheer her life in her old age and helplessness? Can't you find some way of giving her pleasure? some way of amusing a long tedious hour now and then?"

Ellen looked very grave; in her inmost heart she knew this was a duty she shrank from.

"He 'went about doing good.' Keep that in mind. A kind word spoken—a little thing done to smooth the way of one, or lighten the load of another—teaching those who need teaching—entreating those who are walking in the wrong way. Oh, my child, there is work enough!—

'To serve the present age,
My calling to fulfil;
O may it all my powers engage
To do my Maker's will.

Arm me with jealous care,
As in Thy sight to live;
And oh! thy servant, Lord, prepare
A strict account to give,' "

"An account of what?" said Ellen.

"You know what an account is. If I give Thomas a dollar to spend for me at Carra-carra, I expect he will give me an exact account when he comes back, what he has done with every shilling of it. So must we give an account of what we have done with everything our Lord has committed to our care—our hands, our tongue, our time, our minds, our influence; how much we have honoured Him, how much good we have done to others, how fast and how far we have grown holy and fit for heaven."

"It almost frightens me to hear you talk, Miss Alice."

"Not frighten, dear Ellen—that is not the word; sober we ought to be, mindful to do nothing we shall not wish to remember in the great day of account. Do you recollect how that day is described? Where is your Bible?"

She opened at the twentieth chapter of the Revelation.

" 'And I saw a great white throne, and Him that sat on it, from whose face the earth and the heaven flew away; and there was found no place for them.

" 'And I saw the dead, small and great, stand before God; and the books were opened; and another book was opened, which is the book of life: and the dead were judged out of those things which were written in the books, according to their works. And the sea gave up the dead which were in it; and death and hell delivered up the dead which were in them; and they were judged every man according to their works. And death and hell were cast into the lake of fire. This is the second death.

" 'And whosoever was not found written in the book of life was cast into the lake of fire.' "

Ellen shivered. "That is dreadful!" she said.

"It will be a dreadful day to all but those whose names are written in the Lamb's book of life; not dreadful to them, dear Ellen."

"But how shall I be sure, dear Alice, that my name is written there? and I can't be happy if I am not sure."

"My dear child," said Alice tenderly, as Ellen's anxious face and glistening eyes were raised to hers, "if you love Jesus Christ you may know you are His child, and none shall pluck you out of His hand."

"But how can I tell whether I do love him really? sometimes I think I do, and then again sometimes I am afraid I don't at all."

Alice answered in the words of Christ: " 'He that hath My commandments and keepeth them, he it is that loveth Me.' "

"Oh, I don't keep His commandments!" said Ellen, the tears running down her cheeks.

"Perfectly, none of us do. But, dear Ellen, that is not the question. Is it your heart's desire and effort to keep them? Are you grieved when you fail? There is the point. You cannot love Christ without loving to please Him."

Ellen rose and putting both arms round Alice's neck, laid her head there, as her manner sometimes was, tears flowing fast.

"I sometimes think I do love Him a little," she said, "but I do so many wrong things. But he will teach me to love Him if I ask Him, won't He, dear Alice?"

"Indeed He will, dear Ellen," said Alice, folding her arms round her little adopted sister, "indeed he will. He has promised that. Remember what he told somebody who was almost in despair: 'Fear not; only believe.' "

Alice's neck was wet with Ellen's tears; and after they had ceased to flow, her arms kept their hold and her head its resting-place on Alice's shoulder for some time. It was necessary at last for Alice to leave her.

Ellen waited till the sound of her horse's footsteps died away on the road; and then, sinking on her knees beside her rocking-chair, she poured forth her whole heart in prayers and tears. She confessed many a fault and shortcoming that none knew but herself, and most earnestly besought help that "her little rushlight might shine bright." Prayer was to little Ellen what it is to all that know it—the satisfying of doubt, the soothing of care, the quieting of trouble. She had knelt down very uneasy; but she knew that God has promised to be the hearer of prayer, and she rose up very comforted, her mind fixing on those most sweet words Alice had brought to her memory: "Fear not; only believe." When Miss Fortune returned Ellen was quietly asleep again in her rocking-chair, with her face very pale, but calm as an evening sunbeam.

"Well, I declare if that child ain't sleeping her life away!" said Miss Fortune. "She's slept this whole blessed forenoon; I suppose she'll want to be alive and dancing the whole night to pay for it."

"I can tell you what she'll want a sight more," said Mr Van Brunt, who had followed her in; it must have been to see about Ellen, for he was never known to do such a thing before or since; "I'll tell you what she'll want, and that's a right hot supper. She eat as nigh as possible nothing at all this noon. There ain't much danger of her dancing a hole in your floor this some time."

8. HARBINGERS OF THE GOLDEN AGE

And I made a rural pen
And I stain'd the water clear
And I wrote my happy songs
Every child may joy to hear
    —William Blake, "Introduction",
Songs of Innocence (1789)

By the mid-nineteenth century there had appeared several talented writers, working in the same milieu as the Rational Moralists and the Sunday School writers, who began to signal important and long-lasting changes in literature for children. Unlike their doctrinaire contemporaries they were willing to endorse entertainment as a creditable goal in their works for the young, and were capable of fashioning delightful vehicles to ensure success. In special and diverse ways, these poets and storytellers ushered in the Golden Age of children's books.

Happily the numerous poets in this group did not share Mrs Barbauld's fear that adapting poetry to a child's understanding would lessen its strength and beauty. They roamed widely in their poignantly expressive art to create poetry—or, more modestly, colourful ditties—for and about children. Some of this verse is still enjoyed today. Such charming, tuneful simple poems as Jane Taylor's "The Star",

Clement Moore's "A Visit from Saint Nicholas", Sarah Hale's "Mary's Lamb", Mary Howitt's "The Spider and the Fly", and Eliza Follen's "Three Little Kittens" have comforted and amused generations of readers. The act of expressing Christian sentiments in rhyme was carried to truly poetic heights by Christopher Smart in his luminous *Hymns for the Amusement of Children* (1772). William Blake, who etched his texts and illustrations on copper plates, wrote of two separate states that he called "innocence" and "experience". His vision of childhood was profound. This poet-prophet could never be accused of idealizing it as a time of pastoral innocence: he dared, on occasion, to let the child's voice utter harsh social criticisms.

Exploring both joy and sorrow with exquisite delicacy, most of the poets in this group are acute observers of their society and themselves. But their lightness of touch, and in some cases their artistry, remove them almost completely from the world of instruction and preaching, and the stance of complacent moral rectitude, that are associated with their forerunners. They were, in fact, purveyors of delight, as were all the writers in this section; they could never be content with only dry facts or solemn preachments. The tongue-twisters in *Peter Piper's Practical Principles* and the sometimes uproarious cautionary examples in *The English Struwwelpeter* stand learning on its head. Sheer delight characterizes Roscoe's magical account of *The Butterfly's Ball*. And Edward Lear shows in his nonsense limericks the courage and singularity of an artist pursuing entertainment—however wry or quirky—for its own sake.

Several publishers and editors were keenly aware of a mushrooming interest in entertaining the young—though, be it noted, not to the exclusion of instructing them. The London publisher John Harris issued over fifty colour-illustrated books in a series entitled, significantly, *The Cabinet of Amusement and Instruction* (c. 1810-30), which he advertised as "consisting of the most approved Novelties for the Nursery". Such titles as *Peter Piper's Practical Principles, Sir Harry Harold's View of the Dignitaries of England, The Infant's Grammar; or, A Picnic Party of the Parts of Speech, The Picturesque Primer*, and *The Monkey's Frolic* reflect Harris's wish to make every sort of lesson textually and visually amusing. Another influential proponent of attractive and imaginative literature for the young was Henry Cole (1808-82). For his *Home Treasury* (1841-49)—a later series of nursery rhymes, traditional ballads, tales, fables, and fairy stories—he adopted two happy/benign names for his pseudonym, "Felix Summerly". His "Original Announcement" in 1843" stated the purpose of his *Treasury* as "anti-Peter Parleyism", which expressed Cole's opposition to the Parley school of facts without fancy. Speaking of the restricted state of children's literature in his day, he regretted that "the many tales sung or said—from time immemorial, which appealed to the other and certainly not less important elements of a little child's mind, its fancy, imagination, sympathies, affections, are almost all gone out of memory, and are scarcely to be obtained". Cole intended his *Home Treasury* to be the antidote to a "narrow" cultivation of the under-

standing. Inspired by William Blake's book productions, he had his series carefully designed for maximum visual appeal.

In addition to these publishing endeavours, another indication of the considerable energies that were being channelled into the twin objectives of amusing and instructing children is visible in the works of certain literary artists whose reputations extend well beyond the field of children's literature. Charles Lamb is a prominent example of a man of letters who wrote a great deal for the young. Filling what he saw as an unfortunate gap in the experience of children, he paraphrased Chapman's *Odyssey* for them as *The Adventures of Ulysses* (1808) and, with his sister, summarized Shakespeare's plays in *Tales from Shakespeare* (1807). In making these works available Lamb was not only performing a service for the young; he was also counteracting "the cursed Barbauld crew, those Blights & Blasts of all that is human in man and child", as he wrote in a letter to Coleridge (23 October 1802). Lamenting the stranglehold over children's reading of "Mrs Barbauld's stuff" and "Mrs Trimmer's nonsense", he went on to deplore the dismal reality that "Science has succeeded to Poetry no less in the little walks of Children than with Men", and asked: "Is there no possibility of averting this sore evil?" His abridgements and original works for children were a resoundingly affirmative reply.

A further strategy directed against Mrs Barbauld and Mrs Trimmer was the beginning of a modern tradition of the fairy tale. Mr Newbery had deflated the importance of fairies; the Rational Moralists had worried about their misleading children; the Sunday School writers had simply expunged them from juvenile works. But storytellers like Catherine Sinclair and Francis Paget presented charming fairy instructresses—not sententious hired tutors or stern governesses—to convey essential yet entertaining precepts to the young. In *Holiday House: A Series of Tales* (1839) Sinclair used the wise Fairy Teach-All, while in *The Hope of the Katzekopfs: A Fairy Tale* (1844) Paget relied on the prescient Lady Abracadabra to provide much-needed guidance. The presence of fairies in these books, however, does not presuppose idealized youngsters: the juvenile heroes of Sinclair and Paget are far from paragons of sense and virtue. They are often mischievous, and their parents weak-willed and foolish. In fact these writers began a trend of writing about real and therefore imperfect children. As Catherine Sinclair explained in her preface:

In these pages the author has endeavoured to paint that species of noisy, frolicsome, mischievous children which is now almost extinct, wishing to preserve a sort of fabulous remembrance of days long past, when young people were like wild horses on the prairies, rather than like well broken hacks on the road; and when amidst many faults and eccentricities, there was still some individuality of character and feeling allowed to remain.

Writing for the entertainment of her own niece, nephew, and young brother, Miss Sinclair created for the first time a genuinely amusing picture of Victorian children—in this case undisciplined ones. (The novelty of such a subject made the book very popular.) The lessons are imparted by Uncle David and Lady Harriet—as well, in Uncle David's story reproduced below, by Fairy Teach-All—but the fun-loving, even somewhat destructive Graham children learn more through their own experience than through dispensed instruction. Paget's *The Hope of the Katzekopfs*, in contrast, is a fantasy about character formation in which two boys engage in a series of adventures that take place in an allegorical domain and are magically directed by the good fairy Abracadabra.

These fairy instructresses, Teach-All and Abracadabra, were probably known to Charles Kingsley when he introduced Mrs Doasyouwouldbedoneby and Mrs Bedonebyasyoudid to his underwater seminary in

The Water Babies (1863). William Thackeray may have had both Abracadabra and the silly goings-on of the Katzekopf court in mind when, in *The Rose and the Ring* (1854), he created the Fairy Blackstick, the deceptive Angelica, bumbling Bulbo, indolent Giglio, and the surprise heroine Betsinda-Rosalba. Beginning with *At the Back of the North Wind* (1871) and on into the *Curdie* books (1872, 1882), George Macdonald mined the rich vein of the fairy convention. Even Oscar Wilde and Rudyard Kipling used a range of non-corporeal beings, as in "The Happy Prince" and "The Selfish Giant" (1888), and *Puck of Pook's Hill* (1906) and *Rewards and Fairies* (1909).

The writers featured in this chapter were by no means typical of the authors who wrote for children in the pre-1850 period: the moralists and those who pandered to a recently literate market with crude chapbooks were in the majority. But the writings of Smart, Blake, Taylor, Roscoe, Lamb, Peacock, Moore, Sinclair, Paget, Lear, Hoffmann and others exerted an enormous influence because they were poems and stories that tasted more of honey than of medicine and, more significantly, were touched with literary art. Furthermore, by this time a new genre that excluded instruction entirely had been introduced: the action-filled adventure story. (Space limitations have prevented us from including extracts from three of the best of these books: Harriet Martineau's *The Playfellow* (1841) and Captain Frederick Marryat's *Mr Midshipman Easy* (1826) and *Masterman Ready* (1841).) By the opening of the Golden Age a felt need had developed, and was beginning to be satisfied, not just for children's books but for children's literature: works of the imagination clothed in delight.

CHRISTOPHER SMART (1722-1771)
From *Hymns for the Amusement of Children* (1772)

With penury constantly facing him, Smart composed libretti for oratorios, wrote satires under the name of Ebenezer Pentweazle, contributed to a three-penny journal as "Mary Midnight", and found employment in various other forms of hackwork for his father-in-law John Newbery. Although he was known to fall into a kind of religious mania and was twice confined in Bethlehem Hospital (the madhouse, Bedlam), his friend Dr Johnson was not convinced that Smart was mad: "I did not think he ought to be shut up. His infirmities were not noxious to society. He insisted on people praying with him; and I'd as lief pray with Kit Smart as any one else." On the subject of Smart's supposed madness, Boswell quotes Johnson as saying: "Madness frequently discovers itself merely by unnecessary deviation from the usual modes of the world. My poor friend Smart shewed the disturbance of his mind, by falling upon his knees, and saying his prayers in the street, or in any other un-usual place. Now although, rationally speaking, it is greater madness not to pray at all, than to pray as Smart did, I am afraid there are so many who do not pray, that their understanding is not called in question."

In spite of his "unhappy vacillation of mind" (Boswell's words), Smart was capable of writing very beautiful Christian verse. *Hymns for the Amusement of Children*—containing thirty-nine hymns that were written wholly or largely while he was in a debtor's prison (where he died), and were published posthumously—stand as the intermediary text between Watts's *Divine and Moral Songs* and Blake's *Songs of Innocence and Experience*: Smart reflects the gentle Christian spirit of Watts and anticipates the poetic mastery of Blake, and Blake's lyrical rendering of childhood and Christian humility. To follow the hymns, we have included the well-known 'My Cat Jeoffry', in which Smart's Christianity is given a memorable secular expression.

HYMN X
TRUTH

'Tis thus the holy Scriptures ends,
   "Whoever loves or makes a lie,
"On heav'ns felicity depends
   "In vain, for he shall surely die."

The stars, the firmament, the sun,
   God's glorious work, God's great design,
All, all was finish'd as begun,
   By rule, by compass, and by line.

Hence David unto heav'n appeals,
   "Ye heav'ns his righteousness declare;"
His signet their duration seals,
   And bids them be as firm, as fair.

Then give me grace, celestial Sire,
   The truth to love, the truth to tell;
Let everlasting sweets aspire,
   And filth and falshood sink to hell.

HYMN XI
BEAUTY. *For a Damsel.*

Christ, keep me from the self-survey
    Of beauties all thine own;
If there is beauty, let me pray
    And praise the Lord alone.

Pray—that I may the fiend withstand,
    Where'er his serpents be;
Praise—that the Lord's almighty hand
    Is manifest in me.

It is not so—my features are
    Much meaner than the rest;
A glow-worm cannot be a star,
    And I am plain at best.

Then come, my love thy grace impart,
    Great Saviour of mankind;
O come, and purify my heart,
    And beautify my mind.

Then will I thy carnations nurse,
    And cherish every role;
And empty to the poor my purse,
    Till grace to glory grows.

HYMN XVI
LEARNING

Come, come with emulative strife,
To learn the way, the truth, and life,
   Which Jesus is in one;
In all sound doctrine he proceeds,
From Alpha to Omega leads,
   E'en Spirit, Sire, and Son.

Sure of th' exceeding great reward,
Midst all your learning learn the Lord—
   This was thy doctrine, Paul;
And this thy lecture shou'd persuade,
Tho' thou hadst more of human aid,
   Than blest brethren all.

Humanity's a charming thing,
And every science of the ring,
   Good is the classic lore;
For these are helps along the road,
That leads to Zion's blest abode,
   And heav'nly muse's store.

But greater still in each respect,
He that communicates direct
   The tutor of the soul;
Who without pain, degrees or parts,
While he illuminates our hearts,
   Can teach at once the whole.

HYMN XXV
MIRTH

If you are merry sing away,
　　And touch the organs sweet;
This is the Lord's triumphant day,
Ye children in the gall'ries gay,
　　Shout from each goodly seat.

It shall be May to-morrow's morn,
　　A field then let us run,
And deck us in the blooming thorn,
Soon as the cock begins to warn,
　　And long before the sun.

—I give the praise to Christ Alone,
　　My pinks already show;
And my streak'd roses fully blown,
The sweetness of the Lord make known,
　　And to his glory grow.

Ye little prattlers that repair
　　For cowslips in the mead,
Of those exulting colts beware,
But blythe security is there,
　　Where skipping lambkins feed.

With white and crimson laughs the sky,
　　With birds the hedge-rows ring;
To give the praise to God most High,
And all the sulky fiends defy,
　　Is a most joyful thing.

HYMN XXXV
AT DRESSING IN THE MORNING

Now I arise, impow'r'd by Thee,
  The glorious sun to face;
O cloath me with humility,
  Adorn me with thy grace.

All evil of the day forefend,
  Prevent the Tempter's snare;
Thine Angel on my steps attend,
  And give me fruit to pray'r.

O make me useful as I go
  My pilgrimage along;
And sweetly sooth this vale of woe
  By charity and song.

Let me from Christ obedience learn,
  To Christ obedience pay;
Each parent duteous love return,
  And consecrate the day.

HYMN XXXVI
AT UNDRESSING IN THE EVENING

These cloaths, of which I now devest
  Myself, ALL-SEEING EYE,
Must be one day (that day be blest)
  Relinquish'd and laid by.

Thou cordial sleep, to death akin,
  I court thee on my knee;
O let my exit, free from sin,
  Be little more than Thee.

But if much agonizing pain
  My dying hour await,
The Lord be with me to sustain,
  To help and to abate.

O let me meet Thee undeterr'd,
  By no foul stains defil'd!
According to thy Holy Word,
  Receive me as a Child.

MY CAT JEOFFRY

For I will consider my Cat Jeoffry.

For he is the servant of the Living God, duly and daily serving him.

For at the first glance of the glory of God in the East he worships in his way.

For is this done by wreathing his body seven times round with elegant quickness.

For then he leaps up to catch the musk, which is the blessing of God upon his prayer.

For he rolls upon prank to work it in.

For having done duty and received blessing he begins to consider himself.

For this he performs in ten degrees.

For first he looks upon his fore-paws to see if they are clean.

For secondly he kicks up behind to clear away there.

For thirdly he works it upon stretch with the fore-paws extended.

For fourthly he sharpens his paws by wood.

For fifthly he washes himself.

For sixthly he rolls upon wash.

For seventhly he fleas himself, that he may not be interrupted upon the beat.

For eighthly he rubs himself against a post.

For ninthly he looks up for his instructions.

For tenthly he goes in quest of food.

For having consider'd God and himself he will consider his neighbour.

For if he meets another cat he will kiss her in kindness.

For when he takes his prey he plays with it to give it a chance.

For one mouse in seven escapes by his dallying.

For when his day's work is done his business more properly begins.

For he keeps the Lord's watch in the night against the adversary.

For he counteracts the powers of darkness by his electrical skin & glaring eyes.

For he counteracts the Devil, who is death, by brisking about the life.

For in his morning orisons he loves the sun and the sun loves him.

For he is of the tribe of Tiger.

For the Cherub Cat is a term of the Angel Tiger.

For he has the subtlety and hissing of a serpent, which in goodness he suppresses.

For he will not do destruction, if he is well-fed, neither will he spit without provocation.

For he purrs in thankfulness, when God tells him he's a good Cat.

For he is an instrument for the children to learn benevolence upon.

For every house is incompleat without him & a blessing is lacking in the spirit.

For the Lord commanded Moses concerning the cats at the departure
of the Children of Israel from Egypt.

For every family had one cat at least in the bag.

For the English Cats are the best in Europe.

For he is the cleanest in the use of his fore-paws of any quadrupede.

For the dexterity of his defence is an instance of the love of God to him
exceedingly.

For he is the quickest to his mark of any creature.

For he is tenacious of his point.

For he is a mixture of gravity and waggery.

For he knows that God is his Saviour.

For there is nothing sweeter than his peace when at rest.

For there is nothing brisker than his life when in motion.

For he is of the Lord's poor and so indeed is he called by benevolence
perpetually—Poor Jeoffry! poor Jeoffry! the rat has bit thy throat.

For I bless the name of the Lord Jesus that Jeoffry is better.

For the divine spirit comes about his body to sustain it in complete cat.

For his tongue is exceeding pure so that it has in purity what it wants
in music.

For he is docile and can learn certain things.

For he can set up with gravity which is patience upon approbation.

For he can fetch and carry, which is patience in employment.

For he can jump over a stick which is patience upon proof positive.

For he can spraggle upon waggle at the word of command.

For he can jump from an eminence into his master's bosom.

For he can catch the cork and toss it again.

For he is hated by the hypocrite and miser.

For the former is afraid of detection.

For the latter refuses the charge.

For he camels his back to bear the first notion of business.

For he is good to think on, if a man would express himself neatly.

For he made a great figure in Egypt for his signal services.

For he killed the Icneumon-rat very pernicious by land.

For his ears are so acute that they sting again.

For from this proceeds the passing quickness of his attention.

For by stroking of him I have found out electricity.

For I perceived God's light about him both wax and fire.

For the Electrical fire is the spiritual substance, which God sends from
heaven to sustain the bodies both of man and beast.

For God has blessed him in the variety of his movements.

For, though he cannot fly, he is an excellent clamberer.

For his motions upon the face of the earth are more than any other
quadrupede.

For he can tread to all the measures upon the music.

For he can swim for life.

For he can creep.

WILLIAM BLAKE (1757-1827)
From *Songs of Innocence and of Experience*
Shewing the Two Contrary States of the Human Soul (1794)

Poet, engraver, painter, and mystic, Blake spent his life as an obscure, eccentric artist in London and, greatly gifted though he was, was neglected and even ridiculed in his lifetime. For the *Songs* he etched his texts and illustrations together on a copper plate and handcoloured each print, thus producing a harmonious, aesthetic whole.

In 1794 he added Songs of Experience to his Songs of Innocence of 1789. The child-like imagery and lyrical simplicity of these poems, and the importance of the child-figure in representing innocence as well as misery, ensured that many of them would enter children's literature.

Songs of Innocence

THE LAMB

Little Lamb who made thee
Dost thou know who made thee
Gave thee life & bid thee feed,
By the stream & o'er the mead;
Gave thee clothing of delight,
Softest clothing wooly bright;
Gave thee such a tender voice,
Making all the vales rejoice:
Little Lamb who made thee
Dost thou know who made thee

Little Lamb I'll tell thee,
Little Lamb I'll tell thee;
He is called by thy name,
For he calls himself a Lamb:
He is meek & he is mild,
He became a little child:
I a child & thou a lamb,
We are called by his name.
Little Lamb God bless thee,
Little Lamb God bless thee.

INFANT JOY

I have no name
I am but two days old.—
What shall I call thee?
I happy am
Joy is my name,—
Sweet joy befall thee!

Pretty joy!
Sweet joy but two days old.
Sweet joy I call thee:
Thou dost smile.
I sing the while
Sweet joy befall thee.

SPRING

Sound the Flute!
Now it's mute.
Birds delight
Day and Night.
Nightingale
In the dale
Lark in Sky
Merrily
Merrily Merrily to welcome in the Year

Little Boy
Full of joy.
Little Girl
Sweet and small.
Cock does crow
So do you.
Merry voice
Infant noise
Merrily Merrily to welcome in the Year

Little Lamb
Here I am,
Come and lick
My white neck.
Let me pull
Your soft Wool.
Let me kiss
Your soft face.
Merrily Merrily we welcome in the year

HOLY THURSDAY

Twas on a Holy Thursday their innocent faces clean
The children walking two & two in red & blue & green
Grey headed beadles walkd before with wands as white as snow
Till into the high dome of Pauls they like Thames waters flow

O what a multitude they seemd these flowers of London town
Seated in companies they sit with radiance all their own
The hum of multitudes was there but multitudes of lambs
Thousands of little boys & girls raising their innocent hands

Now like a mighty wind they raise to heaven the voice of song
Or like harmonious thunderings the seats of heaven among
Beneath them sit the aged men wise guardians of the poor
Then cherish pity; lest you drive an angel from your door

THE CHIMNEY SWEEPER

When my mother died I was very young,
And my father sold me while yet my tongue,
Could scarcely cry weep weep weep weep.
So your chimneys I sweep & in soot I sleep.

Theres little Tom Dacre, who cried when his head
That curl'd like a lambs back, was shav'd, so I said,
Hush Tom never mind it, for when your head's bare,
You know that the soot cannot spoil your white hair.

And so he was quiet, & that very night,
As Tom was a sleeping he had such a sight,
That thousands of sweepers Dick, Joe, Ned & Jack
Were all of them lock'd up in coffins of black,

And by came an Angel who had a bright key,
And he open'd the coffins & set them all free.
Then down a green plain leaping laughing they run
And wash in a river and shine in the Sun.

Then naked & white, all their bags left behind,
They rise upon clouds, and sport in the wind.
And the Angel told Tom, if he'd be a good boy,
He'd have God for his father & never want joy.

And so Tom awoke and we rose in the dark
And got with our bags & our brushes to work.
Tho' the morning was cold, Tom was happy & warm.
So if all do their duty, they need not fear harm.

Songs of Experience

THE TYGER

Tyger Tyger, burning bright,
In the forests of the night;
What immortal hand or eye,
Could frame thy fearful symmetry?

In what distant deeps or skies,
Burnt the fire of thine eyes?
On what wings dare he aspire?
What the hand, dare sieze the fire?

And what shoulder, & what art,
Could twist the sinews of thy heart?
And when thy heart began to beat,
What dread hand? & what dread feet?

What the hammer? what the chain,
In what furnace was thy brain?
What the anvil? what dread grasp,
Dare its deadly terrors clasp?

When the stars threw down their spears
And water'd heaven with their tears:
Did he smile his work to see?
Did he who made the Lamb make thee?

Tyger Tyger burning bright,
In the forests of the night:
What immortal hand or eye,
Dare frame thy fearful symmetry?

INFANT SORROW

My mother groand! my father wept.
Into the dangerous world I leapt:
Helpless, naked, piping loud:
Like a fiend hid in a cloud.

Struggling in my fathers hands:
Striving against my swadling bands:
Bound and weary I thought best
To sulk upon my mothers breast.

THE CHIMNEY SWEEPER

A little black thing among the snow:
Crying weep, weep, in notes of woe!
Where are thy father & mother? say?
They are both gone up to the church to pray.

Because I was happy upon the heath,
And smil'd among the winters snow:
They clothed me in the clothes of death,
And taught me to sing the notes of woe.

And because I am happy, & dance & sing,
They think they have done me no injury:
And are gone to praise God & his Priest & King
Who make up a heaven of our misery.

HOLY THURSDAY

Is this a holy thing to see,
In a rich and fruitful land,
Babes reducd to misery,
Fed with cold and usurous hand?

Is that trembling cry a song?
Can it be a song of joy?
And so many children poor?
It is a land of poverty!

And their sun does never shine.
And their fields are bleak & bare.
And their ways are fill'd with thorns
It is eternal winter there.

For where-e'er the sun does shine,
And where-e'er the rain does fall:
Babe can never hunger there,
Nor poverty the mind appall.

ANN TAYLOR GILBERT (1782-1866)
and JANE TAYLOR (1783-1824)
From *Original Poems for Infant Minds* (1804-05)
and *Rhymes for the Nursery* (1806)

The daughters of Isaac Taylor were vivacious girls who as children composed stories, plays, and verses for their own amusement. The whole family had an inclination to write; indeed, their father and brother made contributions to *Original Poems*. The publisher Darton and Harvey added further poems by Adelaide O'Keefe (1776-1855) to make up this popular collection of ditties that blend caution, justice, humour, and sentiment, and do so in a graceful conversational style. In their preface to *Rhymes for the Nursery* they asked respectfully to be allowed to show "whether ideas adapted to the comprehension of infancy, admit the restrictions of rhyme and metre". As the illustration from an 1868 edition testifies, their work remained popular for many decades.

MEDDLESOME MATTY

One ugly trick has often spoil'd
    The sweetest and the best;
Matilda, though a pleasant child,
    One ugly trick possess'd,
Which, like a cloud before the skies,
Hid all her better qualities.

Sometimes she'd lift the tea-pot lid,
    To peep at what was in it;
Or tilt the kettle, if you did
    But turn your back a minute.
In vain you told her not to touch,
Her trick of meddling grew so much.

Her grandmamma went out one day,
    And by mistake she laid
Her spectacles and snuff-box gay
    Too near the little maid;
"Ah! well," thought she, "I'll try them on,
As soon as grandmamma is gone."

Forthwith she placed upon her nose
    The glasses large and wide;
And looking round, as I suppose,
    The snuff-box too she spied:
"Oh! what a pretty box is that;
I'll open it," said little Matt.

"I know that grandmamma would say,
    'Don't meddle with it, dear;'
But then, she's far enough away,

And no one else is near:
Besides, what can there be amiss
In opening such a box as this?"

So thumb and finger went to work
    To move the stubborn lid,
And presently a mighty jerk
    The mighty mischief did;
For all at once, ah! woeful case,
The snuff came puffing in her face.

Poor eyes, and nose, and mouth, beside
    A dismal sight presented;
In vain, as bitterly she cried,
    Her folly she repented.
In vain she ran about for ease,
She could do nothing now but sneeze.

She dash'd the spectacles away,
    To wipe her tingling eyes,
And as in twenty bits they lay,
    Her grandmamma she spies.
"Heyday! and what's the matter now?"
Says grandmamma, with lifted brow.

Matilda, smarting with the pain,
    And tingling still, and sore,
Made many a promise to refrain
    From meddling evermore.
And 'tis a fact, as I have heard,
She ever since has kept her word.

THE WOODEN DOLL AND THE WAX DOLL

There were two friends, a very charming pair!
Brunette the brown, and Blanchidine the fair;
And she to love Brunette did constantly incline,
Nor less did Brunette love sweet Blanchidine.
Brunette in dress was neat, yet always plain;
But Blanchidine of finery was vain.

Now Blanchidine a new acquaintance made—
A little girl most sumptuously array'd,
In plumes and ribbons, gaudy to behold,
And India frock, with spots of shining gold.
Said Blanchidine, "A girl so richly dress'd
Should surely be by every one caress'd.
To play with me if she will condescend,
Henceforth 'tis she alone shall be my friend"

And so for this new friend in silks adorn'd,
Her poor Brunette was slighted, left, and scorn'd.
Of Blanchidine's vast stock of pretty toys,
A wooden doll her every thought employs;
Its neck so white, so smooth, its cheeks so red—
She kiss'd, she fondled, and she took to bed.

Mamma now brought her home a doll of wax,
Its hair in ringlets white, and soft as flax;
Its eyes could open and its eyes could shut;
And on it, too, with taste its clothes were put.
"My dear wax doll!" sweet Blanchidine would cry—
Her doll of wood was thrown neglected by.

One summer's day,—'twas in the month of June,—
The sun blazed out in all the heat of noon:
"My waxen doll," she cried, "my dear, my charmer!
What, are you cold? but you shall soon be warmer."
She laid it in the sun—misfortune dire!
The wax ran down as if before the fire!
Each beauteous feature quickly disappear'd,
And melting, left a blank all soil'd and smear'd.

Her doll disfigured she beheld amazed,
And thus express'd her sorrow as she gazed:
"Is it for you my heart I have estranged
From that I fondly loved, which has not changed?
Just so may change my new acquaintance fine,
For whom I left Brunette, that friend of mine.
No more by outside show will I be lured;
Of such capricious whims I think I'm cured:
To plain old friends my heart shall still be true,
Nor change for every face because 'tis new."
Her slighted wooden doll resumed its charms,
And wrong'd Brunette she clasp'd within her arms.

ADELAIDE O'KEEFE

MY MOTHER

Who fed me from her gentle breasts,
And hushed me in her arms to rest,
And on my cheek sweet kisses prest?
              My Mother

When sleep forsook my open eye,
Who was it sung sweet hushaby,
And rocked me that I should not cry?
              My Mother.

Who sat and watched my infant head,
When sleeping on my cradle bed,
And tears of sweet affection shed?
              My Mother.

When pain and sickness made me cry,
Who gazed upon my heavy eye,
And wept, for fear that I should die?
              My Mother.

Who dressed my doll in clothes so gay,
And fondly taught me how to play,
And minded all I had to say?
              My Mother.

Who ran to help me when I fell,
And would some pretty story tell,
Or kiss the place to make it well?
              My Mother.

Who taught my infant lips to pray,
And love God's holy book and day,
And walk in wisdom's pleasant way?
          My Mother.

And can I ever cease to be
Affectionate and kind to thee,
Who was so very kind to me,
          My Mother

Ah no! the thought I cannot bear,
And if God please my life to spare,
I hope I shall reward thy care,
          My Mother.

When thou art feeble, old, and grey,
My healthy arm shall be thy stay,
And I will soothe thy pains away,
          My Mother.

And when I see thee hang thy head,
'Twill be my turn to watch thy bed,
And tears of sweet affection shed,
          My Mother.

For could our Father in the skies
Look down with pleased or loving eyes,
If ever I could dare despise
          My Mother?

From *Rhymes for the Nursery*

THE FIELD DAISY

I'm a pretty little thing,
Always coming with the spring,
In the meadows green, I'm found,
Peeping just above the ground,
And my stalk is cover'd flat,
With a white and yellow hat.

Little lady, when you pass
Lightly o'er the tender grass,
Skip about, but do not tread
On my meek and healthy head,
For I always seem to say,
"Surly winter's gone away."

ANN

THE BABY'S DANCE

Dance little baby, dance up high,
Never mind baby, mother is by;
Crow and caper, caper and crow,
There little baby, there you go;
Up to the ceiling, down to the ground,
Backwards and forwards, round and round;
Dance little baby, and mother shall sing,
With the merry coral, ding, ding, ding.

ANN

THE STAR

Twinkle, twinkle, little star,
How I wonder what you are!
Up above the world so high,
Like a diamond in the sky.

When the blazing sun is gone,
When he nothing shines upon,
Then you show your little light,
Twinkle, twinkle, all the night.

Then the trav'ller in the dark,
Thanks you for your tiny spark,
He could not see which way to go,
If you did not twinkle so.

In the dark blue sky you keep,
And often thro' my curtains peep,
For you never shut your eye,
Till the sun is in the sky.

'Tis your bright and tiny spark,
Lights the trav'ller in the dark:
Tho' I know not what you are,
Twinkle, twinkle, little star.

JANE

THE MICHAELMAS DAISY

I am very pale and dim,
With my faint and bluish rim;
Standing on my narrow stalk,
By the litter'd gravel walk,
And the wither'd leaves, aloft,
Fall upon me, very oft.

But I show my lonely head,
When the other flowers are dead,
And you're even glad to spy
Such a homely thing as I;
For I seem to smile, and say,
"Summer is not quite away."

A. T.

THE LITTLE GIRL TO HER DOLLY

There, go to sleep dolly, in own mother's lap;
I've put on your night-gown and neat little cap;
So sleep, pretty baby, and shut up your eye,
Bye bye, little dolly, lie still, and bye bye.

I'll lay my clean handkerchief over your head,
And then make believe that my lap is your bed;
So hush, little dear, and be sure you don't cry,
Bye bye, little dolly, lie still, and bye bye.

There,—now it is morning, and time to get up,
And I'll crumb you a mess, in my doll's china cup;
So wake little baby, and open your eye,
For I think it high time to have done with bye bye.

A.T.

ELIZABETH TURNER (d. 1846)
From *The Daisy; or, Cautionary Stories in Verse Adapted to the Ideas of Children from Four to Eight years old* (1807)

This book by Elizabeth Turner is a collection of enjoyably facile doggerel with a strong moralistic flavour: the results of misbehaviour are swift and predictable. As the first collection of "Cautionary Stories in Verse", it acquired a degree of fame and was adapted and parodied by Heinrich Hoffmann in *Struwwelpeter* (1848) and by Hilaire Belloc in his light-verse collection, *Cautionary Tales* (1907).

THE GIDDY GIRL

Miss Helen was always too giddy to heed
　What her mother had told her to shun;
For frequently, over the street in full speed,
　She would cross where the carriages run.

And out she would go to a very deep well,
　To look at the water below;
How naughty! to run to a dangerous well,
　Where her mother forbade her to go!

One morning, intending to take but one peep,
　Her foot slipp'd away from the ground;
Unhappy misfortune! the water was deep,
　And giddy Miss Helen was drown'd.

DRESSED OR UNDRESSED

When children are naughty, and will not be dressed,
  Pray, what do you think is the way?
Why, often I really believe it is best
  To keep them in night-clothes all day!

But then they can have no good breakfast to eat,
  Nor walk with their mother or aunt;
At dinner they'll have neither pudding nor meat,
  Nor any thing else that they want.

Then who would be naughty, and sit all the day
  In night-clothes unfit to be seen?
And pray, who would lose all their pudding and play,
  For not being dressed neat and clean?

CARELESS MARIA

Maria was a careless child,
    And grieved her friends by this:
        Where'er she went,
        Her clothes were rent,
    Her hat and bonnet spoil'd,
        A careless little Miss!

Her gloves and mits were often lost,
    Her tippet sadly soil'd;
        You might have seen,
        Where she had been,
    For toys all round were toss'd,
        Oh, what a careless child!

One day her uncle bought a toy,
    That round and round would twirl
        But when he found
        The litter'd ground,
    He said, "I don't tee-totums buy
        For such a careless girl!"

THE NEW PENNY

Miss Ann saw a man,
Quite poor, at a door,
And Ann had a pretty new Penny;
Now this the kind Miss
Threw pat in his hat,
Although she was left without any.

She meant, as she went,
To stop at a shop,
Where cakes she had seen a great many;
And buy a fruit-pie,
Or take home a cake,
By spending her pretty new penny.

But well I can tell,
When Ann gave the man
Her money, she wish'd not for any;
He said, "I've no bread,"
She heard, and preferr'd
To give him her pretty new penny.

DANGEROUS SPORT

Poor Peter was burnt by the poker one day,
  When he made it look pretty and red;
For the beautiful sparks made him think it fine play,
  To lift it as high as his head.

But somehow it happen'd, his finger and thumb
  Were terribly scorch'd by the heat;
And he scream'd out aloud for his Mother to come,
  And stamp'd on the floor with his feet.

Now if Peter had minded his Mother's command,
  His fingers would not have been sore;
And he promised again, as she bound up his hand,
  To play with hot pokers no more.

THE CHIMNEY SWEEPER

Sweep! sweep! sweep! sweep! cries little Jack,
With brush and bag upon his back,
  And black from head to foot;
While daily as he goes along,
Sweep! sweep! sweep! sweep! is all his song,
  Beneath his load of soot.

But then he was not always black,
Oh, no! he once was pretty Jack,
   And had a kind Papa;
But, silly child! he ran to play
Too far from home, a long, long way,
   And did not ask Mamma.

So he was lost, and now must creep
Up chimneys, crying, Sweep! sweep! sweep!

MISS SOPHIA

Miss Sophy, one fine sunny day,
Left her work and ran away;
When soon she reached the garden-gate,
Which finding lock'd, she would not wait,
But tried to climb and scramble o'er
A gate as high as any door.

But little girls should never climb,
And Sophy won't another time;
For when, upon the highest rail,
Her frock was caught upon a nail,
She lost her hold, and, sad to tell,
Was hurt and bruised—for down she fell.

THE GOOD SCHOLAR

Joseph West had been told,
That if, when he grew old,
He had not learnt rightly to spell,
Though his writing were good,
'T would not be understood:
And Joe said, "I will learn my task well."

And he made it a rule
To be silent at school,
And what do you think came to pass?
Why, he learnt it so fast,
That, from being the last,
He soon was the first in the class.

WILLIAM ROSCOE (1753-1831)
The Butterfly's Ball and the Grasshopper's Feast (1807)

Historian, attorney, banker, and rare-book collector, William Roscoe of Liverpool had a keen interest in Italian literature and history and wrote the lives of Lorenzo de Medici (1796) and Leo X (1805). An amateur botanist as well, he was elected a fellow of the Linnean Society (1805); he was also elected as the city's Whig member of Parliament (1806-7). Roscoe wrote *The Butterfly's Ball* as an amusement for his youngest son, Robert, and contributed it to *The Gentleman's Magazine* in 1806. The next year the publisher John Harris issued the rhyme, along with commissioned illustrations by William Mulready, in chapbook form. Whimsical, non-moral, and popular, *The Butterfly's Ball* appeared in many publications in the nineteenth century and was frequently paired in one volume with Catherine Dorset's *The Peacock "At Home"* (pages 252-5). Just as Roscoe's later botanical research led to the naming of an order of one-stamen plants, "Roscoea", his inventiveness in composing *The Butterfly's Ball* was honoured by a whole series of imitations.

THE
BUTTERFLY'S BALL,
and the
GRASSHOPPER'S FEAST

COME, take up your hats, and away let us haste
To the *Butterfly's* Ball and the *Grasshopper's* Feast:
The Trumpeter, *Gadfly*, has summon'd the Crew,
And the Revels are now only waiting for you.
So said little Robert, and pacing along,

His merry Companions came forth in a throng,
And on the smooth Grass, by the side of a Wood,
Beneath a broad Oak that for ages had stood,
Saw the Children of Earth, and the Tenants of Air,
For an Evening's Amusement together repair.
And there came the *Beetle*, so blind and so black,
Who carried the *Emmet*, his Friend, on his back.
And there was the *Gnat*, and the *Dragon-fly* too,
With all their Relations, Green, Orange, and Blue.
And there came the *Moth*, with his plumage of down,
And the *Hornet*, in Jacket of Yellow and Brown,

Who with him the *Wasp*, his Companion, did bring,
But they promised that Evening to lay by their Sting.
And the sly little *Dormouse* crept out of his hole,
And brought to the Feast his blind Brother, the *Mole*.
And the *Snail*, with his Horns peeping out of his Shell,
Came from a great distance, the Length of an Ell.
A Mushroom their Table, and on it was laid
A Water-dock Leaf, which a Table-cloth made.
The Viands were various, to each of their taste,
And the *Bee* brought her Honey to crown the Repast.
Then close on his haunches, so solemn and wise,
The *Frog* from a corner look'd up to the Skies;
And the *Squirrel*, well pleased such diversions to see,

Mounted high over-head, and look'd down from a Tree.
Then out came the *Spider*, with finger so fine,
To shew his dexterity on the tight line.
From one branch to another, his Cobwebs he slung,
Then quick as an arrow he darted along;
But just in the middle,—Oh! shocking to tell,
From his Rope, in an instant, poor Harlequin fell.
Yet he touch'd not the ground, but with talons outspread,
Hung suspended in air, at the end of a thread.
Then the *Grasshopper* came with a jerk and a spring;
Very long was his Leg, though but short was his Wing;

He took but three leaps, and was soon out of sight,
Then chirp'd his own praises the rest of the night.
With step so majestic the *Snail* did advance,
And promised the Gazers a Minuet to dance.
But they all laugh'd so loud that he pull'd in his head,
And went in his own little chamber to bed.
Then, as Evening gave way to the Shadows of Night,
Their Watchman, the *Glow-worm*, came out with a light.
    Then Home let us hasten, while yet we can see,
For no Watchman is waiting for you and for me.
So said little Robert, and pacing along,
His merry Companions return'd in a throng.

CATHERINE ANN DORSET (1750-1817)
The Peacock "At Home" (1807)

The second number of John Harris's *Cabinet of Amusement and Instruction* series, Dorset's *The Peacock "At Home"* presents the rousing response of the birds to Roscoe's insect fête.

THE PEACOCK "AT HOME"

The Butterfly's Ball, and the Grasshopper's Feasts,
Excited the spleen of the Birds and the Beasts:
For their mirth and good cheer—of the Bee was the theme,
And the Gnat blew his horn, as he danc'd in the beam.
'Twas humm'd by the Beetle, 'twas buzz'd by the Fly,
And sung by the myriads that sport 'neath the sky.
The Quadrupeds listen'd with sullen displeasure,
But the Tenants of Air were enrag'd beyond measure.
The Peacock display'd his bright plumes to the Sun,
And, addressing his Mates, thus indignant begun:
"Shall we, like domestic, inelegant Fowls,
"As unpolish'd as Geese, and as stupid as Owls,
"Sit tamely at home, hum drum, with our Spouses,
"While Crickets, and Butterflies, open their houses?
"Shall such mean little Insects pretend to the fashion?
"Cousin Turkey-cock, well may you be in a passion!
"If I suffer such insolent airs to prevail,
"May Juno pluck out all the eyes in my tail;
"So a Fête I will give, and my taste I'll display,
"And send out my cards for Saint Valentine's Day.
—This determin'd, six fleet Carrier Pigeons went out,
To invite all the Birds to Sir Argus's Rout.
The nest-loving TURTLE-DOVE sent an excuse;
DAME PARTLET lay in, as did good Mrs GOOSE.
The TURKEY, poor soul! was confin'd to the rip:
For all her young Brood had just fail'd with the pip.
And the PARTRIDGE was ask'd; but a Neighbour hard by,
Had engag'd a snug party to meet in a Pye;
The WHEAT'EAR declin'd, recollecting her Cousins,
Last year, to a Feast were invited by dozens;
But alas! they return'd not; and she had no taste
To appear in a costume of vine-leaves or paste.
The WOODCOCK preferr'd his lone haunt on the moor;
And the Traveller, SWALLOW, was still on his tour.
The CUCKOO, who should have been one of the guests,
Was rambling on visits to other Birds' Nests.
But the rest, all accepted the kind invitation,

And much bustle it caus'd in the plumed creation:
Such ruffling of feathers, such pruning of coats!
Such chirping, such whistling, such clearing of throats!
Such polishing bills, and such oiling of pinions!
Had never been known in the biped dominions.
The TAYLOR BIRD offer'd to make up new clothes;
For all the young Birdlings, who wish'd to be Beaux:
He made for the ROBIN a doublet of red,
And a new velvet cap for the GOLDFINCH's head;
He added a plume to the WREN'S golden crest,
And spangled with silver the GUINEA-FOWL'S breast;
While the HALCYON bent over the streamlet to view,
How pretty she look'd in her bodice of blue!
Thus adorn'd, they set off for the Peacock's abode,
With the Guide INDICATOR, who shew'd them the road:
From all points of the compass, came Birds of all feather;
And the PARROT can tell who and who were together.
There came LORD CASSOWARY, and General FLAMINGO,
And DON PEROQUETO, escap'd from Domingo;
From his high rock-built eyrie the EAGLE came forth,
And the Duchess of PTARMIGAN flew from the north.
The GREBE and the EIDER DUCK came up by water,
With the SWAN, who brought out the young CYGNET, her daughter.
From his woodland abode came the PHEASANT, to meet
Two kindred, arriv'd by the last India fleet:
The one, like a Nabob, in habit most splendid,
Where gold with each hue of the Rainbow was blended:
In silver and black, like a fair pensive Maid,
Who mourns for her love! was the other array'd.
The CHOUGH came from Cornwall, and brought up his Wife;
The GROUSE travell'd south, from his Lairdship in Fife;
The BUNTING forsook her soft nest in the reeds;
And the WIDOW-BIRD came, though she still wore her weeds;
Sir John HERON, of the Lakes, strutted in a *grand pas*,
But no card had been sent to the pilfering DAW,
As the Peacock kept up his progenitors' quarrel,
Which Esop relates, about cast-off apparel;
For Birds are like Men in their contests together,
And, in questions of right, can dispute for a feather.
      The PEACOCK, Imperial, the pride of his race.
Receiv'd all his guests with an infinite grace,
Wav'd high his blue neck, and his train he display'd,
Embroider'd with gold, and with em'ralds inlaid.
Then with all the gay troup to the shrubb'ry repair'd,
Where the musical Birds had a concert prepar'd;
A holly-bush form'd the Orchestra, and in it
Sat the Black-bird, the Thrush, the Lark, and the Linnet;

A BULL-FINCH, a captive! almost from the nest,
Now escap'd from his cage, and, with liberty blest,
In a sweet mellow tone, join'd the lessons of art
With the accents of nature, which flow'd from his heart.
The CANARY, a much-admir'd foreign musician,
Condescended to sing to the Fowls of condition,
While the NIGHTINGALE warbled, and quaver'd so fine,
That they all clapp'd their wings, and pronounc'd it divine!
The SKY LARK, in extacy, sang from a cloud,
And CHANTICLEER crow'd, and the YAFFIL laugh'd loud.
The dancing began, when the singing was over;
A DOTTERELL first open'd the ball with the PLOVER;
Baron STORK, in a waltz, was allow'd to excel,
With his beautiful Partner, the fair DEMOISELLE;
And a newly-fledg'd GOSLING, so spruce and genteel,
A minuet swam with young Mr. TEAL.
A London-bred SPARROW—a pert forward Cit!
Danc'd a reel with Miss WAGTAIL, and little TOM TIT.
And the Sieur GUILLEMOT next perform'd a *pas seul*,
While the elderly Bipeds were playing a Pool.
The Dowager Lady TOUCAN first cut in,
With old Doctor BUZZARD, and Adm'ral PENGUIN,
From Ivy-bush Tow'r came Dame OWLET the Wise,
And Counsellor CROSSBILL sat by to advise.

Some Birds past their prime, o'er whose *heads* it was fated,
Should pass many St Valentines—yet be unmated,
Look'd on, and remark'd, that the prudent and sage,
Were quite overlook'd in this frivolous age,
When Birds, scarce pen-feather'd, were brought to a rout,
Forward Chits! from the egg-shell but newly come out;
That in their youthful days, they ne'er witness'd such frisking,
And how wrong! in the GREENFINCH to flirt with the SISKIN.
So thought Lady MACKAW, and her Friend COCKATOO,
And the RAVEN foretold that "no good could ensue!"
They censur'd the BANTAM for strutting and crowing,
In those vile pantaloons, which he fancied look'd knowing;
And a want of decorum caus'd many demurs,
Against the GAME CHICKEN, for coming in spurs.
    Old Alderman CORM'RANT, for supper impatient,
At the Eating-room door, for an hour, had been station'd,
Till a MAGPIE, at length, the banquet announcing,
Gave the signal, long wish'd for, a clamouring and pouncing
At the well-furnish'd board all were eager to perch;
But the little Miss CREEPERS were left in the lurch.
    Description must fail; and the pen is unable
To describe all the lux'ries which cover'd the table.
Each delicate viand that taste could denote,
Wasps *a la sauce piquante*, and Flies *en compôte*;
Worms and Frogs *en friture*, for the web-footed Fowl,
And a barbecued Mouse was prepar'd for the Owls.
Nuts, grain, fruit, and fish, to regale ev'ry palate,
And groundsel and chick-weed serv'd up in a salad.
The RAZOR-BILL carv'd for the famishing group,
And the Spoonbill obligingly ladled the soup;
So they fill'd all their crops with the dainties before 'em,
And the tables were clear'd with the utmost decorum.
When they gaily had caroll'd till peep of the dawn,
The Lark gently hinted, 'twas time to be gone;
And his clarion, so shrill, gave the company warning,
That Chanticleer scented the gales of the morning.
So they chirp'd, in full chorus, a friendly adieu;
And, with hearts quite as light as the plumage that grew
On their merry-thought bosoms, away they all flew. . . .
Then long live the PEACOCK, in splendor unmatch'd,
Whose Ball shall be talk'd of, by Birds yet unhatch'd;
His praise let the Trumpeter loudly proclaim,
And the Goose lend her quill to transmit it to Fame.

CHARLES and MARY LAMB (1775-1834; 1764-1847)
From *Poetry for Children* (1809)

Charles Lamb, whose pen-name was Elia, was an essayist, poet, and critic. Devoted companion and custodian, through his whole adult life, of his sometimes mentally unbalanced sister Mary, Lamb enjoyed close friendships with Coleridge, Wordsworth, Hazlitt, and Crabb Robinson. The Lambs had produced some notable works for children prior to the appearance of *Poetry for Children*. Charles had adapted and expanded the familiar nursery rhyme about the exploits of a pack of cards in *The King and Queen of Hearts with The Rogueries of the Knave who stole away the Queen's Pies* (1805). Brother and sister together had composed summaries of Shakespeare's plays, with

Mary doing the comedies and Charles the tragedies, in *Tales from Shakespeare* (1807). Charles had synopsized Chapman's *Odyssey* as *The Adventures of Ulysses* (1808) and had contributed three stories to his sister's collection of stories about young ladies, *Mrs Leicester's School* (1809).

Poetry for Children contains brother-sister dialogues, one of them alluding to William Roscoe, and a slightly uneasy treatment of fairies. For the most part these poems on child-like subjects are contrived and wooden—they lack the light touch and literary grace of the Lambs' prose for children—but the book was well received in its day.

EYES

Lucy, what do you espy
In the cast in Jenny's eye
That should you to laughter move?
I far other feelings prove.
When on me she does advance
Her good-natur'd countenance,
And those eyes which in their way
Saying much, so much would say,
They to me no blemish seem,
Or as none I them esteem;
I their imperfection prize
Above other clearer eyes.

Eyes do not as jewels go
By the brightness and the show,
But the meanings which surround them,
And the sweetness shines around them.

   Isabel's are black as jet,
But she cannot that forget,
And the pains she takes to show them
Robs them of the praise we owe them.
Ann's, though blue, affected fall;
Kate's are bright, but fierce withal;
And the sparklers of her sister
From ill-humour lose their lustre.
Only Jenny's eyes we see,
By their very plainness, free
From the vices which do smother
All the beauties of the other.

CHUSING A NAME

I have got a new-born sister;
I was nigh the first that kiss'd her.
When the nursing woman brought her
To Papa, his infant daughter,
How Papa's dear eyes did glisten!—
She will shortly be to christen:
And Papa has made the offer,
I shall have the naming of her.

Now I wonder what would please her,
Charlotte, Julia, or Louisa.
Ann and Mary, they're too common;
Joan's too formal for a woman;
Jane's a prettier name beside;
But we had a Jane that died.
They would say, if 'twas Rebecca,
That she was a little Quaker.
Edith's pretty, but that looks
Better in old English books;
Ellen's left off long ago;
Blanch is out of fashion now.
None that I have nam'd as yet
Are so good as Margaret.
Emily is neat and fine.
What do you think of Caroline?
How I'm puzzled and perplext
What to chuse or think of next!
I am in a little fever.
Lest the name that I shall give her
Should disgrace her or defame her,
I will leave Papa to name her.

THE DESSERT

With the apples and the plums
Little Carolina comes,
At the time of the dessert she
Comes and drops her last new curt'sy;
Graceful curt'sy, practis'd o'er
In the nursery before.
What shall we compare her to?
The dessert itself will do.
Like preserves she's kept with care,
Like blanch'd almonds she is fair,
Soft as down on peach her hair,
And so soft, so smooth is each
Pretty cheek as that same peach,
Yet more like in hue to cherries;
Then her lips, the sweet strawberries,
Caroline herself shall try them
If they are not like when nigh them;
Her bright eyes are black as sloes,
But I think we've none of those
Common fruit here—and her chin
From a round point does begin,
Like the small end of a pear;
Whiter drapery she does wear
Than the frost on cake; and sweeter
Than the cake itself, and neater,
Though bedeck'd with emblems fine.
Is our little Caroline.

THE FAIRY

Said Ann to Matilda, "I wish that we knew
If what we've been reading of fairies be true.
Do you think that the poet himself had a sight of
The fairies he here does so prettily write of?
O what a sweet sight if he really had seen
The graceful Titania, the Fairy-land Queen!
If I had such dreams, I would sleep a whole year;
I would not wish to wake while a fairy was near.—
Now I'll fancy that I in my sleep have been seeing
A fine little delicate lady-like being,
Whose steps and whose motions so light were and airy,
I knew at one glance that she must be a fairy.
Her eyes they were blue, and her fine curling hair
Of the lightest of browns, her complexion more fair
Than I e'er saw a woman's; and then for her height,
I verily think that she measur'd not quite
Two feet, yet so justly proportion'd withal,
I was almost persuaded to think she was tall.
Her voice was the little thin note of a sprite—
There—d'ye think I have made out a fairy aright?
You'll confess, I believe, I've not done it amiss."
"Pardon me," said Matilda, "I find in all this
Fine description, you've only your young sister Mary
Been taking a copy of her for a fairy."

WHAT IS FANCY?

SISTER

I am to write three lines, and you
Three others that will rhyme.
There—now I've done my task.

BROTHER

Three stupid lines as e'er I knew.
When you've the pen next time,
Some Question of me ask.

SISTER

Then tell me, brother, and pray mind,
Brother, you tell me true:
What sort of thing is *fancy*?

BROTHER

By all that I can ever find,
'Tis something that is very new,
And what no dunces *can see*.

SISTER

That is not half the way to tell
What *fancy* is about;
So pray now tell me more.

BROTHER

Sister, I think 'twere quite as well
That you should find it out;
So think the matter o'er.

SISTER

It's what comes in our heads when we
Play at "Let's make believe,"
And when we play at "Guessing."

BROTHER

And I have heard it said to be
A talent often makes us grieve,
And sometimes proves a blessing.

THE BUTTERFLY

SISTER

Do, my dearest brother John,
Let that Butterfly alone.

BROTHER

What harm now do I do?
You're always making such a noise—

SISTER

O fie, John; none but naughty boys
  Say such rude words as you.

BROTHER

Because you're always speaking sharp:
On the same thing you always harp.
  A bird one may not catch,
Nor find a nest, nor angle neither,
Nor from the peacock pluck a feather,
  But you are on the watch
To moralize and lecture still.

SISTER

And ever lecture, John, I will,
  When such sad things I hear.
But talk not now of what is past;
The moments fly away too fast,
Though endlessly they seem to last
  To that poor soul in fear.

BROTHER

Well, soon (I say) I'll let it loose;
But, sister, you talk like a goose,
  There's no soul in a fly.

SISTER

It has a form and fibres fine,
Were temper'd by the hand divine
  Who dwells beyond the sky.
Look, brother, you have hurt its wing—
And plainly by its fluttering
  You see it's in distress.
Gay painted Coxcomb, spangled Beau,
A Butterfly is call'd you know,
  That's always in full dress;
The finest gentleman of all
Insects he is—he gave a Ball,
  You know the Poet wrote.
Let's fancy this the very same,
And then you'll own you've been to blame
  To spoil his silken coat.

BROTHER

Your dancing, spangled, powder'd Beau,
Look, through the air I've let him go:
  And now we're friends again.
As sure as he is in the air,
From this time, Ann, I will take care,
  And try to be humane.

From *Peter Piper's Practical Principles of Plain and Perfect Pronunciation* (1813)

This ingeniously alliterative abecedary was the eighth number in the *Cabinet of Amusement and Instruction* series published by John Harris. Later additions—*Marmaduke Multiply's Merry Method of Making Minor Mathematicians* (1816) and *Punctuation Personified* (1824)—are simply lessons in rhyme; they lack the rollicking inventiveness and sense of abandoned fun of *Peter Piper's Principles*. The book opens with 'Peter Piper's Polite Preface': 'PETER PIPER Puts Pen to Paper, to produce his Peerless Production, Proudly Presuming it will Please Princes, Peers, and Parlia-ments, and Procure him the Praise and Plaudits of their Progeny and POSTERITY, as he can prove it Positively to be a PARAGON, or Playful, Palatable, Proverbial, Panegyrical, Philosophical, Philanthropical Phaenomenon of Productions.' The excerpts included here are reproduced from the Osborne Collection's edition of 1820, in which the first line of the second rhyme, originally "Bobby Blubber blew a Bullock's Bladder", was changed to the more genteel (and easier to pronounce) "Billy Button bought a butter'd Biscuit".

A a

Andrew Airpump ask'd his Aunt her Ailment:
Did Andrew Airpump ask his Aunt her Ailment?
If Andrew Airpump ask'd his Aunt her Ailment,
Where was the Ailment of Andrew Airpump's
      Aunt?

B   b

Billy Button bought a butter'd Biscuit:
Did Billy Button buy a butter'd Biscuit?
If Billy Button bought a butter'd Biscuit,
Where's the butter'd Biscuit Billy Button bought?

C   c

Captain Crackskull crack'd a Catchpoll's Cockscomb:
Did Captain Crackskull crack a Catchpoll's Cockscomb?
If Captain Crackskull crack'd a Catchpoll's Cockscomb,
Where's the Catchpoll's Cockscomb Captain Crack-
    skull crack'd?

Catchpoll: sheriff's bailiff
Cockscomb: fool's cap or ludicrous term for head

M m

Matthew Mendlegs miss'd a mangled Monkey:
Did Matthew Mendlegs miss a mangled Monkey?
If Matthew Mendlegs miss'd a mangled Monkey,
Where's the mangled Monkey Matthew Mendlegs
    miss'd?

N n

Neddy Noodle nipp'd his Neighbour's Nutmegs:
Did Neddy Noodle nip his Neighbour's Nutmegs?
If Neddy Noodle nipp'd his Neighbour's Nutmegs,
Where are the Neighbour's Nutmegs Neddy Noodle
    nipp'd?

O o

Oliver Oglethorpe ogled an Owl and Oyster:
Did Oliver Oglethorpe ogle an Owl and Oyster?
If Oliver Oglethorpe ogled an Owl and Oyster,
Where are the Owl and Oyster Oliver Oglethorpe
ogled?

P p

Peter Piper pick'd a Peck of Pepper:
Did Peter Piper pick a Peck of Pepper?
If Peter Piper pick'd a Peck of Pepper,
Where's the Peck of Pepper Peter Piper pick'd?

THOMAS LOVE PEACOCK (1785-1866)
From *Sir Hornbook; or, Childe Launcelot's Expedition* (1814)

Well before he had achieved a reputation for his novels or taken up his career with the East India Company, Peacock composed this "grammatico-allegorical ballad", although it was published anonymously— even as late as 1848 in *The Home Treasury* series of his friend Henry Cole. The regular marching stanzas of alternately rhymed lines tell the story of the regiment provided Childe Launcelot by Sir Hornbook and its exploits in the knight's quest of the Muse's "sacred ground". Designed as an adventurous grammar lesson, complete with learned borrowings and explanatory footnotes, *Sir Hornbook* seems a pedantic curiosity today.

VI

Now steeper grew the rising ground,
    And rougher grew the road,
As up the steep ascent they wound
To bold Sir VERB's abode.[1]

Sir VERB was old, and many a year,
    All scenes and climates seeing,
Had run a wild and strange career
    Through every mode of being.

And every aspect, shape, and change
    Of *action*, and of *passion*:
And known to him was all the range
    Of feeling, taste, and fashion.

He was an Augur, quite at home
    In all things present done,[2]
Deeds past, and every act to come
    In ages yet to run.

Entrenched in intricacies strong,
    Ditch, fort, and palisado,
He marked with scorn the coming throng,
    And breathed a bold bravado:

—"Ho! who are you that dare invade
    My turrets, moats, and fences?
Soon will your vaunting courage fade,
When on the walls, in lines array'd,
You see me marshal undismay'd
    My host of moods and tenses."[3]—

[1] A VERB is a word which signifies to BE, to DO, or to SUFFER; as, "*I am, I love, I am loved.*"

[2] The two lines in *Italics* are taken from Chapman's Homer.

[3] Verbs have five moods: The INDICATIVE, IMPERATIVE, POTENTIAL, SUBJUNCTIVE, and INFINITIVE.

"In vain,"—Childe LAUNCELOT cried in scorn,—
—"On them is your reliance;"—
Sir HORNBOOK wound his bugle horn,
And twang'd a loud defiance.

They swam the moat, they scal'd the wall,
Sir VERB, with rage and shame,
Beheld his valiant *general* fall,
INFINITIVE by name.[4]

INDICATIVE *declar'd* the foes[5]
Should perish by his hand;
And stout IMPERATIVE arose,[6]
The squadron to *command*.

POTENTIAL[7] and SUBJUNCTIVE[8] then
Came forth with *doubt* and *chance*:
All fell alike, with all their men,
Before Sir HORNBOOK's lance.

ACTION and PASSION nought could do
To save Sir VERB from fate;
Whose doom poor PARTICIPLE knew,[9]
He must *participate*.

The ADVERB, who had skulk'd behind,[10]
To shun the mighty jar,
Came forward, and himself resign'd
A prisoner of war.

Three children of IMPERATIVE,
Full strong, though somewhat small,
Next forward came, themselves to give
To conquering LAUNCELOT's thrall.

---

[4] The INFINITIVE mood expresses a thing in a *general* and unlimited manner: as, *"To love, to walk, to be ruled."*

[5] The INDICATIVE mood simply *indicates* or *declares* a thing: as, "He loves:" "he is loved:" or asks a question: as, "Does he love?"—"Is he loved?"

[6] The imperative mood *commands* or *entreats*: as, "Depart:" "Come hither:"—"Forgive me."

[7] The POTENTIAL mood implies *possibility* or *obligation*: as, "It may rain:"—"They should learn."

[8] The SUBJUNCTIVE mood implies *contingency*: as, "If he *were* good, he would be happy."

[9] The PARTICIPLE is a certain form of the verb, and is so called from participating the nature of a verb and an adjective: as: *"he is an* ADMIRED *character; she is a* LOVING *child."*

[10] The adverb is joined to verbs, to adjectives, and to other adverbs, to qualify their signification: as, *that is a* REMARKABLY *swift horse: It is* EXTREMELY WELL *done."*

CONJUNCTION press'd to join the crowd;[11]
But PREPOSITION swore,[12]
Though INTERJECTION sobb'd aloud,[13]
That he would *go before*.

Again his horn Sir HORNBOOK blew,
Full long, and loud, and shrill;
His merrymen all, so stout and true,
Went marching up the hill.

VII

Sir SYNTAX dwelt in thick fir-grove,[14]
All strown with scraps of flowers,[15]
Which he had pluck'd, to please his love,
Among the Muses' bowers.

His love was gentle PROSODY,[16]
More fair than morning beam;
Who liv'd beneath a flowering tree,
Beside a falling stream.

And these two claim'd, with high pretence,
The whole Parnassian ground,
Albeit some little difference
Between their taste was found:
Sir SYNTAX he was all for sense,
And PROSODY for sound.

Yet in them both the MUSES fair
Exceedingly delighted;
And thought no earthly thing so rare,
That might with that fond twain compare,
When they were both *united*.

---

[11] A CONJUNCTION is a part of speech chiefly used to connect words: as, *"King* AND *constitution;"* or sentences: as, *"I went to the theatre, AND saw the new pantomime."*

[12] A PREPOSITION is most commonly *set before* another word to show its relation to some word or sentence preceding: as, *"The fisherman went* DOWN *the river* WITH *his boat."*
    Conjunctions and *Prepositions* are for the most part *Imperative moods of obsolete verbs: Thus, AND signifies ADD; John and Peter—John add Peter:"*—"The fisherman *with his* boat—The fisherman, *join* his boat."

[13] INTERJECTIONS are words *thrown in* between the parts of a sentence, to express passions or emotions: as, *"Oh! Alas!"*

[14] SYNTAX is that part of grammar, which treats of the agreement and construction of words in a sentence.

[15] I allude to the poetical fragments with which syntax is illustrated.

[16] PROSODY is that part of grammar which treats of the true pronunciation of words, and the rules of versification.

—"Ho! yield, Sir SYNTAX!"—HORNBOOK cried,
   "This youth must pass thy grove,
Led on by me, his faithful guide,
   In yonder bowers to rove."—

There ETYMOLOGY they found,[17]
   Who scorn'd surrounding fruits;
And ever dug in deepest ground,
   For old and mouldy ROOTS.

Sir HORNBOOK took Childe LAUNCELOT's hand,
   And tears at parting fell:
—"Sir CHILDE,"—he said—"with all my band
   I bid you here farewell.

"Then wander through these sacred bowers,
   Unfearing and alone:
All shrubs are here, and fruits, and flowers,
   To happiest climates known."—

Thereat full much, Sir SYNTAX said,
   But found resistance vain:
And through his grove Childe LAUNCELOT sped,
   With all Sir HORNBOOK's train.

They reach'd the tree where PROSODY
   Was singing in the shade:
Great joy Childe LAUNCELOT had to see,
   And hear that lovely maid.

Now, onward as they press'd along,
   Did nought their course oppose;
'Till full before the martial throng
   The MUSE's gates arose.

Once more his horn Sir HORNBOOK blew,
   A parting signal shrill:
His merrymen all, so stout and true,
   Went marching down the hill.

Childe LAUNCELOT pressed the sacred ground,
   With hope's exulting glow;
Some future song perchance may sound
   The wondrous things which there he found,
If you the same would know.

---

[17] ETYMOLOGY is that part of grammar, which investigates the *roots*, or *derivation*, of
words.

CLEMENT CLARKE MOORE (1779-1863)
"A Visit from Saint Nicholas" (1823)

An instructor at the General Theological Seminary in New York, Moore wrote this poem for his own children. "A Visit from Saint Nicholas" appeared anonymously in *The Troy Sentinel* on 23 December 1823. Whether submitted to faltering recitation at children's Christmas concerts or to the grand declamation of an important actor, it continues to charm with its dramatic narrative, rollicking metre, and vivid diction: Moore's images nest securely in our minds.

A VISIT FROM SAINT NICHOLAS

'Twas the night before Christmas, when all through the house
Not a creature was stirring, not even a mouse;
The stockings were hung by the chimney with care,
In hopes that St Nicholas soon would be there;
The children were nestled all snug in their beds,
While visions of sugar plums danced in their heads;
And mamma in her 'kerchief, and I in my cap,
Had just settled our brains for a long winter's nap,
When out on the lawn there arose such a clatter,
I sprang from the bed to see what was the matter.
Away to the window I flew like a flash,
Tore open the shutters and threw up the sash.

The moon on the breast of the new-fallen snow
Gave the lustre of midday to objects below,
When, what to my wondering eyes should appear,
But a miniature sleigh, and eight tiny reindeer,
With a little old driver, so lively and quick,
I knew in a moment it must be St Nick.
More rapid than eagles his coursers they came,
And he whistled, and shouted, and called them by name:
'Now, Dasher! now, Dancer! now, Prancer and Vixen!
On, Comet! on, Cupid! on, Donder and Blitzen!
To the top of the porch! to the top of the wall!
Now dash away! dash away! dash away all!'
As dry leaves that before the wild hurricane fly,
When they meet with an obstacle, mount to the sky,
So up to the house-top the coursers they flew,
With the sleigh full of toys, and St Nicholas too.

And then, in a twinkling, I heard on the roof
The prancing and pawing of each little hoof.
As I drew in my head, and was turning around,
Down the chimney St Nicholas came with a bound.
He was dressed all in fur, from his head to his foot,
And his clothes were all tarnished with ashes and soot;
A bundle of toys he had flung on his back,
And he looked like a peddler just opening his pack.
His eyes—how they twinkled, his dimples how merry!
His cheeks were like roses, his nose like a cherry!
His droll little mouth was drawn up like a bow,
And the beard of his chin was as white as the snow;
The stump of a pipe he held tight in his teeth,
And the smoke it encircled his head like a wreath;
He had a broad face and a little round belly,
That shook, when he laughed, like a bowlful of jelly.
He was chubby and plump, a right jolly old elf,
And I laughed when I saw him, in spite of myself:

A wink of his eyes and a twist of his head,
Soon gave me to know I had nothing to dread;
He spoke not a word, but went straight to his work,
And filled all the stockings, then turned with a jerk,
And laying his finger aside of his nose,
And giving a nod, up the chimney he rose;
He sprang to his sleigh, to his team gave a whistle,
And away they all flew like the down of a thistle.
But I heard him exclaim, ere he drove out of sight,
'Happy Christmas to all, and to all a good night.'

SARAH JOSEPHA HALE (1788-1879)
From *Poems for Our Children* (1830)

A Boston parent and a promoter of children's literature, Mrs Hale included "Mary Had a Little Lamb" in the American periodical she edited, *Juvenile Miscellany*, in 1830. Later that year the poem became part of her collection, *Poems for Our Children Designed for Families, Sabbath Schools and Infant Schools*. Within two years it had been set to music. Any comment about its being sentimental is irrelevant because it has been implanting itself in the consciousness of infants for 150 years and will do so far into the future.

MARY'S LAMB

Mary had a little lamb,
    Its fleece was white as snow,
And everywhere that Mary went
    The lamb was sure to go;
He followed her to school one day—
    That was against the rule,
It made the children laugh and play
    To see a lamb at school.

And so the teacher turned him out,
    But still he lingered near,
And waited patiently about,
    Till Mary did appear.
And then he ran to her and laid
    His head upon her arm,
As if he said, 'I'm not afraid—
    You'll shield me from all harm.'

'What makes the lamb love Mary so?'
    The little children cry;
'Oh, Mary loves the lamb, you know,'
    The teacher did reply,
'And you each gentle animal
    In confidence may bind,
And make it follow at your call,
    If you are always kind.'

ELEANOR MURE (1779-1885)
The Story of the Three Bears (1831)

As the dedication page of her illustrated manuscript declares, this was Miss Mure's "Birthday Present to Horace Broke, Sept: 26: 1831". Four-year-old Horace or "Horbook", as he called himself, was the nephew of the author-illustrator, "Aunt Nello". Her *Three Bears* pre-dates Robert Southey's prose version in *The Doctor* (vol. IV, chapter CXXIX) by six years. Both Mure and Southey have a meddlesome old woman as the central character. The young fair-haired heroine familiar to today's children did not appear until Joseph Cundall's version of the story in *A Treasury of Pleasure Books* (1850), and she did not receive the name "Goldilocks" until the early twentieth century. Southey sent the old woman "to the House of Correction for a vagrant as she was", but Miss Mure devised a farcical ending.

THE STORY OF THE THREE BEARS

Many ages ago, it was common, I find,
For dumb creatures to talk just as well as mankind:
Birds and Beasts met together t'arrange their affairs;
Nay! the Frogs of the day, must needs give themselves airs,
And apeing their betters, not pleas'd with their station,
Talk'd of having a King to rule over their nation.

In these curious days, it did raise no surprise,
(Though now 'twould make ev'ry one open their eyes)
That three Bears, very sick of their woods and their den,
Should fancy a home 'mongst the dwellings of men;
So not caring a fig for what any one said,
They bought a large house already furnished.

An old woman liv'd near them, who to their house went,
As to make their acquaintance she was fully bent.
They refused to receive her; and at this rebuff,
The angry old woman went home in a huff;
"Adzooks!" she exclaim'd, "what impertinent Bears!
"I would fain know their title to give themselves airs."

She, without more reflection, resolv'd not to let
The matter rest here; and work'd into a pet.
She made up her mind to watch them safe out,
Then not at all thinking what she was about,
She determin'd, without the Bears' leave, to explore
Each part of the house; so popp'd in at the door.

She went to the parlour; and there she did see
Some bowls of good milk, by one, two, and three:
She tasted the first, and then spit it about;
She drank some of the second, and threw it all out,
But when of the third, she had taken one sup,
Oh! greedy old woman! she drank it all up.

She went to the drawing-room, and she found there,
For each of the Bears, a most ponderous chair;
She sat down in the first, but she found it too rough;
She sat down in the second but that she felt tough;
She sat down in the third, without much ado;
When, good lack-a-day! the bottom burst through.

She went to the bedrooms, and there she did find
Three nice-looking beds, the best of their kind;
She lay down in the first; but she found little ease:
She lay down in the second, which still less did please;
She lay down in the third, without much ado,
When, good lack-a-day! the bottom burst through!

She look'd out of the window, and there she descried
The bears coming homewards, with dignified stride.
"Oh!" quoth she, I am lost, if the bears find me here."
So forthwith in a closet, all trembling with fear,
She hid herself; hoping she might get away,
Before the three Bruins could find where she lay.

Meanwhile the poor bears who had been out to roam,
Were coming as fast as they could to their home:
Tired, hungry, and longing for food and rest,
Unsuspicious of harm, to the parlour they prest;
As they opened the door, a sight greeted their eyes,
Which fill'd their rough breasts both with wrath & surprise.

The first bear, roaring loud, exclaim'd, "What do I see?"
"Who's been tasting my good milk, without leave of me?"
The second more gently said; "I can't conceive
"Who's been drinking my milk without asking my leave?"
The little bear scream'd, looking into his cup,
"Who's been drinking my milk, and drunk it all up?"

They went to the drawing-room; where the first bear
Roar'd, "Who, without leave, has sat down in my chair?"
The second, astonish'd, more mildly did say,
"Who's been sitting in my chair when I was away?"
The little bear madly cried; "What shall I do?
"Who has sat in my chair, and the bottom burst thro'?"

To the bedroom they went; and the first bear then said
"Who since I've been out, has lain down in my bed?"
The second bear, quite aghast, fiercely did say,
"Who has had the presumption in my bed to lay?"
The little bear scream'd out, "Oh! What shall I do?"
"Who in my bed has lain, and the bottom burst thro'?"

Indignant they run the delinquent to find;
Each corner they search, and each door look behind:
The closet they open, exclaiming; "She's here!"
And drag forth the dame, half expiring with fear;
Quite determin'd to punish her, long they debate
What, in justice, should be their old enemy's fate.

On the fire they throw her, but burn her they couldn't;
In the water they put her, but drown there she wouldn't;
They seize her before all the wondering people,
And chuck her aloft on St Paul's churchyard steeple;
And if she's still there when you earnestly look,
You will see her quite plainly.—my dear little Horbook!

MARY BOTHAM HOWITT (1799-1888)
From *Sketches of Natural History* (1834)

As Quakers and professional writers, both Mrs Howitt and her husband William, author of *The Boy's Country Book* (1839), made distinctive contributions to children's literature. In addition to serving as an early translator of Hans Andersen's *Fairy Tales*, Mary edited a collection of cautionary poems *(The Pink)* by the redoubtable moralist Elizabeth Turner, and herself wrote much popular verse and the well-liked *Strive and Thrive* (1840) and *Little Coin, Much Care* (1842), two children's novels that, as the titles suggest, have a strongly moral tone. The moral envoi of "The Spider and the Fly"—whose sub-title, "An Apologue", means moral fable—is thus entirely fitting for her time and outlook. The verse first appeared in *The New Year's Gift* of 1829 and was later incorporated in *Sketches of Natural History*, a collection of poems about animals and insects that was illustrated with the finely detailed engravings of Ebenezer Landells. Mrs Howitt sought to introduce the leavening agents of charm and humour to strict cautionary preachments, and because of this the dialogue between the wily, flattering spider and the cautious but gullible fly has been a timeless nursery favourite.

The Howitts pressed for reforms within the Society of Friends and, growing less and less content with its restrictions, eventually withdrew.

THE SPIDER AND THE FLY

AN APOLOGUE

A NEW VERSION OF AN OLD STORY

"Will you walk into my parlour?" said the Spider to the Fly,
" 'Tis the prettiest little parlour that ever you did spy;
The way into my parlour is up a winding stair,
And I've a many curious thing to shew when you are there."
"Oh no, no," said the little Fly, "to ask me is in vain,
For who goes up your winding stair can ne'er come down again."

"I'm sure you must be weary, dear, with soaring up so high;
Will you rest upon my little bed?" said the Spider to the Fly.
"There are pretty curtains drawn around; the sheets are fine and thin,
And if you like to rest awhile, I'll snugly tuck you in!"
"Oh no, no," said the little Fly, "for I've often heard it said,
They never, never wake again, who sleep upon your bed!"

Said the cunning Spider to the Fly, "Dear friend what can I do,
To prove the warm affection I've always felt for you?
I have within my pantry, good store of all that's nice;
I'm sure you're very welcome—will you please to take a slice?"
"Oh no, no," said the little Fly, "kind sir, that cannot be,
I've heard what's in your pantry, and I do not wish to see!"

"Sweet creature!" said the Spider, "you're witty and you're wise,
How handsome are your gauzy wings, how brilliant are your eyes!
I've a little looking-glass upon my parlour shelf,
If you'll step in one moment, dear, you shall behold yourself."
"I thank you, gentle sir," she said, "for what you're pleased to say,
And bidding you good morning now, I'll call another day."

The Spider turned him round about, and went into his den,
For well he knew the silly Fly would soon come back again:
So he wove a subtle web, in a little corner sly,
And set his table ready, to dine upon the Fly.
Then he came out to his door again, and merrily did sing,
"Come hither, hither, pretty Fly, with the pearl and silver wing;
Your robes are green and purple—there's a crest upon your head;
Your eyes are like the diamond bright, but mine are dull as lead!"

Alas, alas! how very soon this silly little Fly,
Hearing his wily, flattering words, came slowly flitting by;
With buzzing wings she hung aloft, then near and nearer drew,
Thinking only of her brilliant eyes, and green and purple hue—
Thinking only of her crested head—poor foolish thing! At last,
Up jumped the cunning Spider, and fiercely held her fast.
He dragged her up his winding stair, into his dismal den,
Within his little parlour—but she ne'er came out again!

And now dear little children, who may this story read,
To idle, silly flattering words, I pray you ne'er give heed:
Unto an evil counsellor, close heart and ear and eye,
And take a lesson from this tale, of the Spider and the Fly.

CATHERINE SINCLAIR (1800-1864)
From *Holiday House: A Series of Tales* (1839)

These are stories about the extremely lively Graham children, Laura and Harry, who live with their grandmother, Lady Harriet, a fond Uncle David, and a demanding nurse called Crabtree, whose sternness is usually modified by avuncular indulgence and the calm wisdom of Lady Harriet. As the children grow older and the book nears its end, the madcap tenor of domestic adventures lessens. In fact *Holiday House* closes with the most sobering of all experiences. Laura and Harry, along with Crabtree and their invalid father, gather round the deathbed of their older brother, Frank, a fatally wounded midshipman.

At the time of Uncle David's fairy story, reproduced below, high seriousness and pathos of this order have not yet overtaken the narrative of *Holiday House*. Master No-book, Giant Snap 'em up, and Fairy Teach-all draw on the well-established Newbery tradition of personified abstractions like Graspall, Gripe, and Meanwell—though Sinclair's characters are exaggerated. This "nonsensical story about giants and fairies" transmits Uncle David's lesson about the importance of reading books with absolute clarity. It is convincing and somehow reassuring that the younger Grahams do not convert immediately to his cause.

CHAPTER IX
UNCLE DAVID'S NONSENSICAL STORY
ABOUT GIANTS AND FAIRIES

"Pie-crust and pastry-crust, that was the wall;
The windows were made of black-puddings and white,
And slated with pancakes—you ne'er saw the like!"

In the days of yore, children were not all such clever, good sensible people as they are now! Lessons were then considered rather a plague—sugar-plums were still in demand—holidays continued yet in fashion—and toys were not then made to teach mathematics, nor story-books to give instruction in chemistry and navigation. These were very strange times, and there existed at that period, a very idle, greedy, naughty boy, such as we never hear of in the present day. His papa and mama were—no matter who,—and he lived, no matter where. His name was Master No-book, and he seemed to think his eyes were made for nothing but to stare out of the windows, and his mouth for no other purpose but to eat. This young gentleman hated lessons like mustard, both of which brought tears into his eyes, and during school-hours, he sat gazing at his books, pretending to be busy, while his mind wandered away to wish impatiently for dinner, and to consider where he could get the nicest pies, pastry, ices, and jellies, while he smacked his lips at the very thoughts of them. I think he must have been first cousin to Peter Grey, but that is not perfectly certain.

Whenever Master No-book spoke, it was always to ask for something, and you might continually hear him say, in a whining tone of voice, "Papa! may I take this piece of cake? Aunt Sarah! will you give me an apple? Mama! do send me the whole of that plum-pudding!" Indeed, very frequently when he did not get permission to gormandize, this naughty glutton helped himself without leave. Even his dreams were like his waking hours, for he had often a horrible nightmare about lessons, thinking he was smothered with Greek Lexicons, or pelted out of the school with a shower of English Grammars, while one night he fancied himself sitting down to devour an enormous plum-cake, and that all on a sudden it became transformed into a Latin Dictionary!

One afternoon, Master No-book, having played truant all day from school, was lolling on his mama's best sofa in the drawing-room, with his leather boots tucked up on the satin cushions, and nothing to do, but to suck a few oranges, and nothing to think of but how much sugar to put upon them, when suddenly an event took place which filled him with astonishment.

A sound of soft music stole into the room, becoming louder and louder the longer he listened, till at length, in a few moments afterwards, a large hole burst open in the wall of his room, and there stepped into his presence two magnificent fairies, just arrived from their castles in the air, to pay him a visit. They had travelled all the way on purpose to have some conversation with Master No-book, and immediately introduced themselves in a very ceremonious manner.

The fairy Do-nothing was gorgeously dressed with a wreath of flaming gas round her head, a robe of gold tissue, a necklace of rubies, and a bouquet in her hand, of glittering diamonds. Her cheeks were rouged to the very eyes,—her teeth were set in gold, and her hair was of a most brilliant purple; in short, so fine and fashionable-looking a fairy never was seen in a drawing-room before.

The fairy Teach-all, who followed next, was simply dressed in white muslin, with bunches of natural flowers in her light brown hair, and she carried in her hand a few neat small books, which Master No-book looked at with a shudder of aversion.

The two fairies now informed him, that they very often invited large parties of children to spend some time at their palaces, but as they lived in quite an opposite direction, it was necessary for their young guests to choose which it would be best to visit first; therefore now they had come to inquire of Master No-book, whom he thought it would be most agreeable to accompany on the present occasion.

"In my house," said the fairy Teach-all, speaking with a very sweet smile, and a soft, pleasing voice, "you shall be taught to find pleasure in every sort of exertion, for I delight in activity and diligence. My young friends rise at seven every morning, and amuse themselves with working in a beautiful garden of flowers,—rearing whatever fruit they wish to eat,—visiting among the poor,—associating pleasantly together,—studying the arts and sciences,—and learning to know the world in which they live, and to fulfil the purposes for which they have been brought into it. In short, all our amusements tend to some useful object, either for our own improvement or the good of others, and you will grow wiser, better, and happier every day you remain in the Palace of Knowledge."

"But in Castle Needless, where I live," interrupted the fairy Do-nothing, rudely pushing her companion aside, with an angry contemptuous look, "we never think of exerting ourselves for anything. You may put your head in your pocket, and your hands in your sides as long as you choose to stay. No one is ever even asked a question, that he may be spared the trouble of answering. We lead the most fashionable life imaginable, for nobody speaks to anybody! Each of my visitors is quite an exclusive, and sits with his back to as many of the company as possible, in the most comfortable arm-chair that can be contrived. There, if you are only so good as to take the trouble of wishing for anything, it is yours, without even turning an eye round to look where it comes from. Dresses are provided of the most magnificent kind, which go on of themselves, without your having the smallest annoyance with either buttons or strings,—games which you can play without an effort of thought,—and dishes dressed by a French cook, smoking hot under your nose, from morning till night,—while any rain we have, is either made of cherry brandy, lemonade, or lavender water,—and in winter it generally snows iced-punch for an hour during the forenoon."

Nobody need be told which fairy Master No-book preferred; and quite charmed at his own good fortune in receiving so agreeable an invitation, he eagerly gave his hand to the splendid new acquaintance who promised him so much pleasure and ease, and gladly proceeded, in a carriage lined with velvet, stuffed with downy pillows, and drawn by milk-white swans, to that magnificent residence Castle Needless, which was lighted by a thousand windows during the day, and by a million of lamps every night.

Here Master No-book enjoyed a constant holiday and a constant feast, while a beautiful lady covered with jewels, was ready to tell him stories from morning till night, and servants waited to pick up his playthings if they fell, or to draw out his purse or his pocket-handkerchief when he wished to use them.

Thus Master No-book lay dozing for hours and days on rich embroidered cushions, never stirring from his place, but admiring the view of trees covered with the richest burned almonds, grottoes of sugar-candy, a jet d'eau of champagne, a wide sea which tasted of sugar instead of salt, and a bright clear pond, filled with gold-fish, that let themselves be caught whenever he pleased. Nothing could be more complete, and yet, very strange to say, Master No-book did not seem particularly happy! This appears exceedingly unreasonable, when so much trouble was taken to please him; but the truth is, that every day he became more fretful and peevish. No sweet-meats were worth the trouble of eating, nothing was pleasant to play at, and in the end he wished it were possible to sleep all day, as well as all night.

Not a hundred miles from the fairy Do-nothing's palace, there lived a most cruel monster called the giant Snap-'em-up, who looked, when he stood up, like the tall steeple of a great church, raising his head so high, that he could peep over the loftiest mountains, and was obliged to climb up a ladder to comb his own hair.

Every morning regularly, this prodigiously great giant walked round the world before breakfast for an appetite, after which, he made tea in a large lake, used the sea as a slop-basin, and boiled his kettle on Mount Vesuvius. He lived in great style, and his dinners were most magnificent, consisting very often of an elephant roasted whole, ostrich patties, a tiger smothered in onions, stewed lions, and whale soup; but for a side-dish his greatest favourite consisted of little boys, as fat as possible, fried in crumbs of bread, with plenty of pepper and salt.

No children were so well fed, or in such good condition for eating as those in the fairy Do-nothing's garden, who was a very particular friend of the giant Snap-'em-up's, and who sometimes laughingly said she would give him a license, and call her own garden his "preserve," because she allowed him to help himself, whenever he pleased, to as many of her visitors as he chose, without taking the trouble even to count them, and in return for such extreme civility, the giant very frequently invited her to dinner.

Snap-'em-up's favourite sport was, to see how many brace of little boys he could bag in a morning; so in passing along the streets, he peeped into all the drawing-rooms without having occasion to get upon tiptoe, and picked up every young gentleman who was idly looking out of the windows, and even a few occasionally who were playing truant from school, but busy children seemed always somehow quite out of his reach.

One day, when Master No-book felt even more lazy, more idle, and more miserable than ever, he lay beside a perfect mountain of toys and cakes, wondering what to wish for next, and hating the very sight of everything and everybody. At last he gave so loud a yawn of weariness and disgust, that his jaw very nearly fell out of joint, and then he sighed so deeply, that the giant Snap-'em-up heard the sound as he passed along the road after breakfast, and instantly stepped into the garden, with his glass at his eye, to see what was the matter. Immediately on observing a large, fat, over-grown boy, as round as a dumpling, lying on a bed of roses, he gave a cry of delight, followed by a gigantic peal of laughter, which was heard three miles off, and picking up Master No-book between his finger and his thumb, with a pinch that very nearly broke his ribs, he carried him rapidly towards his own castle, while the fairy Do-nothing laughingly shook her head as he passed, saying, "That little man does me great credit!—he has only been fed for a week, and is as fat already as a prize ox! What a dainty morsel he will be! When do you dine to-day, in case I should have time to look in upon you?"

On reaching home, the giant immediately hung up Master No-book by the hair of his head, on a prodigious hook in the larder, having first taken some large lumps of nasty suet, forcing them down his throat to make him become still fatter, and then stirring the fire, that he might be almost melted with heat, to make his liver grow larger. On a shelf quite near, Master No-book perceived the dead bodies of six other boys, whom he remembered to have seen fattening in the fair Do-nothing's garden, while he recollected how some of them had rejoiced at thoughts of leading a long, useless, idle life, with no one to please but themselves.

The enormous cook now seized hold of Master No-book, brandishing her knife, with an aspect of horrible determination, intending to kill him, while he took the trouble of screaming and kicking in the most desperate manner, when the giant turned gravely round and said, that as pigs were considered a much greater dainty when whipped to death than killed in any other way, he meant to see whether children might not be improved by it also; therefore she might leave that great hog of a boy till he had time to try the experiment, especially as his own appetite would be improved by the exercise. This was a dreadful prospect for the unhappy prisoner; but meantime it prolonged his life a few hours, as he was immediately hung up again in the larder, and left to himself. There, in torture of mind and body,—like a fish upon a hook, the wretched boy began at last to reflect seriously upon his former ways, and to consider what a happy home he might have had, if he could only have been satisfied with business and pleasure succeeding each other, like day and night, while lessons might have come in, as a pleasant sauce to his play-hours, and his play-hours as a sauce to his lessons.

In the midst of many reflections, which were all very sensible, though rather too late, Master No-book's attention became attracted by the sound of many voices laughing, talking, and singing, which caused him to turn his eyes in a new direction, when, for the first time, he observed that the fairy Teach-all's garden lay upon a beautiful sloping bank not far off. There a crowd of merry, noisy, rosy-cheeked boys, were busily employed, and seemed happier than the day was long; while poor Master No-book watched them during his own miserable hours, envying the enjoyment with which they raked the flower borders, gathered the fruit, carried baskets of vegetables to the poor, worked with carpenter's tools, drew pictures, shot with bows and arrows, played at cricket, and then sat in the sunny arbours learning their tasks, or talking agreeably together, till at length, a dinner-bell having been rung, the whole party sat merrily down with hearty appetites, and cheerful good-humour, to an entertainment of plain roast meat and pudding, where the fairy Teach-all presided herself, and helped her guests moderately, to as much as was good for each.

Large tears rolled down the cheeks of Master No-book while watching this scene; and remembering that if he had known what was best for him, he might have been as happy as the happiest of these excellent boys, instead of suffering ennui and weariness, as he had done at the fairy Do-nothing's, ending in a miserable death; but his attention was soon after most alarmingly roused by hearing the giant Snap-'em-up again in conversation with his cook, who said, that if he wished for a good large dish of scolloped children at dinner, it would be necessary to catch a few more, as those he had already provided would scarcely be a mouthful.

As the giant kept very fashionable hours, and always waited dinner for himself till nine o'clock, there was still plenty of time; so, with a loud grumble about the trouble, he seized a large basket in his hand, and set off at a rapid pace towards the fairy Teach-all's garden. It was very seldom that Snap-'em-up ventured to think of foraging in this direction, as he had never once succeeded in carrying off a single captive from the enclosure, it was so well fortified and so bravely defended; but on this occasion, being desperately hungry, he felt as bold as a lion, and walked, with outstretched hands, straight towards the fairy Teach-all's dinner-table, taking such prodigious strides, that he seemed almost as if he would trample on himself.

A cry of consternation arose the instant this tremendous giant appeared; and as usual on such occasions, when he had made the same attempt before, a dreadful battle took place. Fifty active little boys bravely flew upon the enemy, armed with their dinner knives, and looked like a nest of hornets, stinging him in every direction, till he roared with pain, and would have run away, but the fairy Teach-all, seeing his intention, rushed forward with the carving knife, and brandishing it high over her head, she most courageously stabbed him to the heart!

If a great mountain had fallen to the earth, it would have seemed like nothing in comparison of the giant Snap-'em-up, who crushed two or three houses to powder beneath him, and upset several fine monuments that were to have made people remembered for ever; but all this would have seemed scarcely worth mentioning, had it not been for a still greater event which occurred on the occasion, no less than the death of the fairy Do-nothing, who had been indolently looking on at this great battle, without taking the trouble to interfere, or even to care who was victorious, but being also lazy about running away, when the giant fell, his sword came with so violent a stroke on her head, that she instantly expired.

Thus, luckily for the whole world, the fairy Teach-all got possession of immense property, which she proceeded without delay to make the best use of in her power.

In the first place, however, she lost no time in liberating Master No-book from his hook in the larder, and gave him a lecture on activity, moderation, and good conduct, which he never afterwards forgot; and it was astonishing to see the change that took place immediately in his whole thoughts and actions. From this very hour, Master No-book became the most diligent, active, happy boy in the fairy Teach-all's garden; and on returning home a month afterwards, he astonished all the masters at school by his extraordinary reformation. The most difficult lessons were a pleasure to him,—he scarcely ever stirred without a book in his hand,—never lay on a sofa again,—would scarcely even sit on a chair with a back to it, but preferred a three-legged stool,—detested holidays,—never thought any exertion a trouble,—preferred climbing over the top of a hill to creeping round the bottom,—always ate the plainest food in very small quantities,—joined a Temperance Society!—and never tasted a morsel till he had worked very hard and got an appetite.

Not long after this, an old uncle, who had formerly been ashamed of Master No-book's indolence and gluttony, became so pleased at the wonderful change, that, on his death, he left him a magnificent estate, desiring that he should take his name; therefore, instead of being any longer one of the No-book family, he is now called Sir Timothy Bluestocking,—a pattern to the whole country round, for the good he does to every one, and especially for his extraordinary activity, appearing as if he could do twenty things at once. Though generally very good natured and agreeable, Sir Timothy is occasionally observed in a violent passion, laying about him with his walking-stick in the most terrific manner, and beating little boys within an inch of their lives; but on inquiry, it invariably appears that he has found them out to be lazy, idle, or greedy, for all the industrious boys in the parish are sent to get employment from him, while he assures them that they are far happier breaking stones on the road, than if they were sitting idly in a drawingroom with nothing to do. Sir Timothy cares very little for poetry in general; but the following are his favourite verses, which he has placed over the chimney-piece at a school that he built for the poor, and every scholar is obliged, the very day he begins his education, to learn them:—

> Some people complain they have nothing to do,
> And time passes slowly away;
>
> They saunter about with no object in view,
> And long for the end of the day.
>
> In vain are the trifles and toys they desire,
> For nothing they truly enjoy;
> Of trifles, and toys, and amusements they tire,
> For want of some useful employ.
>
> Although for transgression the ground was accursed,
> Yet gratefully man must allow,
> 'Twas really a blessing which doom'd him at first,
> To live by the sweat of his brow.

ELIZA LEE FOLLEN (1787-1860)
From *New Nursery Songs for all Good Children* (1843)

Mrs Follen was a New Englander dedicated to the cause of preserving traditional nursery rhymes and using them as models for her own ditties for children. In her preface to *Little Songs* (1856), she observed: "It has been my object . . . to endeavour to catch something of the good-humoured pleasantry, the musical nonsense which make Mother Goose so attractive to all ages." It is to Mrs Follen's credit that in her collection of mediocre verse one poem has entered oral literature: "Three Little Kittens". As in the exploits of Mrs Trimmer's young Redbreasts, Mrs Follen's cat family experiences both rewards and punishments. In contrast to the sentimentally charged narrative of Mrs Trimmer, however, the tidy marching rhythm with which the kittens' deeds are related evokes the reader's smiles rather than emotional involvement.

THREE LITTLE KITTENS

Three little kittens they lost their mittens,
    And they began to cry,
Oh, mother dear, we sadly fear
    Our mittens we have lost.
What! lost your mittens, you naughty kittens!
    Then you shall have no pie.
Mee-ow, mee-ow, mee-ow.
    No, you shall have no pie.

The three little kittens they found their mittens,
    And they began to cry,
Oh, mother dear, see here, see here,
    Our mittens we have found!
Put on your mittens, you silly kittens,
    And you shall have some pie.
Purr-r, purr-r, purr-r.
    Oh, let us have some pie.

The three little kittens put on their mittens,
    And soon ate up the pie;
Oh, mother dear, we greatly fear
    Our mittens we have soiled.
What! soiled your mittens, you naughty kittens!
    Then they began to sigh.
    Mee-ow, mee-ow, mee-ow.
    Then they began to sigh.

The three little kittens they washed their mittens,
    And hung them out to dry;
Oh! mother dear, do you not hear,
    Our mittens we have washed!
What! washed your mittens, then you're good kittens,
    But I smell a rat close by.
    Mee-ow, mee-ow, mee-ow.
    We smell a rat close by.

THE REVEREND FRANCIS EDWARD PAGET (1806-1882)
From *The Hope of the Katzekopfs: A Fairy Tale* (1844)

Under the pseudonym of "William Churne, of Staffordshire", the rector of Elford wrote this tale while—in addition to his pastoral duties—he was also editing *The Juvenile Englishman's Library*. Paget had very fixed views about the damage done in writing down to children. In the preface to the second series of *Tales of Village Children* (1847), he said: "Children are as capable of understanding deep things as adults, in some respects, more so." In *The Hope of the Katzekopfs* an only son is born to doting parents, who foolishly indulge his every whim. Paget's allegorical narrative shows that this wilful boy is capable of reforming and disciplining himself—with magical help. Though filled with fantastic characters and events, and entertainingly recounted, this fairy tale has a very practical theme: the formation of character.

From Chapter 1: THE HEIR AND MANY FRIENDS

So when her Majesty was tired of crying, she ceased: and, in the course of the afternoon, wrote a note to her "dearest Lady Abracadabra," expressing the intensity of her satisfaction at the fact that her sweet baby had secured the protection of such an amiable and powerful patroness.

Then she sent for the Baroness Yellowlily, and told her that, as she had reason to fear that a malicious old Fairy was disposed to do the child a mischief, and, perhaps, carry him off altogether, she must immediately anoint him all over with an unguent, made of three black spiders, the gall of a brindled cat, the fat of a white hen, and the blood of a screech owl; and that his cradle must be watched night and day until after the christening. It was lucky for Queen Ninnilinda that the Lady Abracadabra wished nothing but well to the little prince, and knew nothing of these proceedings.

It is not necessary to fatigue the reader with the details of the fête, which was given a few weeks after the events which have just been recorded. There were firing of cannon, and ringing of bells, and beating of drums, and blowing of trumpets. And there were long processions of high officers of state, and nobles, and foreign ambassadors, dressed in gorgeous robes, and glittering with gold and jewels. And there was the arrival of the Fairy sponsor, in a coach made of a single pearl, and drawn by a matchless pair of white cockatrices from the mountains of Samarcand; and there was the flight of birds of Paradise that accompanied her, each bearing round its neck a chain of gold and diamonds, from which depended a casket, containing some costly offering for the Hope of the House of Katzekopf. And there was the Lady Abracadabra herself, no longer stamping the floor with anger, and wearing that frightful, unbecoming, ill-tempered dress of yellow and black, but arrayed in the most delicate fabrics of the fairy-loom, and bearing upon her shoulders a mantle of gossamer, spangled all over with dew-drops, sparkling with the colours of a hundred rainbows. No look of age or ill-nature had she. The refulgence of her veil had obliterated her wrinkles, and as she passed along the gallery of the palace, side by side with the Archduchess of Klopsteinhesseschloffengrozen, even Queen Ninnilinda herself was forced to confess that she looked very amiable, that her manners were exceedingly good, and that, on the whole, she was a captivating person,—when she chose it.

When the child was to be named, the Queen gave a supplicatory glance at her kinswoman, and gently whispered in an appealing tone, "Have you *really* any objection to the charming name originally proposed? Conrad-Adalbert-Willibald. . . ."

But the Lady Abracadabra cut the catalogue short, with saying the word "Eigenwillig" in so decided a tone, that the prince was named Eigenwillig directly, and there was an end of the matter.

And then followed the royal banquet, and then a ball, and then the town was illuminated, and at midnight the fête terminated with a most magnificent display of fireworks.

Just, however, before the amusements of the evening were concluded, the old Fairy called her niece and the King into the royal closet, and thus addressed them: "Kinsmen mine," said she, "I have shewn you this day that I bear a most hearty good-will both to you and your's; and therefore if ye be wise,—which I think ye are not—you will listen to what I now say to you. You have got a fair son: for that you must thank Providence; and your son has got the fairest gifts that were to be found in all Fairy-land: for them you must thank me. But if, in spite of these gifts, your son turns out a wilful, disagreeable, selfish monkey, for that you will have to thank yourselves. Queen Ninnilinda, if ever I saw a mother that was likely to spoil a child, you are that person. King Katzekopf, if ever I saw a father who was likely to let his son lead him by the nose, you are that man. But attend to what I say," continued the Fairy, with a look of great severity, "I don't intend to have my godchild a selfish little brat, who shall be a bad man, and a bad king, and a bad son, whom everybody shall dislike, and whose faults shall be all attributed to his having a Fairy godmother. No: I have named the child according to his natural temper. I have called him Eigenwillig, because his disposition is to be self-willed. And of this it is fit that you should be reminded continually, even by his name, in order that you may discipline his mind, and make him the reverse of what he is now called. Poor child! he has everything around him to make him selfish. Let it be the object of your life, to make him unselfish. This is my injunction, and remember I have both the will and the power to enforce it. I am his godmother, and I am a Fairy besides, so I have a right to insist. And mark my words, I shall do *my* duty by the prince, let who will neglect their's. I shall watch over him night and day, and shall be among you when least you expect me. If you manage him properly, you may expect my help; if you shew yourselves unfit for the charge, I shall take the reins of discipline into my own hands; and if you then resist me . . . but I will not allow myself to imagine that such infatuation and insanity were possible. Sweet niece, I must take my leave. May I trouble your Majesty to open the window. Kiss my godchild for me. Good night."

As the Lady Abracadabra took her leave, there was a rustling of wings in the air, the chariot of pearl, with its attendant cockatrices, appeared on a level with the window: the Fairy sprung into her seat, and, preceded by a cloud of lantern flies, each insect sparkling with a different coloured flame, blue, or crimson, or violet, or green, and followed by myriads of elves, each crowned with asteroids of lambent light, she wended on her way to Fairy-land, her track through the sky being marked by a long train of sparks, whose dazzling brilliancy waxed fainter and fainter as she receded from earth, till it mingled with, and became lost in the pallid hues of the Milky Way.

It is needless to say that Queen Ninnilinda did not relish the parting admonitions of her Fairy kinswoman. First, she (being a Queen) did not like to submit to dictation; next, she persuaded herself that she had a full right to do as she pleased, and to spoil her own child as much as she liked; lastly, being rather timid, she felt very uncomfortable at the notion of being watched by a Fairy, and still more so at the possibility of incurring that Fairy's vengeance. So, as usual, she vented all her anger on her husband, and then went to bed and sobbed herself to sleep. King Katzekopf was not easily perturbed; and the chronicles of the kingdom assure us that he slept as well as usual on the night after the fête; but upon awaking next morning he felt the necessity of something being done, and therefore called together once more his trusty councillors, who, after much grave discussion, determined that the best method of securing the further favour of the Lady Abracadabra would be, by immediately appointing proper instructors for the royal infant.

Accordingly a commission was issued to inquire who would be the proper persons to undertake so responsible an office, and after a year and a half of diligent investigation, it was decided that the three cleverest women in the kingdom should be charged with the prince's education until such time as he should exchange his petticoats for jacket and trousers. So the Lady Brigida was appointed to teach him how to feed himself, and to instruct him in *Belles Lettres*, and the—ologies: the Lady Frigida was to make him an adept in prudence and etiquette: while the Lady Rigida was directed to enlighten his mind on the science of political economy, and to teach him the art of governing the country.

But alas! nobody thought of appointing a preceptress, who should instruct him in the art of governing *himself*.

Meanwhile, Queen Ninnilinda, finding that her husband had become highly popular in consequence of the pains he was taking to have his heir properly educated, determined that she would do something which should set her own character in a favourable light as a wise and discreet mother. She, therefore, after much careful consideration, drew up the following rules for the nursery, which were immediately printed in an Extraordinary Gazette, and which were received with so much applause, that almost all the ladies in the kingdom adopted them immediately in their own families, and have, in fact, been guided by them ever since, even though they have not followed Queen Ninnilinda's plan of having them framed and glazed.

RULES FOR THE NURSERY

1. The Prince Eigenwillig is never to be contradicted; for contradiction is depressing to the spirits.

2. His Royal Highness is to have everything he cries for; else he will grow peevish and discontented.

3. He is to be allowed to eat and drink when, what, and as much as he pleases; hunger being a call of nature, and whatever nature dictates is natural.

4. His Royal Highness is to be dissuaded from speaking to any one below the rank of Baron; as it is highly desirable that he should acquire a proper pride.

5. It is to be impressed on the Prince's mind continually that he is an object of the first consequence, and that his first duty is to take good care of himself.

Such being the plan laid down for Prince Eigenwillig's education, it is not to be wondered at that, by the time he was two years old, he had a very fair notion of the drift of his mother's rules, and that they found great favour in his eyes; insomuch that at three, when the Ladies Brigida, Frigida, and Rigida commenced the task of tuition, he contrived to inspire them with the notion that their office, for the present, at least, was likely to be a sinecure. He even resisted the efforts which the Lady Brigida made to induce him to feed himself with a fork and a spoon, and adhered upon principle to the use of his fingers, lest, by yielding the point, he should seem to allow himself to be contradicted.

At four years old the precocity of his talents had greatly developed themselves. He had mingled mustard with the Lady Frigida's chocolate; he had pulled the chair from under his father, just as the King was about to sit down, whereby his Majesty got a tumble, and the Prince got his ears boxed; he had killed nurse Yellowlily's cockatoo by endeavouring to ascertain whether it was as fond of stewed mushrooms as he was himself, and he had even gone the length of singing in her presence, and of course in allusion to her bereavement,

> "Dame what made your ducks to die?
> Ducks to die? ducks to die? ducks to die?
> Eating o' polly-wigs! Eating o' polly-wigs."

But if truth must be told, the prince had acquired by this time many worse habits than that of mischief. And these had their origin in his being permitted to have his own way in everything. For, indeed, it might be said, that this spoilt child was the person who ruled the entire kingdom. The prince ruled his nurse, and his three instructresses; they ruled the Queen; the Queen ruled the King; the King ruled his Ministers; and the Ministers ruled the country.

O Lady Abracadabra, Lady Abracadabra, how could you allow things to come to such a pass? You must have known right well that Queen Ninnilinda was very silly; and that King Katzekopf was one of those folks who are too indolent to exert themselves about anything which is likely to be troublesome or unpleasant; and you must have been quite sure that the nurses and governesses were all going the wrong way to work; you must have foreseen that at the end of four years of misman-agement the poor child would be a torment to himself and to everybody else. Why did you not interfere?

This is a hard question to answer; but perhaps the Lady Abracadabra's object was to convince both parties of this fact by actual experience, as being aware that in such experience lay the best hope of a remedy.

From Chapter VI: EXPERIMENTS ON THE HEIR

"My son, none ever mastered that odious sprite, but he received as-sistance from me. It is only by the aid of DISCIPLINE that any one can hope to conquer SELF!"

Then the Prince knew the old man's name, and he ceased to wonder why he had been so unwilling, on a former occasion, to make it known; for it has a stern, repulsive sound in it, which is sure to disgust the thoughtless and the pleasure-seeking.

"Father," said the Prince, "if thy name be Discipline, then will I be thy Disciple. Had I known thee sooner, from what faults and errors should I have been saved! If thou hadst but taken a part in the education of my earliest years, how different should I now be from what, alas! I am."

"Prince," replied his venerable friend, "heretofore you have been greatly to be pitied, for you have deserved as well as possessed the name of Self-willed. But sharp trials have brought you to your senses, and I trust that you have already laid the foundations of a character in which shall be united all the best qualities of your race. But you have still an arduous task before you, and your first and most pressing duty is, to effect the entire subjugation of that hateful sprite whom I still see cling-ing to you."

"Father," said the Prince, "will you now be my companion, and will you advise and help me to master Selbst?"

"That will I gladly, my child," answered Discipline, and forthwith they wended on their way.

Steep, and rugged, and narrow was the route; now among tangled thickets of thorns and briers, now over parched and arid sands, now in a waste and howling wilderness. Often, when the Prince was most hungry and thirsty, did Discipline enjoin him to go without food or drink, or, just as he was about to partake of them, to give them to some wayfarer on the road. Often, when most weary, was he advised to pass the night in watching. Often when he desired to go one way, was he recommended to pursue another.

Now all this was done in order to master Selbst, and make him glad to relax his hold, and quit a companion who would give him nothing to eat, and who led him through thorns and briers for the purpose of wounding and hurting him.

And all this Prince Eigenwillig continued to do day after day, and still he found the wisdom of those oft repeated sayings of his aged companion: "Learn to live hardly; Deny yourself in things lawful; Love not comforts; Think of others first, and of yourself last." And thus, when they drew near to their journey's end, and the palace of the Lady Abracadabra was in sight, the sprite Selbst, who had exercised such tyranny over the little boy, was no longer to be seen. For some time,—much longer than the sanguine Prince had expected,—for it was when Discipline had been for some time his companion, he continued to feel inconvenience from the presence of the malicious elf. But in due time, *starving* and *contradiction* did their promised work. The evil creature dwindled, and withered, and shrank, till at length, from sheer weakness and exhaustion, he relaxed his hold round the Prince's throat, and fell to the ground.

The Prince himself was not aware of the precise moment when this event took place, and Discipline did not think good to make him acquainted with it immediately. And even when he made the circumstance known, he accompanied it with a word of caution.

"Prince," said he, "you are released from the grasp of your adversary. He has fallen to the ground, mastered by your perseverance and resolution. But I intreat you bear this in mind, that, though invisible, he still runs at your side; and if ever you give him opportunity or encouragement, he will yet again be your master!"

They had now reached the palace of the Lady Abracadabra, and as they stood before its portals, the Fairy godmother came out to receive them. Once more she was radiant with smiles; the flame-coloured petticoat had faded into the palest primrose, and instead of seeming haggard and wrinkled, her complexion had that dazzling lustre which is peculiar to Fairy-land. She threw her arms round her Godson and embraced him with tenderness.

"I have been a secret witness," she said, "of all your trials and struggles. I have watched your endeavours to rid yourself of your selfish, and self-willed habits, and being satisfied of the pains you have taken, and are taking with yourself, I am not afraid to restore you to your family. The Court of King Katzekopf is not a wholesome atmosphere for you; but every place has its trials, and I am satisfied that you will profit by your past experience."

"Lady," replied the Prince, "the time has been that I have feared you, and even hated you; but I now know how much I owe to you. You have taught me that the secret of happiness is in myself, and that I am most happy when I am showing most consideration to others. I hope, dear Lady, that now you are about to send me home, you will not cease to befriend me, and that this venerable man may accompany me to the upper world."

"Follow the rules he has given you here, and you will not need his bodily presence. They that dwell in kings' houses, and the rich, and the indolent, and the lovers of comforts, bear a deadly hatred to him, and therefore he is not wont to expose himself to their insults. You, however, he has adopted as one of his children, and so long as you do not forget him, he will not forget you. For myself you may count on my protection. If I loved you because I saw the elements of good in you, when I brought you into this country seven years ago, how much more do I love you now, when I have witnessed your endeavours to become master of yourself."

"*Seven years ago!*" These were almost the only words in the sentence which the Prince heard. Why, the time he had spent in Fairy-land seemed hardly as many days. But so it was; and when he came to reflect, he remembered to have heard, over and over again, that nobody who enters Fairy-land is allowed to return under seven years.

So it was; and when he arrived at his father's court (where he found himself already expected; for, little as Queen Ninnilinda deserved it, the Lady Abracadabra had never kept her in ignorance about her son's place of abode, and general well-doing)—when he arrived at his father's court, he saw changes which soon satisfied him that a long period had elapsed since he had quitted it. King Katzekopf had become quite childish, and Queen Ninnilinda was so occupied with her lap-dogs and parrots, that, though very glad to see her son, she was not likely to spoil him again. The Baroness Yellowlily was dead, and the Ladies Rigida, Frigida and Brigida had quitted the court for scenes more congenial to their taste.

But the greatest surprise of all to Prince Eigenwillig, was to hear himself spoken to as if he were almost a young man. It seemed but the other day, since he was a little naughty child, and now grave counsellors were discussing the propriety of appointing him Regent of the kingdom, and easing poor old King Katzekopf's shoulders from the burden and cares of state.

Prince Eigenwillig had, however, too much distrust of himself, and felt the responsibilities of the position too deeply to desire such a charge; but when he saw that the welfare of the nation in a great measure depended on it, and found that the Lady Abracadabra heartily approved of it, he consented to become Regent.

And his first act, when he assumed the office, was to write an affectionate letter to Witikind, intreating him to forgive him his past misconduct, and come and give him his assistance in ruling the country.

Count Rudolf had been dead some years, and Witikind was in possession of his father's estates, and he found such abundant scope for the best energies of his mind in contributing to the welfare of his neighbours and vassals, that he could not (especially after his past experience) make up his mind to quit his beloved Taubennest for a court. So he declined the Prince's offer of place and power; but was, through life, his sound adviser and faithful friend.

As for the Prince, though he could not shake off the *name* of Eigenwillig, he entirely ceased to be the *thing*: in a few years he became king in his father's place; reigned long and happily; ruled his subjects well; his family better still; and himself best of all: so that his name was cherished in his native land long after his bones were mouldering in the grave; and it is mentioned in the Chronicles of Carivaldus of Cologne, that he whose real name was Eigenwillig, and who for some years of his life was called the Hope of the Katzekopfs, is now only remembered by that name which the universal consent of his countrymen assigned him while still living, and that his designation in the annals of Christendom is that of King Katzekopf *the GOOD*.

EDWARD LEAR (1812-1888)
From *The Book of Nonsense* (1846)

The English painter Edward Lear wrote and illustrated these first nonsense limericks for the grandchildren of his early patron, the Earl of Derby. He had already gained some respect for his precisely detailed and coloured ornithological drawings; and since 1837, and the start of his European and Asian travels, he had sketched landscapes and compiled travel journals. He was esteemed by such contemporaries as Queen Victoria, to whom in 1845 he gave drawing lessons, and Tennyson, with whom he kept up a lengthy correspondence. Lear is remembered most often today for his nonsense literature—works he wrote for diversion and amusement. His limericks, songs, alphabets, "botanies", and stories—all marked by his inimitable whimsy and absurd humour—continue to divert young and old readers alike.

There was an Old Man of Coblenz,
The length of whose legs was immense;
He went with one prance, from Turkey to France,
That surprising Old Man of Coblenz.

There was an Old Man of the West,
Who never could get any rest;
So they set him to spin, on his nose and his chin,
Which cured that Old Man of the West.

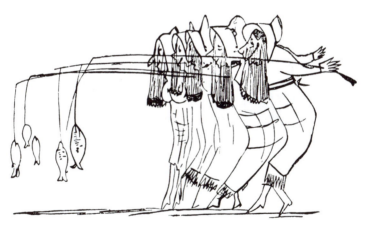

There was an Old Man of Marseilles,
Whose daughters wore bottle-green veils;
They caught several Fish, which they put in a dish,
And sent to their Pa' at Marseilles.

There was an Old Person of Sparta,
Who had twenty-five sons and one daughter;
He fed them on snails, and weighed them in scales,
That wonderful person of Sparta.

There was a young Lady of Tyre,
Who swept the loud chords of a lyre;
At the sound of each sweep, she enraptured the deep,
And enchanted the city of Tyre.

There was a Young Lady of Welling,
Whose praise all the world was a telling;
She played on the harp, and caught several carp,
That accomplished Young Lady of Welling.

(Overleaf)

HEINRICH HOFFMANN (1809-1894)
From *The English Struwwelpeter; or, Pretty Stories and Funny Pictures for Little Children* (1848)

A Frankfurt pediatrician, psychiatrist, and watercolourist, Hoffmann composed and illustrated *Lustige Geschichten und drolige Bilder* (Pretty Stories and Funny Pictures) for his three-year-old son in 1844. He wrote five works for children in all and expressed his preference for *Koenig Nussknacker und der Arme Rheinhold* (King Nutcracker or the Dream of Poor Reinhold). But his reputation among English readers rests firmly on his first book. After friends had convinced him to publish it, the ten stories—in particular the last about Slovenly Peter—became so popular that by its fifth edition in 1847 the title was changed to *Der Struwwelpeter*. English translations in Britain (1848) and America (1850) followed shortly; the book has since been translated into a total of thirty-one languages and has inspired a number of political satires, the most memorable being *Struwwelhitler*. Parents frequently find these exaggerated cautionary tales frightening and disturbing; children, on the other hand, usually warm to their humorous, albeit grisly, caricature of wrong-doing.

SLOVENLY PETER

See Slovenly Peter! Here he stands,
With his dirty hair and hands.
See! his nails are never cut;
They are grim'd as black as soot;
No water for many weeks,
Has been near his cheeks;
And the sloven, I declare,
Not once this year has combed his hair!
Anything to me is sweeter
Than to see shock-headed Peter.

THE DREADFUL STORY OF PAULINE AND THE MATCHES

Mamma and Nurse went out one day,
And left Pauline alone at play;
Around the room she gayly sprung,
Clapp'd her hands, and danced, and sung.
Now, on the table close at hand,
A box of matches chanc'd to stand,
And kind Mamma and Nurse had told her,
That if she touch'd them they would scold
   her;
But Pauline said, "Oh, what a pity!
For, when they burn, it is so pretty;
They crackle so, and spit, and flame;
And Mamma often burns the same.
I'll just light a match or two
As I have often seen my mother do."

When Minz and Maunz, the pussy-cats,
   heard this
They held up their paws and began to hiss.
"Me-ow!" they said, "me-ow, me-o!
You'll burn to death, if you do so,
Your parents have forbidden you, you
   know."

But Pauline would not take advice,
She lit a match, it was so nice!
It crackled so, it burn'd so clear,—
Exactly like the picture here.
She jump'd for joy and ran about,
And was too pleas'd to put it out.

When Minz and Maunz, the little cats,
   saw this,
They said, "Oh, naughty, naughty Miss!"
And stretch'd their claws,
And rais'd their paws;
" 'Tis very, very wrong, you know;
Me-ow, me-o, me-ow, me-o!
You will be burnt if you do so,
Your mother has forbidden you, you
   know."

Now see! oh! see, what a dreadful thing
The fire has caught her apron-string;
Her apron burns, her arms, her hair;
She burns all over, everywhere.

Then how the pussy-cats did mew,
What else, poor pussies, could they do?
They scream'd for help, 'twas all in vain,
So then, they said, "We'll scream again.
Make haste, make haste! me-ow! me-o!
She'll burn to death,—we told her so."

So she was burnt with all her clothes,
And arms and hands, and eyes and nose;
Till she had nothing more to lose
Except her little scarlet shoes;
And nothing else but these was found
Among her ashes on the ground.

And when the good cats sat beside
The smoking ashes, how they cried!
"Me-ow, me-o! Me-ow, me-oo!
What will Mamma and Nursy do?"
Their tears ran down their cheeks so fast,
They made a little pond at last.

THE STORY OF AUGUSTUS WHO WOULD NOT HAVE ANY SOUP

Augustus was a chubby lad;
Fat ruddy cheeks Augustus had;
And everybody saw with joy
The plump and hearty healthy boy.
He ate and drank as he was told,
And never let his soup get cold.
But one day, one cold winter's day,
He threw away the spoon and screamed:
"O take the nasty soup away!
I won't have any soup to-day:
I will not, will not eat my soup!
I will not eat it, no!"

Next day, now look, the picture shows
How lank and lean Augustus grows!
Yet, though he feels so weak and ill,
The naughty fellow cries out still—
"Not any soup for me, I say!
O take the nasty soup away!
I will not, will not eat my soup!
I will not eat it, no!"

The third day comes. O what a sin!
To make himself so pale and thin.
Yet, when the soup is put on table,
He screams, as loud as he is able—
"Not any soup for me, I say!
O take the nasty soup away!
I won't have any soup to-day!"

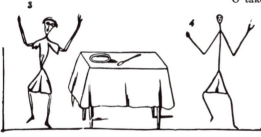

Look at him, now the fourth
day's come!
He scarce outweighs a sugar-plum;
He's like a little bit of thread;
And on the fifth day he was—dead!

BIBLIOGRAPHY

CRITICAL AND HISTORICAL STUDIES

Ariès, Philippe. *Centuries of Childhood: A Social History of Family Life.* Trans. R. Baldick. London: Jonathan Cape, 1962.

Boas, George. *The Cult of Childhood.* London: The Warburg Institute, 1966.

Coveney, Peter. *Poor Monkey: The Child in Literature.* London: Rockliff, 1957.

Darton, F.J.Harvey. *Children's Books in England: Five Centuries of Social Life.* Cambridge: At the University Press, 1932; 1958.

de Mause, Lloyd, ed. *The History of Childhood.* New York: Psychohistory Press, 1974.

Egoff, Sheila. *The Republic of Childhood: A Critical Guide to Canadian Children's Literature in English.* Second Edition. Toronto: Oxford University Press, 1975.

Ellis, Alec. *A History of Children's Reading and Literature.* Oxford: Pergamon Press, 1968.

Field, Mrs E.M. *The Child and His Book: Some Account of the History and Progress of Children's Literature in England.* London: Wells Gardner, Darton & Co., 1892.

Fraser, James H., editor. *Society and Children's Literature.* Boston: David R. Godine, in association with the American Library Association, 1978.

Green, Roger Lancelyn. *Tellers of Tales: Children's Books and their Authors from 1800 to 1968.* London: Kaye & Ward Ltd., 1969.

Hazard, Paul. *Books, Children and Men.* Trans. M. Mitchell. Boston: The Horn Book, 1947.

Hürlimann, Bettina. *Three Centuries of Children's Books in Europe.* Trans. and ed. B.W. Alderson. New York: The World Publishing Company, 1959.

Kiefer, Monica. *American Children Through their Books, 1700-1835.* Philadelphia: University of Pennsylvania Press, 1948.

MacLeod, Anne Scott. *A Moral Tale: Children's Fiction and American Culture, 1820-1860.* Hamden: The Shoe String Press, 1975.

Meigs, Cornelia, A. Eaton, E. Nesbitt, R.G. Viguers. *A Critical History of Children's Literature in English from Earliest Times to the Present.* New York: Macmillan, 1953.

Muir, Percy. *English Children's Books 1600 to 1900.* New York: Frederick A. Praeger, 1954.

Pinchbeck, Ivy and M. Hewitt. *Children in English Society From Tudor Times to the Eighteenth Century.* London: Routledge and Kegan Paul, 1969.

Saxby, H.M. *A History of Australian Children's Literature, 1841-1941.* Sydney: Wentworth Books, 1969.

Smith, James Steel. *A Critical Approach to Children's Literature.* New York: McGraw Hill, 1967.

Thwaite, Mary F. *From Primer to Pleasure in Reading: An Introduction to the History of Children's Books in England from the Invention of Printing to 1914 with an outline of some developments in other countries.* Boston: The Horn Book, 1972.

Townsend, John Rowe. *Written for Children: An Outline of English Children's Literature.* London: Garnet Miller, 1965.

Whalley, Joyce Irene. *Cobwebs to Catch Flies: Illustrated Books for the Nursery and Schoolroom 1700-1900.* London: Elek Books, 1974.

ANTHOLOGIES AND REPRINTS OF EARLY CHILDREN'S LITERATURE

Arnold, Arnold. *Pictures and Stories from Forgotten Children's Books.* New York: Dover Publications, 1969.

Barry, Florence V. *A Century of Children's Books.* London: Methuen, 1922.

Brand, Christiana, ed. *Naughty Children.* London: Victor Gollancz, 1968.

de Vries, Leonard, ed. *Flowers of Delight culled from the Osborne Collection of Early Children's Books: An Agreeable Garland of Prose and Poetry for the instruction and amusement of little masters and misses and their distinguished parents*. London: Dennis Dobson, 1965.

_____. *Little Wide-Awake: An Anthology from Victorian Children's Books and Periodicals in the Collection of Anne and Fernand G. Renier*. London: Arthur Barker Ltd., 1967.

Early Children's Books and Their Illustration. The Pierpont Morgan Library, New York. With a preface by Charles Ryskamp. Boston: David R. Godine, 1975.

Freeman, Ruth S. *Yesterday's School Books: A Looking Glass for Teachers of Today*. Watkins Glen, N.Y.: Century House, 1960.

Haviland, Virginia. *Yankee Doodle's Literary Sampler of Prose, Poetry and Pictures Being an anthology of diverse works published for the edification and/or entertainment of young readers in America before 1900 selected from Rare Book Collections of the Library of Congress*. Washington: Library of Congress, 1974.

Johnson, Clifton. *Old-Time Schools and School-Books*. New York: Macmillan, 1904.

Opie, Iona and Peter. *A Nursery Companion*. London: Oxford University Press, 1980.

Seymour-Smith, Martin, ed. *A Cupful of Tears: Sixteen Victorian Novelettes*. London: Wolfe Publishing, 1965.

Temple, Nigel. *Seen and Not Heard: A Garland of Fancies for Victorian Children*. London: Hutchinson, 1970.

Tuer, Andrew W. *Forgotten Children's Books*. New York: Benjamin Blom, 1898.

_____. *Stories from old-fashioned Children's Books*. London: Leadenhall Press, 1899-1900.

1. EARLY LESSONS AND COURTESY BOOKS

Adamson, John William. *'The Illiterate Anglo-Saxon' and other Essays on Education, Medieval and Modern*. Cambridge: At the University Press, 1946.

Ascham, Roger. *The Scholemaster*. Ed. D.C. Whimster. London: Methuen, 1934.

Butterworth, Charles C. *The English Primers (1529-1545): Their Publication and Connection with the English Bible and the Reformation in England*. Philadelphia: University of Pennsylvania Press, 1953.

Cassidy, Rev. Frank P. *Molders of the Medieval Mind: The Influence of the Fathers of the Church on the Medieval Schoolmen*. Port Washington: Kennikat Press, 1966.

Charlton, Kenneth. *Education in Renaissance England*. London: Routledge and Kegan Paul, 1965.

Comenius, John Amos. *Orbis Pictus*. A facsimile of the first English edition of 1659 introduced by John E. Sadler. London: Oxford University Press, 1968.

Folmsbee, Beulah. *A Little History of the Horn-book*. Boston: The Horn Book, Inc., 1942.

Ford, Paul Leicester, ed. *The New England Primer; A History of its Origin and Development with a reprint of the unique copy of the earliest known edition and many facsimile illustrations and reproductions*. New York: Dodd & Mead, 1897. Rpt. Columbia University, 1962.

Furnivall, Frederick J., ed. *The Babees Book*. Early English Text Society. London: Trübner & Co., 1868.

_____. *Caxton's Book of Curteyse 1477-8*. E.E.T.S. London: Trübner & Co., 1868.

Garmonsway, G.N., ed. *Ælfric's Colloquy*. London: Methuen, 1939.

Harris, Benjamin. *The Protestant Tutor*. With a preface for the Garland Edition by Daniel A. Cohen. New York: Garland Publishing, Inc., 1977.

Heartman, Charles F. *The New-England Primer Issued Prior to 1830: A Bibliographical Check-List*. New York: R.R. Bowker Company, 1934.

Kozik, Frantisek. *Johan Amos Comenius*. Trans. S.E. Fink-Myhre. Prague: SNTL, 1958.

Leach, A.F. *The Schools of Medieval England*. London: Methuen, 1915.

Lenaghan, R.T., ed. *Caxton's Aesop*. Cambridge: Harvard University Press, 1967.

Littlefield, George Emory. *Early Schools and School-Books of New England*. New York: Russell & Russell, 1965.

Plimpton, G.A. *The Education of Chaucer Illustrated from the Schoolbooks in Use in His Time*. London: Oxford University Press, 1935.

Rickert, Edith. *The Babees Book: Medieval Manners for the Young: Done into Modern English from Dr. Furnivall's Text*. New York: Cooper Square, 1966.

Tuer, Andrew White. *History of the Horn-book*. London: Leadenhall Press, 1896.

2. PURITAN 'HELL-FIRE' TALES

Bunyan, John. *A Book for Boys and Girls; or, Country Rhymes for Children. Being a facsimile of the unique first edition, published in 1686, deposited in the British Museum.* With an introduction giving an account of the work, by John Brown. London: E. Stock, 1889.

Coats, R.G., "John Bunyan as a Writer for Children," *The Westminster Review*, 176 (1911), 303-7.

Elliott, Emory. *Puritan Influences in American Literature.* Urbana: University of Illinois Press, 1979.

Frye, Ronald M. *God, Man, and Satan: Patterns of Christian Thought and Life in Paradise Lost, Pilgrim's Progress, and The Great Theologians.* Princeton: Princeton University Press, 1960.

Hensley, Jeannine, ed. *The Works of Anne Bradstreet.* Cambridge: Harvard University Press, 1967.

Hill, Christopher. *Change and Continuity in Seventeenth-Century England.* London: Weidenfeld and Nicolson, 1974.

————. *Society and Puritanism in Pre-Revolutionary England.* London: Secker & Warburg, 1964.

————. *The World Turned Upside Down; Radical Ideas during the English Revolution.* London: Temple Smith, 1972.

Janeway, James. *A Token for Children, being an exact account of the conversion, holy and exemplary lives and joyful deaths of several young children.* London: Simpkin & Marshall, 1821.

Jones, P.M. and N.R. Jones, eds. *Salvation in New England: Selections from the Sermons of the First Preachers.* Austin: University of Texas Press, 1977.

Kaufman, U. Milo. *The Pilgrim's Progress and Traditions in Puritan Meditation.* New Haven: Yale University Press, 1966.

Marcus, Leah S. *Childhood and Cultural Despair: A Theme and Variation in Seventeenth-Century Literature.* Pittsburgh: University of Pittsburgh Press, 1978.

Morgan, Edmund S. *The Puritan Family: Religion and Domestic Relations in New England.* New York: Harper & Row, 1944.

Morison, Samuel E. *The Puritan Pronaos: Studies in the Intellectual Life of New England in the Seventeenth Century.* New York: New York University Press, 1936.

3. THE LYRICAL INSTRUCTION OF ISAAC WATTS

Bishop, Selma L. *Isaac Watts Hymns and Spiritual Songs 1707-1748: A Study in Early Eighteenth Century Language Changes.* London: The Faith Press, 1962.

Davis, Arthur P. *Isaac Watts, His Life and Works.* Virginia Union University, 1943.

Escott, Harry. *Isaac Watts Hymnographer: A Study of the Beginnings, Development, and Philosophy of the English Hymn.* London: Independent Press, 1962.

Watts, Isaac. *Divine Songs Attempted in Easy Language for the Use of Children; facsimile reproductions of the first edition of 1715 and an illustrated edition of circa 1840.* With an introduction and bibliography by J.H.P. Pafford. London: Oxford University Press, 1971.

————. *Reliquiae Juveniles. Miscellaneous Thoughts in Prose and Verse (1734).* With an introduction by S.J. Rogal. Gainesville: Scholars' Facsimiles & Reprints, 1968.

4. CHAPBOOKS AND PENNY HISTORIES

Ashton, John. *Chap-Books of the Eighteenth Century.* New York: Benjamin Blom, 1882.

Federer, Charles A., ed. *Yorkshire Chap-Books.* London: Elliot Stock, 1889.

Neuberg, Victor E. *Chapbooks: A Bibliography of References to English and American Chapbook Literature of the Eighteenth and Nineteenth Centuries.* London: The Vine Press, 1964.

Nursery Rhymes and Chapbooks 1805-1814. With a preface for the Garland Edition by Justin G. Schiller. New York: Garland Publishing, Inc., 1978.

The Penny Histories: A Study of Chapbooks for young readers over two centuries. With an introduction by Victor E. Neuberg. London: Oxford University Press, 1968.

Thompson, Roger, ed. *Samuel Pepys' Penny Merriments.* New York: Columbia University Press, 1977.

Zall, P.M., ed. *A Nest of Ninnies and Other English Jestbooks of the Seventeenth Century.* Lincoln: University of Nebraska Press, 1970.

5. JOHN NEWBERY: INSTRUCTION
WITH DELIGHT

Boreman, Thomas. *The Gigantick History of the Two Famous Giants and Other Curiosities in Guildhall, London.* With a preface for the Garland Edition by M.H. Platt. New York: Garland Publishing, Inc., 1977.

The History of Little Goody Two-Shoes. A Facsimile Reproduction of the 1766 Edition. With an introduction by Charles Welsh. London: Griffith & Farran, 1881.

Newbery, John. *A Little Pretty Pocket-Book.* A Facsimile with an introductory essay and bibliography by M.F. Thwaite. London: Oxford University Press, 1966.

Roscoe, S. *John Newbery and His Successors 1740-1814, A Bibliography.* Wormley: The Five Owls Press, 1973.

———. *Newbery, Carnan, Power.* London: Dawsons of Pall Mall, 1966.

Whitmore, William H., ed. *The Original Mother Goose's Melody As First Issued by John Newbery, of London Reproduced in facsimile from edition as reprinted by Isaiah Thomas, of Worcester, Mass.* Albany: Joel Munsell's Sons, 1889.

6. RATIONAL MORALISTS

Abbott, Rev. Jacob. *Rollo at School.* London: James S. Hodson, 1839.

Avery, Gillian. *Nineteenth Century Children: Heroes and Heroines in English Children's Stories 1780-1900.* London: Hodder and Stoughton, 1965.

Day, Thomas. *The History of Sandford and Merton.* London: George Routledge & Sons, n.d.

Edgeworth, Maria. *Early Lessons.* London: Routledge, Warne & Routledge, 1859.

Fenn, Lady Eleanor. *Cobwebs to Catch Flies: or, Dialogues in Short Sentences Adapted to children from the Age of three to eight years.* London: Juvenile Library, 1822.

Fielding, Sarah. *The Governess or, Little Female Academy. A facsimile reproduction of the first edition of 1749.* With an introduction and bibliography by Jill E. Gray. London: Oxford University Press, 1968.

Goodrich, S.G., ed. *Robert Merry's Museum.* Volumes XI and XII. New York: D. Mead, 1846.

Hofland, Barbara. *Farewell Tales Founded on Facts.* New York: W.E. Dean, n.d.

Horsley, Henry S. *The Affectionate Parent's Gift, and the Good Child's Reward; Consisting of a Series of Poems and Essays, on Natural, Moral, and Religious Subjects.* London: Printed for T. Kelly, 1828 (Osborne Collection).

Inglis-Jones, Elisabeth. *The Great Maria: A Portrait of Maria Edgeworth.* London: Faber and Faber, 1959.

Jordan, Alice M. *From Rollo to Tom Sawyer.* Boston: The Horn Book, 1948.

Locke, John. *Some Thoughts Concerning Education.* With an Introduction and Notes by R.H. Quick. Cambridge: At the University Press, 1880, rpt., 1934.

Marcet, Jane. *Mary's Grammar Interspersed with Stories and Intended for the Use of Children.* London: Longmans, Green, and Co., n.d.

Parley, Peter, pseud. *Make the Best of It, or Cheerful Cherry, and Other Tales.* New York: Sheldon & Co., 1863.

Patterson, Sylvia W. *Rousseau's Emile and Early Children's Literature.* Metuchen, N.J.: Scarecrow Press, 1971.

Peck, Dorothy Abbott. "A Study of the Life and Selected Works of Jacob Abbott (1803-1879), Early American Children's Author." M.A. Thesis. Washington: Catholic University of America, 1969.

Roselle, Daniel. *Samuel Griswold Goodrich, Creator of Peter Parley: A Study of His Life and Work.* Albany: State University of New York Press, 1968.

Rousseau, Jean-Jacques. *Emile.* Trans. B. Foxley. London: J.M. Dent & Sons, 1911.

Traill, Catharine Parr. *The Canadian Crusoes: A Tale of The Rice Lake Plains.* Boston: Crosby & Nichols, 1862.

———. *The Young Emigrants or Pictures of Canada. A Facsimile of the 1826 anonymous edition.* New York: Johnson Reprint Corporation, 1969.

Wollstonecraft, Mary. *Original Stories From Real Life. With Conversations Calculated to Regulate the Affections, and Form the Mind to Truth and Goodness.* With five illustrations by Wm Blake. Introduction E.V. Lucas. London: H. Frowde, 1906.

7. SUNDAY SCHOOL MORALISTS

Barbauld, Anna Laetitia. *Hymns in Prose for Children.* London: John Murray, 1880.

Cutt, Margaret Nancy. *Ministering Angels: A Study of Nineteenth Century Evangelical Writing for Children*. Wormley: The Five Owls Press, 1979.

_____. *Mrs Sherwood and Her Books for Children*. London: Oxford University Press, 1974.

Elliott-Binns, L.E. *The Early Evangelicals: A Religious and Social Study*. London: Lutterworth Press, 1953.

Jones, M.G. *The Charity School Movement: A Study of Eighteenth Century Puritanism in Action*. Cambridge: Cambridge University Press, 1938.

More, Hannah. *The Shepherd of Salisbury Plain, Parts I and II*. With a preface for the Garland Edition by James Silverman. New York: Garland Publications, 1977.

_____. *Domestic Tales and Allegories; Illustrating Human Life*. New York: D. Appleton & Company, 1865.

Rede, Lucy Leman. *Flowers That Never Fade*. London: Dean and Munday, 1838.

Sherwood, Mary Martha. *The History of the Fairchild Family; or, The Child's Manual: Being a Collection of Stories Calculated to Show the Importance and Effects of a Religious Education*. London: James Nisbet & Co., n.d.

Smith, Naomi Royde. *The State of Mind of Mrs Sherwood*. London: Macmillan, 1946.

Taylor, E.R. *Methodism and Politics 1791-1851*. Cambridge: At the University Press, 1935.

Toon, Peter. *Evangelical Theology 1833-1856: A Response to Tractarianism*. London: Marshall, Morgan & Scott, 1979.

Trimmer, Sarah Kirby. *The Robins; or, Domestic Life Among the Birds Designed for the Instruction of Children Respecting their Treatment of Animals*. New York: C.S. Francis, 1851.

Warner, Susan. *The Wide, Wide World*. New York: Grosset and Dunlap, n.d.

8. HARBINGERS OF THE GOLDEN AGE

Blake, William. *Songs of Innocence and of Experience Shewing the Two Contrary States of the Human Soul*. With an introduction and commentary by Sir Geoffrey Keynes. London: Rupert Hart-Davies Ltd., 1967.

Davidson, Angus. *Edward Lear Landscape Painter and Nonsense Poet (1812-1888)*. London: John Murray, 1938.

Dorset, Catherine A. *The Peacock At Home*. Illustrated and Illuminated. London: Cundall & Addey, 1851.

Hoffmann, Heinrich. *Slovenly Peter or Cheerful Stories and Funny Pictures for Good Little Folks*. With Colored Illustrations After the Original Style. Philadelphia: John C. Winston Company, n.d.

Howitt, Mary. *Sketches of Natural History*. Boston: Weeks, Jordan & Co., 1839.

Lamb, Charles and Mary. *Poetry for Children*. London: Leadenhall Press, 1892.

Lear, Edward. *A Book of Nonsense*. Fourteenth Edition. London: Dalziel Brothers, 1863.

Mure, Eleanor. *The Story of the Three Bears*. Toronto: Oxford University Press, 1967. For the Friends of the Osborne and Lillian H. Smith Collections.

Ober, Warren U., ed. *The Story of the Three Bears: The Evolution of an International Classic*. Delmar, New York: Scholars' Facsimiles & Reprints, 1981.

Paget, Rev. Francis E. *The Hope of the Katzekopfs; A Fairy Tale*. New York: Johnson Reprint Corporation, 1968.

Peacock, T.L. *The Works of T.L. Peacock*, ed. Henry Cole. In three volumes. London: Richard Bentley and Son, 1875.

Peter Piper's Practical Principles of Plain and Perfect Pronunciation. To which is added, A Collection of moral and entertaining conundrums. London: J. Harris, 1820. (Osborne Collection).

Roscoe, William. *The Butterfly's Ball, and the Grasshopper's Feast*. London: J. Harris, 1807. (Osborne Collection).

Salway, Lance, ed. *A Peculiar Gift; Nineteenth Century Writings on Books for Children*. Harmondsworth: Kestrel Books, 1976.

Sinclair, Catherine. *Holiday House: A Series of Tales*. Edinburgh: William Whyte and Co., 1851.

Smart, Christopher. *Hymns for the Amusement of Children (1772)*. London: Scolar Press, 1973.

Taylor, Ann and Jane. *Hymns for Infant Minds*. A New Edition. London: Jackson and Walford, 1846.

_____. *Original Poems*. Illustrated. London and New York: George Routledge & Sons, 1868.

Turner, Elizabeth. *The Daisy; or, Cautionary Stories in Verse*. Adapted to the Ideas of Children from Four to Eight Years Old. London: J. Harris, 1807.

INDEX